CW00666136

HETERARCHY IN WORLD POLITICS

Heterarchy in World Politics challenges the fundamental framing of international relations and world politics. IR theory has always been dominated by the presumption that world politics is, at its core, a system of states. However, this has always been problematic, challengeable, time-bound, and increasingly anachronistic.

In the 21st century, world politics is becoming increasingly multi-nodal and characterized by "heterarchy"—the coexistence and conflict between differently structured micro- and meso- quasi-hierarchies that compete and overlap not only across borders but also across economic-financial sectors and social groupings. Thinking about international order in terms of heterarchy is a paradigm shift away from the mainstream "competing paradigms" of realism, liberalism, and constructivism. This book explores how, since the mid-20th century, the dialectic of globalization and fragmentation has caught states and the interstate system in the complex evolutionary process toward heterarchy. These heterarchical institutions and processes are characterized by increasing autonomy and special interest capture. The process of heterarchy empowers strategically situated agents—especially agents with substantial autonomous resources and, in particular, economic resources—in multi-nodal competing institutions with overlapping jurisdictions. The result is the decreasing capacity of macro-states to control both domestic and transnational political/economic processes. In this book, the authors demonstrate that this is not a simple breakdown of states and the states system; it is in fact the early stages of a structural evolution of world politics.

This book will interest students, scholars and researchers of international relations theory. It will also have significant appeal in the fields of world politics, security studies, war studies, peace studies, global governance studies, political science, political economy, political power studies and the social sciences more generally.

Philip G. Cerny is Professor Emeritus of Politics and Global Affairs at the University of Manchester, UK, and Rutgers University-Newark, USA. His research interests are the theory of world politics and political economy.

Innovations in International Affairs

Series Editor: Raffaele Marchetti

LUISS Guido Carli, Italy

Innovations in International Affairs aims to provide cutting-edge analyses of controversial trends in international affairs with the intent to innovate our understanding of global politics. Hosting mainstream as well as alternative stances, the series promotes both the re-assessment of traditional topics and the exploration of new aspects.

The series invites both engaged scholars and reflective practitioners, and is committed to bringing non-western voices into current debates.

Innovations in International Affairs is keen to consider new book proposals in the following key areas:

- **Innovative topics**: related to aspects that have remained marginal in scholarly and public debates
- **International crises**: related to the most urgent contemporary phenomena and how to interpret and tackle them
- **World perspectives**: related mostly to non-western points of view

Titles in this series include:

Megatrends of World Politics
Globalization, Integration and Democratization
Edited by Marina M. Lebedeva and Denis A. Kuznetsov

Africa–Europe Cooperation and Digital Transformation
Edited by Chux Daniels, Benedikt Erforth and Chloe Teevan

Heterarchy in World Politics
Edited by Philip G. Cerny

For more information about this series, please visit: www.routledge.com/Innova tions-in-International-Affairs/book-series/IIA

HETERARCHY IN WORLD POLITICS

Edited by Philip G. Cerny

Routledge
Taylor & Francis Group

LONDON AND NEW YORK

First published 2023
by Routledge
4 Park Square, Milton Park, Abingdon, Oxon OX14 4RN

and by Routledge
605 Third Avenue, New York, NY 10158

Routledge is an imprint of the Taylor & Francis Group, an informa business

© 2023 selection and editorial matter, Philip G. Cerny; individual chapters, the contributors

The right of Philip G. Cerny to be identified as the author of the editorial material, and of the authors for their individual chapters, has been asserted in accordance with sections 77 and 78 of the Copyright, Designs and Patents Act 1988.

All rights reserved. No part of this book may be reprinted or reproduced or utilised in any form or by any electronic, mechanical, or other means, now known or hereafter invented, including photocopying and recording, or in any information storage or retrieval system, without permission in writing from the publishers.

Trademark notice: Product or corporate names may be trademarks or registered trademarks, and are used only for identification and explanation without intent to infringe.

British Library Cataloguing-in-Publication Data
A catalogue record for this book is available from the British Library

ISBN: 978-1-032-39875-4 (hbk)
ISBN: 978-1-032-40341-0 (pbk)
ISBN: 978-1-003-35261-7 (ebk)

DOI: 10.4324/9781003352617

Typeset in Times New Roman
by Apex CoVantage, LLC

CONTENTS

NOTES ON CONTRIBUTORS

Mădălina Virginia Antonescu is a scientific researcher at Bucharest University, Romania. Her research interests are urban politics, cultural anthropology, and international relations.

Rosalba Belmonte is a postdoctoral researcher in political sociology at Tuscia University in Viterbo, Italy. Her research interests are the distribution of political power, the state and extra-state authorities, gender relations, and gender-based violence.

Alexandre Bohas is Professor at the ESSCA School of Management in Angers, France, and research associate at CERGAM in Aix-Marseille. His research interests are cultural globalization, politics, and business, and transnational governance.

Philip G. Cerny is Professor Emeritus of Politics and Global Affairs at the University of Manchester, UK, and Rutgers University-Newark, USA. His research interests are the theory of world politics and political economy.

Carole L. Crumley is Professor Emerita of Anthropology at the University of North Carolina, Chapel Hill. Her research interests are complex adaptive systems in the social sciences, especially governance, and historical ecology.

Judit Fabian is currently a post-doctoral visiting researcher at the Graduate School of Public and International Affairs at the University of Ottawa, a fellow at the Canadian Global Affairs Institute, and a core and founding member of the Gender Research Hub of the World Trade Organization. Judit's overall work centers upon the idea of democratic global economic governance, and her current research focus is world trade politics.

Shahar Hameiri is Professor of International Politics in the School of Political Science and International Studies, University of Queensland, Australia. His research mainly examines the politics of state transformation, with a particular focus on Southeast Asia, China, and the Pacific.

Lee Jones is Professor of Political Economy and International Relations at Queen Mary University of London. His research interests are political economy and the transformation of states and governance, with a particular focus on Southeast Asia and China.

Hortense Jongen is Assistant Professor of Politics at the Vrije University Amsterdam and researcher at the University of Gothenburg. Her research interests are the new modes of global governance, with a specific interest in global and regional internet governance and the global fight against corruption.

Gabriela Kütting is Professor of Politics and Global Affairs at Rutgers University-Newark, New Jersey. Her research interests are in environmental justice, coloniality and the global environment, global governance, and environmental politics.

Michael J. Morley is Professor of Management at the Kemmy Business School, University of Limerick, Ireland. His research interests are international and cross-cultural management.

Dana-Marie Ramjit is Professor of Public Policy and Administration at Adler University, Vancouver, Canada. Her research interests are postinternationalism, heterarchy, and contemporary governance.

Peter Rutland is Professor of Government at Wesleyan University, Middletown, Connecticut. His research interests are nationalism and Russian and East European politics.

Richard Sakwa is Professor of Russian and European Politics at the University of Kent at Canterbury, Senior Research Fellow at the National Research University— Higher School of Economics, Moscow, and Honorary Professor in the Faculty of Political Science at Moscow State University. His research interests are Russian politics and international relations.

Alejandra Salas Porras is Professor of Political Science at the National Autonomous University of Mexico, Mexico City. Her research interests are national and global elites, the political economy of development, and think tanks.

Aleksandra Spalińska is a doctoral student in the Faculty of Political Science and International Studies at the University of Warsaw, Poland. Her research interests are theorizing world order, international relations theory, research design, non-state actors, and postmodernity.

Gita Subrahmanyam is a part-time lecturer at Birkbeck College and other University of London institutions, and a part-time international development policy consultant whose clients include UNESCO, African Development Bank, Sida, and GIZ. Her academic research focuses on empires and state theory, while her practical policy work focuses on education and employment.

SECTION I
Theory and History

1

HETERARCHY

Toward Paradigm Shift in World Politics

Philip G. Cerny

Introduction: Beyond State-Centrism

Since the study of IR formally began at the University of Wales, Aberystwyth, in 1919, international relations theory has been dominated by the presumption that world politics is at its core a system of states. However, this way of conceiving world politics was always problematic, challengeable, time-bound, and increasingly anachronistic. In the 21st century, world politics is becoming increasingly *multi-nodal* and characterized by *heterarchy*—the predominance of cross-cutting sectoral mini- and meso-hierarchies above, below, and cutting across states. These heterarchical institutions and processes are characterized by increasing autonomy and special interest capture. States today are no longer primarily "proactive states" but more and more "reactive states." State capacity is not simply eroded but entangled in hybrid structures and processes. A fundamental paradigm shift is required in our understanding of how world politics works.

In recent decades, there have been three mainstream "competing paradigms" in the study of "inter-national" relations—realism, liberalism, and constructivism (Wolin 2016). All assume that the dominant independent variables are states and the inter-state system—that is, methodological state-centrism. Indeed, even contemporary analytical/theoretical frameworks focused on the complexity and coupling of networks assume that states are still the basic "nodes" of the system (cf. Guillén 2015). Since the mid-20th century, however, a dialectic of globalization and fragmentation (Cerny and Prichard 2018) has caught states and the interstate system in a complex evolutionary process toward what is called "heterarchy"—the coexistence and conflict between differently structured micro- and meso- quasi-hierarchies that compete and overlap not only across borders but also across economic-financial sectors and social groupings. This process empowers strategically situated agents—especially agents with substantial autonomous

DOI: 10.4324/9781003352617-2

resources, especially economic resources—in multinodal "competing institutions with overlapping jurisdictions." The core of this process is the triangulation of (a) the "disaggregated state" (Slaughter 2004), where policymaking processes and bureaucratic institutions are embedded in distinct issue-areas and sectors rather than centripetal state structures, (b) fragmented global governance and "regime complexes" (Alter and Raustiala 2018), and (c) the shift of the world economy to the Third (or Fourth) Industrial Revolution, sometimes called "functional differentiation." This process is leading to an uneven spectrum of market/hierarchy or public/private *de facto* policymaking processes and diverse types of "capture" between a range of private actors and meso- and micro-hierarchies, institutions, and processes. State structures and state actors have less and less "state capacity" to act as "unit actors" in world politics. Multilevel and multi-nodal policymaking and implementation processes are evolving above, below, and cutting across states caught up in the dialectic of globalization and fragmentation.

1. State-Centrism in International Relations Theory

State-centrism has a complex history. On the one hand, it has been seen to evolve from the political unification of specific territories by ruling cliques and/or mass movements through a consolidation of internal power structures and the role of both civil and external warfare in transforming multilevel, tribal, or feudal structures into institutionalized sovereign entities, mainly since the 18th and 19th centuries but increasingly consolidated in the 20th, especially after the Treaties of Versailles and Sevres after the end of the First World War. Complex, shifting frontiers—empires and tribes—were replaced by more clearly demarcated borders (Schain 2019). The ideological rationale for state consolidation has been to identify states sociologically with specific, identifiable social units called "nations," that Benedict Anderson (1983) defines as "imagined political communities." The concept of "nation" in the pre-modern world was more localized and tribal (Leon 1973); in the modern age, it would come to be seen as an ethnically consolidated grouping providing bottom-up legitimacy to emerging nation-states.

However, it can be argued that economic factors came to be the most significant variable in the consolidation of nation-states. The First Industrial Revolution enabled political and economic elites in England to transform what became the United Kingdom into the first economic superpower, in terms of both domestic consolidation and the expansion of British economic power in the world. This led other proto-states to consolidate in competition with other emerging states on both levels, especially in Europe, where the nation-state system developed and spread its organizational model internationally through innovation, trade, and empire (Kennedy 1988; see Subrahmanyam, this book). More important historically, however, was the Second Industrial Revolution, in which the combination of the consolidation of nation-states and the large factory system in a range of cutting-edge industries, such as steel, railways, energy production and distribution, shipbuilding, and later automobiles—a structure that would come to be called "Fordism"—led to new, more intense forms of international competition. It was also at the core of Stalinism. These developments, both market-based and monopolistic/oligopolistic, gave rise to state–economic complexes and, indeed, to social and institutional reorganization along the interacting lines of capitalist hierarchies and Weberian bureaucratization. The interstate economic conflict/ competition that resulted played a leading role in two World Wars and later the Cold War. The state and the interstate system therefore came to be seen as the apogee of a secular process of ordering political systems, starting from hunter-gatherer societies and evolving through city-states and empires to statist modernity.

In this context, the development of international relations as an academic discipline has been dominated by state-centric paradigms (cf. Jackson and Sørensen 2010; Wolin 2016, Daddow 2017). This approach is referred to as "two-level games" (Putnam 1988). The most state-centric paradigms have been so-called "realism" and its later spinoff, "neorealism" (Waltz 1979). Neorealism is rooted in the methodological assertion that states are inherently constructed domestically in a hierarchical mode—that is, that they are analytically distinct, endogenously sovereign, and bureaucratically ordered units. In contrast, the "inter-national" system is "anarchical" in that there is no overarching hierarchical order. States operate as "unit actors" and must compete and/or cooperate *as if* they were internally organized as effective hierarchies, leading to a preordained hierarchy-within-anarchy set of games. The other two "mainstream" paradigms, liberalism, and constructivism, also posit the structural predominance of states and the inter-state system. Other non-mainstream paradigms, such as Marxism, world systems theory, critical theory, feminism, poststructuralism, postcolonialism, and green international theory (Daddow 2017), deal with important subcategories rather than the macrostructure of world politics. The state, therefore, whether or not it was effectively *centralized*, has nevertheless been seen as *centripetal* in the evolution of sociopolitical life (Birnbaum 1982). In fact, however, the role of imperial heterarchical structures was also a crucial part of this process (Subrahmanyam, this book). This flawed conceptualization of the state has, of course, been dominated not only by quasi-imperial state-building processes themselves but also by the perception among mass publics that states, despite their disadvantages, are *normatively* the best way to organize political life. Furthermore, state-building has long been associated, at least since the Enlightenment, with notions of progress and modernity, whether liberal, capitalist, or socialist.

2. Beyond State-centrism: The Dialectic of Globalization and Fragmentation

However, the dialectic of globalization and fragmentation is increasingly undermining the "segmentary" differentiation of state/interstate-centrism and is superseding it with "functional" and/or "sectoral" differentiation (Albert et al. 2013) above, below, and cutting across states. Furthermore, globalization itself is all too often perceived to be a structurally homogenizing process, requiring new forms of intergovernmental cooperation or global governance. Dimensions of homogenization are said to include economic globalization, the ideological hegemony of neoliberalism (Cerny 2020), socio-cultural convergence, technological innovation and change, liberal internationalism and global governance, and the emergence of a so-called "flat world" (Friedman 2005). Normative calls for a quasi-world state follow this logic, called "global governance" (see Cerny, this book). However, supposed global-level developments are increasingly challenged by structural tensions and contradictions across multiple dimensions. Theorists have identified these processes using concepts like "functional differentiation," "multiscalarity" (Scholte 2000), "deterritorialization," disparate "landscapes" (Root 2013), "neomedievalism" (Spalińska, this book), "fragmegration" (Rosenau 1990), "state transformation" (Hameiri and Jones, this book), or a "pluralist world order" (Macdonald and Macdonald 2020; see Belmonte, this book). Diverse differentiated structures become more co-dependent and complementary—more "functional"—in a postmodern world.

Among the dimensions of functional differentiation, economic activities and roles tend to underlie wider social and political processes of structuration (Albert et al. 2013). Social bonds too are increasingly fractionated and multicultural, often localized, regionalized, and, indeed, dispersed through material and immaterial transborder linkages, especially information and communications technology, social media, migration, and diasporas, and religious and ethnic, rather than "national," identities. The best-known form of functional differentiation is economic, including multinational firms, financial markets and institutions, as well as a growing transnational division of labor among linked production processes or "supply chains" or "value chains." The integration and differentiation of these structures makes them prone to systemic shocks, as witnessed in the 2008 financial crisis. Related to this turn from the state is "deterritorialization," in many cases more analogous to fluid, pre-modern "frontiers" (De Wilde et al. 2019). Indeed, the state itself is being transformed into a heterarchical structure (Hameiri and Jones, this book; Sakwa, this book). Today it seems more and more apposite to talk of the complex interaction not only of "competing institutions with overlapping jurisdictions," but also the interaction of localities, regions, and different social and economic groups (see Antonescu, this book). Recent scholarship has suggested that up to 80% of the world's population lives in areas of limited, failed, or contested statehood (Geldenhuys 2009; Risse 2011).

One way to conceptualize these processes is what James N. Rosenau called "fragmegration" (Rosenau 1990; see Ramjit, this book). This is an ongoing *process*. The European Union, for example, is in continual structural quasi-crisis, trying to deal centrally with plural tensions between the local and the transnational, as demonstrated by the Brexit issue and the setting up of a Eurozone bailout fund at the end of November 2020, which also involved difficult compromises between the E.U. and the "illiberal democracies" of Hungary and Poland on various social and taxation issues. In the United States and in the rest of the developed and developing worlds, economic growth may well be slowing down as the Third Industrial Revolution runs out of steam (Gordon 2016; Stiglitz 2019), while inequality increases (Piketty 2017; Milanovic 2016). Furthermore, austerity and the erosion of the rights of labor are undermining the mid-20th century social contract on which the welfare state and liberal democracy have been based (Blyth 2013). Political leaders in unstable states are either engaged in attempting to restore authoritarian repression, as in Russia, China, Egypt, and Turkey, or are ensnared in the breakdown of the political system, as in Brazil, Venezuela, and a range of African countries. The number of what are called "failed states" is increasing, and the plurality of ways in which they are doing so is cause for alarm. Today disenchantment with the providential rhetoric of the Enlightenment is the norm. Rationalities of marginal economic utility have transformed statehood into a marketizing, *commodifying* process. The neoliberal state in particular sees people themselves as personalized *enterprises* in permanent competition with each other (Davidson and Rees-Mogg 1997; Dardot and Laval 2014; Cerny 1990, 1998, 2009, 2010), rather than the social animals of other versions of political thought. Furthermore, the state has become a promoter of financialization rather than welfare or social democracy, prompting the financialization of society itself—undermining the potential for what has been called the "entrepreneurial state" concerned with providing public goods (Tiberghien 2007; Block and Keller 2011; Herman 2012; Mazzuccato 2013). Nevertheless, the state remains the primary provider of welfare programs, and finance cannot do without it for a host of public goods that rely on finance for credit. Social democracy has been replaced by the supposed "democratization of finance" and "financial inclusion" (see Litan and Rauch 1998; Shiller 2003). The state itself has in turn become a globalizing agent—a "competition state," promoting its own disaggregation (Cerny 1997; Genschel and Seelkopf 2015).

3. Dimensions of Heterarchy: From the Sub-National to the Transnational

World politics is now better understood as a complex set of meso- and mini-hierarchies, including individuals and social groups, classes and vested interests, tribes and religions, and economic structures and processes that cut across state and regional boundaries, mediated at different speeds by different technologies, social bonds, and identities and in different forms of marketization and oligopolization/monopolization. All this produces territories without governments, authorities without states, shifting boundaries, regulatory systems transcending borders, and increasingly powerful but sectorally splintered supranational authorities (Cassese 2016). From this perspective, "levels" are an oversimplification. So, for example, while semi-dematerialized price mechanisms by which markets and institutions relate to each other and to the wider economy, society, and polity shape our interactions, they do so through people and material processes that connect them (Coole and Frost 2010; Srnicek 2013). They take place through our interactions with the computers, logistics, and groups of people "next" to us in an increasingly "intangible" world of "capitalism without capital" (Haskel and Westlake 2018). Actors and political processes can only increasingly *react* to price changes that are independently produced by market and institutional transactions, many of which are automated. Strategically situated actors are able to mobilize and manage material resources, influential contacts, ideologies and mind sets, and knowledge.

This has led to the consolidation of a range of "extra-state authorities" (Belmonte, this book) and "regime complexes" (Alter and Raustiala 2018) across a range of institutions and processes, including "low capacity states," fragmented global governance, and oligopolistic, sectorally differentiated quasi-corporatist policymaking, regulatory, and policy implementation processes. These embed the "privileged position of business" (Lindblom 1977) and transnationally powerful interest groups, including intangible sectors such as information technology (with firms such as Facebook, Apple, Amazon, Netflix, and Google, referred to as FAANGs), banking and finance, etc., as well as transnational corporations, supply chains and other linkages transcending and undermining state territorial and economic boundaries. States themselves have sought to benefit from these structural transformations by sponsoring the international competitiveness of domestically located firms, leading to transnational oligopolization and rent-seeking. Recent history suggests that the development of an effective global governance structure as a way to reorganize world politics is increasingly unlikely, even moving in the opposite direction. In other words, the processes of capture and reverse capture explored by Dauvergne and Lebaron (2014) in the case of nongovernmental organizations (NGOs) have, if anything, proliferated more widely in the transnational sphere precisely because of the fragmented institutionalization and crosscutting linkages and networks characteristic of that sphere. Davies, in a seminal history of international non-governmental organizations (INGOs), argues that the burgeoning constellation of such organizations in the 1980s and 1990s has been declining and fragmenting in the 21st century (Davies 2014). Global governance can be even more vulnerable to whipsawing, bypassing, capture and manipulation, and even corruption than the traditional domestic public policy sphere.

At the core of these processes, furthermore, is the *hybridization* of the public and private. Key actors—the more powerful economic interest groups, state actors in particular issue areas, certain NGOs, etc.—have differing and sometimes incompatible interests as well as common interests and engage in processes of conflict, competition, and coalition-building in order to pursue those interests. Actors depend upon the capacities of real-world, crosscutting "interest" groups—including both "sectional" (or "material interest") and "value" groups (Key 1953), civil society groups, non-governmental organizations (NGOs), and social movements—to manipulate constraints, to identify and take advantage of opportunities, and to shape new directions. What is new, however, are the rapidly evolving transnational linkages among groups in a growing range of overlapping transnational webs of power. The most influential actors are those who can coordinate their activities across borders, at multiple levels, and linking multiple nodes of power. *Governance* itself is therefore being transformed into a "polycentric" or "multinucleated" global political system.

The multinationalization of industry, the expansion of trade, and the globalization of financial markets, along with the development of a transnational consumer society, have transformed many sectoral groups into transnational interest groups, operating across borders and involved in complex competition and coalition-building with each other, with state actors, with so-called "global governance" regimes, and increasingly with mass publics. Within and across states, too, bureaucrats, politicians, and other officials or state actors have become more and more imbricated with groups of their counterparts in other countries through transgovernmental networks, policy communities, and the like. In the economic sphere, post-Fordist forms of production based on flexibilization have transformed "techniques of industry," labor markets, finance, and the like (Haskel and Westlake 2018, Frey 2019).

4. Capture and Networking

Key sets of groups that have in the past been closely bound up with the territorial nation-state are increasingly experimenting with new forms of quasi-private regulation of their activities. And state actors themselves, once said to be "captured" by large, well-organized domestic constituencies, are increasingly captured instead by transnationally linked sectors. These actors do not merely set state agencies and international regimes against each other—a process sometimes called "venue shopping" (or "forum shopping") or "regulatory arbitrage"—but they also cause them to try to network in an increasingly dense fashion with their peers in other states and simultaneously instill them and their transnational private/public links in state elites. Among the major losers are trade unions and other groups with few transnational linkages, although they are sometimes still in a position to obtain compensatory side payments from national governments.

Major social movements and cause groups are increasingly focused on transnational issues, such as the environment, human rights, women's issues, the international banning of landmines, opposition to holding political prisoners, promoting "sustainable development," eliminating poor countries' international debts, and the like (see Rutland, this book). Operating in such a changing world is leading to new problems of management and control, or "the privatization of governance" (Lake 1999; Kahler and Lake 2003), or the emergence of "private authority" in international affairs. Private actors decide more independently the rules of their conduct and act to ensure order in the markets, facilitate trade, and protect private property (Claire et al. 1999; Ronit and Schneider 2000; Hall and Biersteker 2003; Stringham 2015). In this world, even small firms that seem ostensibly "local" are not immune, being dependent upon "foreign" raw materials, export markets, investment finance, migrant labor, and the like, and both increasingly form nodes of wider networks and coordinate their actions.

Less formal networks and more formal interaction among firms, "private regimes," "alliance capitalism," and the ability of non-state actors in general to develop a range of formal and informal interconnections have led to significant degrees of "policy transfer" both across states and in terms of shaping the evolution of global governance more broadly (Higgott et al. 2000; Evans 2005; Gemzik-Salwach & Opolski, 2017). Significant issue-areas, including accountancy, auditing, corporate governance, regulation of the internet (Jongen, this book), etc., have witnessed ongoing negotiation processes among firms, private sector organizations representing particular industrial, financial, and commercial sectors, as well as governments and international regimes, in order to reconcile conflicting standards and move toward a more level playing field (Mügge 2006). Those actors that will be most effective at influencing and shaping politics and policy outcomes are those who: perceive and define their goals, interests and values in international, transnational, and translocal contexts; build cross-border networks, coalitions, and power bases among a range of potential allies and adversaries; and are able to coordinate and organize their strategic action on a range of international, transnational, and translocal scales in such a way as to pursue transnational policy agendas and institutional *bricolage*, although recent examples of the growth of populism and the persistence of anomie (Bohas and Morley, this book) demonstrate the strength of resistance. Meanwhile, recent attempts to reform financial regulation, for example, are increasingly facing obstacles stemming from the lack of a coherent transnational response (Goldbach 2015; Cerny, this book).

Major international meetings such as the G20 or the COP26 climate change conference not only demonstrate differences among states; they are immediately faced with domestic pressures, making the transnationalization of policy something that often has to be pursued surreptitiously and legitimated indirectly—or "depoliticized"—especially when the light of crisis or disruptive change is shone on particular domestic sectors and interests (Roberts 2010). Those new actors— what Belmonte calls "extra-state authorities"—increasingly compete with the state's ability to establish rules, control borders, formulate, and implement public policies autonomously, and go beyond states' boundaries and create their own sovereign system—i.e., self-government authorities, illegal authorities, civil society authorities, and economic-financial authorities. At one end, we find so-called "natural monopolies" and, of course, oligopolies, especially where they are transnationally linked, characterized by "specific assets" (Durkheim, 1893/1933; Williamson 1975, 1985) that are basically indivisible, like the big factory system, aircraft manufacturing, Fordism, etc.; and, at the other end, those characterized by structurally competitive, divisible, and inherently tradable "non-specific assets." In the 21st century, however, there has been rapid and far-reaching *technological* change that is profoundly transforming both domestic and transnational economic structures and processes from small businesses to global finance. In particular, there is an ongoing debate about whether these changes lead to a growing tendency for the abstract financial economy to become divorced from the "real" economy of production, which has been called "capitalism without capital" (Haskel and Westlake 2018; see Cerny, this book), creating new groups of social and economic *"winners"* and *"losers."* Three kinds of structuring dimensions, taken together, differentiate these issue-areas and distinguish the forms of governance most likely to develop in each of a range of "policy domains."

5. Dimensions of Heterarchy

The first is a mainly *economic–structural dimension*. Where a particular industry or activity is characterized predominantly by specific assets, then government intervention, whether through public ownership, direct control, subsidization and/ or traditional "hands-on" forms of regulation, is more likely to lead to relatively efficient outcomes compared with pure privatization or marketization. In contrast, where an industry or activity is characterized predominantly by non-specific assets—say, a flexible, post-Fordist steel mini-mill, a small business that does not attract takeovers by large, especially transnationally organized firms, some high-tech companies, service industries, etc.—then not only will it be more efficiently organized through private markets, but also, in public policy terms, arms'-length regulation. The second dimension concerns the configuration of interests characteristic of the industry or activity concerned. On the one hand, patterns of cross-border sectional or economic-utilitarian politics of specific agricultural sectors will be very different from those of a rapidly changing steel industry, varied high-tech sectors, textiles, and other consumer goods, or the commercial aircraft industry. On the other hand, new forms of value politics on a range of globalizing non-economic issue areas like AIDS prevention, poverty reduction, criminal law, and the like, have been growing, where transnational pressure groups, advocacy coalitions, and non-governmental organizations (NGOs) seek new ways to compete and cooperate. The third dimension concerns the relative sensitivity and vulnerability of the industry or activity to specific transnational economic trends—in particular export potential, import vulnerability, position in an international production chain, exposure to internationally mobile capital, and the like. When an industry or activity is insulated from such cross-border structures and processes, lobbying pressure and "iron triangles" in that sector are likely to favor traditional redistributive/protective policy measures. However, firms and sectors that are highly integrated or linked into such structures and processes, especially where there is a "world market price" for a good or asset that determines local prices, then lobbying pressure from firms in that sector and from industry organizations is likely to be organized through flexible coalitions that include transnational actors from outside the national "container" and that operate at the transnational level to influence global governance processes.

These dimensions might potentially be applied to assess the likelihood and shape of policy innovation and coalition-building across a range of contrasting, differently structured issue areas and policy domains, and the actors that populate them, including:

- financial systems and regulation,
- international monetary policy and exchange rate management,
- macroeconomic—fiscal and monetary—policy,
- microeconomic and strategic industrial policy,
- public and social services,
- trade policy,
- corporate governance,
- labor markets,
- welfare states, and
- the most informal, diffuse and unorganized—but nonetheless increasingly marketized—issue area of all, consumption.

It is ultimately the *mix* of policy measures that is the core *problématique* of the fragile transnational political process and heterarchical coalition-building. The politics of certain key issue areas like financial regulation can play a distinct catalytic role in reshaping global economics and politics *as a whole*, imposing their particular market and policy structure on other sectors and issue areas too.

6. 21st Century Scenarios

There are several complex—and interactive—potential outcomes to these developments. The first is "durable disorder" (Minc 1993), in which actors are continually attempting to experiment with pragmatic reactions to manage these developments through such processes as bringing economic sectors and activities into the public sector, as with responses to the COVID-19 pandemic. The second involves complex, uneven issue-areas—triangulated assemblages of vested interests, hubs, brokerage, "sectoral corporatism," etc., in differentiated sectors; this is probably the closest to heterarchy. The third leads to anomie, possibly even *dystopia*, leading to a fundamental destabilization of world politics. The most likely outcome will be an uneven and unstable mixture of these scenarios—muddling through. Heterarchy therefore is still in an early stage of development. But given the dialectic of globalization and fragmentation, it appears to be the way the world is being restructured. The late 20th and early 21st centuries would appear to be a critical—secular—*branching point* in the path dependency of world politics and political economy, with a more uneven and unstable form of transnational capitalism unfolding that will increasingly be dominated by complex special interests. This restructuration process requires a new paradigm—heterarchy.

References

Albert, M., Buzan, B., and Zürn, M., eds., 2013. *Bringing sociology to international relations: world politics as differentiation theory*. Cambridge: Cambridge University Press.

Alter, K.J., and Raustiala, K., 2018. "The Rise of International Regime Complexity". *Annual Review of Law and Social Science*, 14 (no. 1), 18.2–18.21. 27 June.

Anderson, B., 1983. *Imagined communities: reflections on the origin and spread of nationalism*. London: Verso.

Birnbaum, P., 1982. *La logique de l'État*. Paris: Fayard.

Block, F.L., and Keller, M.R., 2011. *State of innovation: the U.S. government's role in technology development*. London: Routledge.

Blyth, M., 2013. *Austerity: the history of a dangerous idea*. New York: Oxford University Press.

Cassese, S., 2016. *Territori e potere*. Bologna: Il Mulino.

Cerny, P.G., 1990. *The changing architecture of politics: structure, agency and the future of the state*. London: Sage.

Cerny, P.G., 1997. "Paradoxes of the Competition State: The Dynamics of Political Globalization". *Government and Opposition*, 32 (no. 2), 251–274. Spring.

Cerny, P.G., 1998. "Neomedievalism, Civil War and the New Security Dilemma: Globalisation as Durable Disorder". *Civil Wars*, 1 (no. 1), 36–64. Spring.

Cerny, P.G., 2009. "Multi-Nodal Politics: Globalisation is What Actors Make of It". *Review of International Studies*, 35 (no. 2), 421–449. April.

Cerny, P.G., 2010. *Rethinking world politics: a theory of transnational neopluralism*. New York and Oxford: Oxford University Press.

Cerny, P.G. and Prichard, A., 2018. "The New Anarchy: Globalisation and Fragmentation in 21st Century World Politics, Special Issue on Anarchy and International Relations Theory". *Journal of International Political Theory*, 13 (no. 3), 378–394. October.

Coole, D.H. and Frost, S., 2010. *New materialisms. Ontology, agency, and politics*. Durham, NC: Duke University Press.

Cutler, A. Claire, Virginia Haufler and Tony Porter, eds. (1999). *Private Authority and International Affairs* (Albany, NY: State University of New York Press).

Daddow, O., 2017. *International relations theory*. 3rd edition. London: Sage.

Dardot, P. and Laval, C., 2014. *La nouvelle raison du monde*. Paris: la Découverte/Poche; English language edition *The new way of the world: on neoliberal society*. London: Verso. (2013).

Dauvergne, P. and Lebaron, G., 2014. *Protest Inc.: the corporatization of activism*. Cambridge: Polity Press.

Davidson, J.D. and Rees-Mogg, W., 1997. *The sovereign individual: mastering the transformation to the information age*. New York: Simon & Schuster.

Davies, T., 2014. *NGOs: a new history of transnational civil society*. London: C. Hurst.

De Wilde, P., et al., eds., 2019. *The struggle over borders: cosmopolitanism and communitarianism*. Cambridge: Cambridge University Press.

Durkheim, É., 1893/1933. *The division of labor in society*, trans. George Simpson. New York: Free Press.

Evans, M.G., 2005. *Policy transfer in global perspective*. London: Ashgate.

Frey, C.B., 2019. *The technology trap: capital, labor and power in the age of automation*. Princeton, NJ: Princeton University Press.

Friedman, T.L., 2005. *The world is flat: a brief history of the 21st century*. 1st edition. New York: Farrar, Straus and Giroux.

Geldenhuys, D., 2009. *Contested states in world politics*. London: Palgrave Macmillan.

Gemzik-Salwach, A. and Opolski, K., eds., 2017. *Financialization and the economy*. London and New York: Routledge.

Genschel, P. and Seelkopf, L., 2015. "The Competition State". In: S. Leibfried, et al., eds. *The Oxford handbook of transformations of the state*. Oxford: Oxford University Press, 1–23.

Goldbach, R., 2015. *Global governance and regulatory failure: the political economy of banking*. Basingstoke, Hants: Palgrave Macmillan.

Gordon, R.J., 2016. *The rise and fall of American growth: the U.S. standard of living since the Civil War*. Princeton, NJ: Princeton University Press.

Guillén, M.F., 2015. *The architecture of collapse: the global system in the 21st century*. Oxford: Oxford University Press.

Haas, P., ed., 1997. *Knowledge, power, and international policy coordination*, special issue of International Organization. Vol. 46, no. 1. Columbia, SC: University of South Carolina Press. Winter.

Hall, R.B. and Biersteker, T.J., eds., 2003. *The emergence of private authority in global governance*. Cambridge: Cambridge University Press.

Hardt, M. and Negri, A., 2000. *Empire*. Cambridge, MA: Harvard University Press.

Haskel, J. and Westlake, S., 2018. *Capitalism without capital: the rise of the intangible economy*. Princeton, NJ: Princeton University Press.

Herman, A., 2012. *Freedom's forge: how American business produced victory in World War II*. New York: Random House.

Higgott, R.A., Underhill, G.R. and Bieler, A. 2000. *Non-state actors and authority in the global system*. London: Routledge.

Holloway, J., 2002. *Change the world without taking power: the meaning of revolution today*. London: Pluto Press.

Jackson, P.T. and Nexon, D.H., 1999. "Relations Before States: Substance, Process and the Study of World Politics". *European Journal of International Relations*, 3 (no. 5), 291–332.

Jackson, R. and Sørensen, G., 2010. *Introduction to international relations: theories and approaches*. 4th edition. Oxford: Oxford University Press.

Kahler, M. and Lake, D.A., eds., 2003. *Governance in a global economy: political authority in transition*. Princeton, NJ: Princeton University Press.

Kanter, R.M., 1985. *The change masters: innovation and entrepreneurship in the American corporation*. Glencoe, IL: Free Press.

Kennedy, P., 1988. *The rise and fall of the great powers*. New York: Random House.

Key, V.O., Jr., 1953. *Politics, parties, and pressure groups*. New York: Thomas Y. Crowell.

Lake, D.A., 1999. "Global Governance: A Relational Contracting Approach". In: A. Prakash and J.A. Hart, eds. *Globalization and governance*. London: Routledge, 31–53.

Leon, T.C., 1973. *Nationalism in the middle ages*. Malabar, FL: Krieger Publishing.

Lindblom, C.E., 1977. *Politics and markets: the world's political-economic systems*. New |York: Basic Books.

Litan, R.E. and Rauch, J., 1998. *American finance for the 21st century*. Washington, DC: Brookings Institution Press.

Macdonald, T. and Macdonald, K., 2020. "Towards a 'Pluralist' World Order: Creative Agency and Legitimacy in Global Institutions". *European Journal of International Relations*, 26 (no. 2), 518–544.

Mazzuccato, M., 2013. *The entrepreneurial state: debunking public vs. private sector myths*. New York: Anthem Press.

Milanovic, B., 2016. *Global inequality: a new approach for the age of globalization*. Cambridge, MA: Belknap Press for Harvard University Press.

Minc, A., 1993. *Le nouveau Moyen Âge*. Paris: Gallimard.

Mügge, D., 2006. "Private-Public Puzzles: Inter-Firm Competition and Transnational Private Regulation". *New Political Economy*, 11 (no. 2), 177–200. June.

Piketty, T., 2017. *Capital in the twenty-first century*. Cambridge, MA: Harvard University Press.

Putnam, R.D., 1988. "Diplomacy and Domestic Policy: The Logic of Two-Level Games". *International Organization*, 42 (no. 3), 427–460. Summer.

Risse, T., 2011. "Governance in Areas of Limited Statehood: Introduction and Overview". In: T. Risse, ed. *Governance without a state?: policies and politics in areas of limited statehood*. New York: Columbia University Press, 1–38.

Roberts, A., 2010. *The logic of discipline: global capitalism and the architecture of government*. New York and Oxford: Oxford University Press. London: Routledge.

Ronit, K. and Schneider, V., eds., 2000. *Private organisations in global politics*. London and New York: Routledge.

Root, H.L., 2013. *Dynamics among nations: the evolution of legitimacy and development in modern states*. Cambridge, MA: MIT Press.

Rosenau, J.N., 1990. *The governance of fragmegration: neither a world republic nor a global interstate system*. Paper Presented at the World Congress of the International Political Science Association, Quebec City. 1–5 August.

Schain, M.A., 2019. *The border: policy and politics in Europe and the United States*. New York: Oxford University Press.

Scholte, J.A., 2000. *Globalization: a critical introduction*. London: Palgrave Macmillan.

Shiller, R.J., 2003. *The new financial order: risk in the 21st century*. Princeton, NJ: Princeton University Press.

Slaughter, A.-M., 2004. *A new world order*. Princeton, NJ: Princeton University Press.

Srnicek, N., 2013. *Representing complexity: the material construction of world politics. International relations*. Unpublished PhD Thesis. London: London School of Economics and Political Science.

Stiglitz, J.E., 2019. *People, power, and profits: progressive capitalism in an age of discontent*. New York: W.W. Norton.

Stringham, E.P., 2015. *Private governance: creating order in economic and social life*. Oxford: Oxford University Press.

Tiberghien, Y., 2007. *Entrepreneurial states: reforming corporate governance in France, Japan, and Korea*. Ithaca, NY: Cornell University Press.

Waltz, K., 1979. *Theory of international politics*. Reading, MA: Addison-Wesley.

Williamson, O.E., 1975. *Markets and hierarchies*. New York: Free Press.

Williamson, O.E., 1985. *The economic institutions of capitalism*. New York: Free Press.

Wolin, S., 2016. (1966/2016). *Politics and vision: continuity and innovation in western political thought. Princeton*. Expanded edition. Princeton, NJ: Princeton University Press.

2

FROM POSTINTERNATIONALISM TO HETERARCHY

Turbulence and Distance Proximities in a World of Globalization and Fragmentation

Dana-Marie Ramjit

Introduction: Beyond Postinternationalism

It is indisputable that we are living in a politically, socially, and economically chaotic era. Looking at recent developments heightened by global crises, we witness drastic shifts in structures, uncertainty, and socio-political innovations. The entities that make up society appear to be fragmented, conflicted, and unrestricted. As states struggle to maintain sovereignty, business and technology giants have become influential and dominant. With the growth, dependence, and contribution of the nonprofit sector, allegiances are spent, and concepts like legitimacy and authority are being redefined. Lines between traditional and global, domestic, and international are becoming increasingly hazy and perhaps soon imperceptible. Moreover, the onset of the global pandemic has authorized the virtual workspace, speeding up the impact of globalization on political structures and policymaking. These developments have created turbulence and instability, central features of the contemporary world.

In the pre-international era, politics was dictated by territoriality, but this arrangement is losing relevance as modern authority structures have become diverse, overlapping, and numerous. Contrastingly, the postinternational world is leading toward heteronomous authority in which power is allocated among numerous actors based on obstacles instead of spaces to achieve international functionalism.

Heterarchy is described as the cohabitation among varied and convoluted structures across society, a process that decreases state capacity and advances multi-nodal structuration (Belmonte & Cerny, 2021). There is no monopoly on knowledge, practice, or agency, but each is dispersed according to specialties, resulting from swift innovation and new knowledge. The idea of organizational knowledge leads to social change and global reshuffling.

DOI: 10.4324/9781003352617-3

Politics today requires a new perspective that accounts for dynamic changes before us. This chapter outlines global turbulence and instability distinctive of the existing political environment and presents the institutionalization of heterarchy as an alluring solution to the shakiness and confusion. These ideas lay the groundwork for theorizing beyond the postinternational to the heterarchical to depict what the new political frontier looks like.

1. The Postinternational Realm: Turbulence and Distant Proximities

After World War II, society endured several turns. Some of these are the growth in specialized labor, collective action, altered identities, growth in actors, fluctuating authority structures, assorted goals and new arrangements, short-lived partnerships, policy setbacks, and a faster, more connected, and challenging world (Ansell et al., 2017; Rosenau, 1990; Weatherby et al., 2017). Voting rights in the 19th century, along with the mass media, ushered society into liberty and democracy (McNair, 2017). These occurrences slowly but surely expunged boundaries, pushing out systems in prolonged disequilibrium or cognitive disequilibrium, a state of tension between what people understood (local) and what was newly confronted (global) (Kibbler, 2011; Rosenau, 2003).

Postinternationalism describes this modern, dynamic, interdependent political environment in which state-centric realist philosophies have lost relevance in solving complex global problems (Ferguson & Mansbach, 2007; Rosenau, 1990, 2003). The postinternational concepts of turbulence and distant proximities provide an exhaustive account of global volatility.

Turbulence

Global instability triggered turbulence that transpired at the micro (individuals and groups) and macro (new technologies) levels, hence the reason postinternationalism was referred to as a micro theory of macro change (Hobbs, 2000; Rosenau, 1990; Weatherby et al., 2017). Change was characterized by opposing forces such as stagnation and transformation, past and future, interdependence and dependence, and centralization and decentralization (Ansell et al., 2017; Ferguson & Mansbach, 2007; Hobbs, 2000; Rogers, 2009; Rosenau, 1990). The idea of turbulence realistically portrayed contemporary society.

Turbulence can be defined as erratic, inconsistent, unexpected, and unpredictable activity that creates a complex environment. Complexity is the result of demands made by pertinent actors who ought to be adapted and involved in policymaking (Ansell et al., 2017; Bubolz & Sontag, 2009; Maull, 2011). Examples of turbulence include climate change, global terrorism, financial meltdowns, pandemics, nuclear weapons, humanitarian crises and conflicts, poverty, migration, and failed states (Karns et al., 2015). Turbulence became a key element in a modern society muddled with state incompetence and ultimately, insignificance (Ansell et al., 2017; Webster, 2017; Worth, 2017).

The most striking element of turbulence is political transformation. A turbulent system accommodates an increase in diverse actors or polities, their targets, activities, and movements (Hobbs, 2000; Ferguson & Mansbach, 2007; Kibbler, 2011; Rosenau, 1990, 2003). The rise of non-state actors puts a dent in national sovereignty and engenders a bifurcated or pluricentric realm where states and multiple actors exist (Ansell et al., 2017; Bellamy, 2017; Rogers, 2009; Rosenau, 1990, 2003; Weatherby et al., 2017). The world has now recognized multicentrism as a replacement for state centrism.

The slow evaporation of the state, whose jurisdictional authority is dispersed, has resulted in an emergent, multilevel system of globalizing governance (Rosenau, 2003; Lipschutz, 2000; Hobbs, 2000; Trondal & Bauer, 2017). While postinternational intellectuals debated the precise role of the state, there was common ground in the belief that it had already begun to lose impact and appeal. Authority in postinternational society transferred down to the regional and local levels but up to the global level. This meant that passive individuals were converted into active players, as communication and technology mobilized people to acquire the expertise needed to make politically sound decisions (Hobbs, 2000; Rosenau, 1990; Weatherby et al., 2017). The newly found autonomy of the postinternational citizen created a capacity for self-determination, self-governance, and freedom, a potential state rival.

Today, societies are dissatisfied with the effectiveness of the state on a range of critical policy issues and with increasing cross-border connections, interest, transnational, and non-profit networks are building horizontal and diagonal relationships (Belmonte & Cerny, 2021).

Distant Proximities

Distant proximities are concurrent feelings of distance and proximity. Distant proximities describe how the local unfolds into the global and modern tension represents the friction between localization and globalization (Andaya, 2017; Guy, 2009; Rosenau, 2003). These tensions arise between core and peripheral countries, national and transnational, community and cosmopolitan, cultures and subcultures, centralization and decentralization, space and pace, universalism, and particularism, the global and local (Rosenau, 2003; Weatherby et al., 2017).

An appealing understanding of distant proximities employs the image of a violin. A poorly built violin restricts its notes in the same way the pre-international world constrained society by maintaining localization (Rosenau, 2003). Conversely, a well-built violin bolsters its notes much like the postinternational world, which reinvented spaces to achieve a globally interdependent system that challenges localization by liberating entities (Andaya, 2017; Gordon, 2017; Prichard & Cerny, 2017; Rosenau, 2003; Weatherby et al., 2017).

Contemporary pressures lead to fragmegration, a strong relationship between fragmentation and integration in society caused by globalization (Ansell et al., 2017; Rosenau, 2003). As social and geographic gaps become narrow, people become both integrated and fragmented or distant and proximate. A collapse of ideological beliefs due to growth in technology and science marks a fragmegrative world (Rosenau, 2003). People discard old identities and embrace new ideas and realities, which extends division between individualism and collectivism (Rosenau, 2003; Weatherby, et al., 2017).

Fragmegration portrays a new and different atmosphere of global units. As traditional approaches fail, norms and rules that champion society decline, and people become flexible, advanced, autonomous individuals with several ever-changing identities; the distant becomes proximate (Galaz & Pierre, 2017; Rosenau, 2003). Proximity represents the local world that emphasized landscapes, while distant represents the global world focused on ethnoscapes, technoscapes, financescapes, mediascapes, and ideoscapes (Rosenau, 2003). Postinternational fragmegration observed the popularity of the global amid the disappearance of the local.

Two significant revolutions are attributed to fragmegration. An organizational revolution redefined traditional authority, influence, and power, and an economic revolution modified the movement of goods, services, and wealth, creating a hyperconnected, complex, and ultrafast economy (Prichard & Cerny, 2017; Galaz & Pierre, 2017; Rosenau, 2003; Weatherby et al., 2017). These innovations eliminated boundaries and integrated the world. As the attachment to regions waned, societies became independent, skilled, and powerful while states became weak and forced to share authority with new polities (Ferguson & Mansbach, 2007; Rosenau, 2003; Weatherby et al., 2017). Individuality and liberality broadened societal horizons.

The global effect of fragmegration is undeniable. First, state power and territoriality concepts became increasingly unpopular (Prichard & Cerny, 2017; Rosenau, 2003). Though states are valid, feasible, and robust, society is witnessing their incapacity to manage the dynamics of change, which only leads to greater fragmegration (Ansell et al., 2017; Rosenau, 2003). As state supremacy dwindles, travel increases, cultural ties become broken, and value transmission lessens, hence, the notion of deterritorialization. Simultaneously, spikes in movement, migration, and the establishment of diasporas introduce the notion of reterritorialization (Gordon, 2017; Prichard & Cerny, 2017; Rosenau, 2003).

Second, fragmegration confuses allegiances. The gradual disappearance of citizen loyalty and the rise of a pulsating community of non-state actors have threatened state sovereignty (Prichard & Cerny, 2017; Rosenau, 2003; Weatherby et al., 2017). Decentralization replaced centralization, which resulted in unguarded power spaces waiting to be occupied by organizations seeking recognition. Our societies are facing *bureaucratic disarray* or *decisional paralysis* (Karns et al., 2015; Rosenau, 2003). People are now competent to address their own needs, have squandered their hope in the state, and are seeking unconventional options like heterarchical systems.

Economic globalization forms a third consequence of fragmegration. The postinternational world is an interdependent, multicentric complex system in which economic independence is unlikely (Andaya, 2017; Ansell et al., 2017; Rosenau, 2003; Prichard & Cerny, 2017). The conflict between the individual and the national is one in which the individual increasingly appears victorious.

Distant proximities underline two crucial realities facing us: the boundary-blurring global and the boundary-preserving local (Prichard & Cerny, 2017; Rosenau, 2003). This antagonism climaxes to shepherd society into an emerging age of *glocalization* or *dochakaku*, a Japanese term for global localization (Andaya, 2017; Guy, 2009; Rosenau, 2003).

A fragmegrated world characterizes a new space to deal with contemporary global challenges, such as environmental pollution, currency crunches, the drug trade, terrorism, AIDS, and illegal immigration. These problems are beyond the reach of states and require varied ways to consider the intricate mutually constituting political processes unfolding. The notion of *functional differentiation* or heterarchy provides some useful perspectives.

2. The Heterarchical Realm

Politics in a multi-centric, bifurcated world is complex, and complex politics comprises global, regional, sub-regional, national, provincial, local, and individual. This new multistoried formation results from technological innovation, environmental collapse, global socio-economic and paradigm shifts (Hobbs, 2000; Trondal & Bauer, 2017; Rosenau, 2003; Rogers, 2009). It is helpful to view contemporary politics as dynamic, contradictory, and shocking.

While the Westphalian system denoted ideas of internationalism, postinternationalism saw the end of those ideas as sovereign states joined by several macro actors (Hobbs, 2000; Bellamy, 2017; Ferguson & Mansbach, 2007; Rogers, 2009; Weatherby et al., 2017). Hybrid sovereignty or participatory politics suggest that diverse actors negotiate autonomy and territoriality (Ramadan & Fregonese, 2017). Scale shifting considers a dispersion of power among different networks (Tarrow, 2010). Cheesy authority explores empty power spaces much like the holes in blocks of Swiss cheese, waiting to be occupied by private, governmental, nongovernmental, transnational, and supranational actors (Hobbs, 2000). Unmistakably, a relevant definition of contemporary politics explores the contribution of multiple actors that pique our interest amid the confusion.

Crucially, the challenge policymakers face in the 21st century is their capacity to detect, understand, and solve modern-day problems that are progressively super-wicked, complex, and multidimensional (Ansell et al., 2017; Hobbs, 2000; Karns et al., 2015). Some of these are security, wealth, markets, and human dignity. With its focus on diverse relationships among elements in a system, heterarchy offers prospects for effectively managing the modern political environment with its perspective of change that involves spatial, temporal, and cognitive proportions.

Heterarchy was first described as the organization of cognitive structures in the brain not arranged hierarchically, but adapts to a re-classification of values when human situations change (McCulloch, 1945). Minsky and Papert (1972) used heterarchy to explain the organization of computer sub-rules. Hofstadter (1979) classified heterarchy as a system in which no highest level exists. Stark (2010) explained heterarchy as an organizational construct of multiple organizing rules. Kontopoulos (1993) understood heterarchy as an interactional structure of high complexity. These definitions acutely describe postinternational change and conflict.

The heterarchical configuration is dialectic, which means that both heterarchical and hierarchical structures co-exist, much like the postinternational dialectical relationship between globalization and localization (Byrne, 1998; Harvey & Reed, 1996; Kontopoulos, 1993; Mouzelis, 1995). This flexibility is a crucial feature of complex and dynamic systems. The heterarchical perspective aligns with the postinternational concepts of turbulence and distant proximities to explore three critical ideas consistent with vigorous social philosophy: 1) an account of the micro (individual) and macro (social) change, a micro theory of macro change; 2) the activity of social actors who make up the social structure of society; 3) an explanation for intermittent structural transformation (Rosenau, 1990; Harvey & Reed, 1996).

Heterarchy is a response to complexity. In a postinternational world, innovation functions alongside adaptation as society adjusts to the new global political and economic environment predominantly through interdependence. While hierarchical systems involve dependence, heterarchical forms function with minimal hierarchy and organizational heterogeneity (Stark, 2010). Instead of focusing on a narrow set of entities or delegating tasks to specialized groups in uncertain environments, innovation is accomplished with decentralization and generalization. Contemporary problems are no longer designated to specific entities but distributed across entities to cope with turbulence.

Since this approach can create further complexity and confusion, hierarchical rules are applied to maintain coordination and control. The result of this approach is increased autonomy as authority is no longer delegated vertically but laterally (Stark, 2010). This design advances a reliable perspective of contemporary politics as actors are not just answerable to a finite set of superiors but numerous sectors of society. The idea of *mutual monitoring*, which enables entities to work cooperatively to solve problems, is attractive because it increases transparency, socialization, and complementarity (Stark, 2010, 2018).

In a volatile and uncertain environment, systems are dependent on networks and strategic alliances, which create opportunities for *distributed intelligence* or *distributed cognition* (Stark, 2010). Boundaries are re-traced, actors are regrouped, and systems are reinvented. The linking of ideas and resources across boundaries establishes bonds that can reduce isolation and incapacity and promote knowledge transfer and increased skill.

The postinternational world is highly technological, making it unstable; hence, there is no one best solution. Instead, spaces remain open, fused, and revisited, and progress is dependent on reorganization. The heterarchical political world can be seen as a complex adaptive system because of its array of management principles (Wang, 2010). In modern society, values have shifted, and performance is dependent on successful communication and collaboration across distinctive identities and cultures. Heterarchical organization enables systems to maintain diversity and individuality.

Modern politics is challenged by systemic change and must build resilient systems capable of introspection, learning, and the flexibility to reconceptualize and revise. Heterarchy offers a new, open, and inclusive approach to managing the postinternational political domain.

3. The Battle Between Continuity and Change

Change is the driving force of the postinternational world. It is continual, intense, transformative, and dramatic (Pierre & Galaz, 2017; Rosenau, 1990; Weatherby et al., 2017). A fitting example is the shift from the industrial to the post-industrial world, furthering structural transfers from a tight bipolar to a loose bipolar to a multipolar political world (Ansell et al., 2017; Rosenau, 1990, 2003). Global change is endogenous and exogenous and can be observed in three broad areas: orientational, structural, and relational (Ansell et al., 2017; Rosenau, 2003). Orientational or skill change saw variations in people's analytical skills, degrees of conformity, views on legitimacy, and emotional swings. Structural change impacted the laws of governance (informal regimes, formal alliances, and legal conventions). Relational change such as class and status shifted power, balance, and trust. These changes can be attributed to five occurrences.

First, technology and the microelectronic revolution diminished distances and accelerated communication (Gordon, 2017; Rosenau, 1990; Weatherby et al., 2017). Second, contemporary problems like terrorism, trafficking, AIDS and other disasters, interdependence, and multinational interactions (Karns et al., 2015; Rosenau, 1990). Third, the continued incapacity of states to solve new problems resulted in a lack of control over populations (Karns et al., 2015; Rosenau, 1990, 2003). Fourth, as states became weak, subsystems gained prominence, and decentralization replaced centralization (Ansell et al., 2017; Gordon, 2017; Rosenau, 2003). Fifth, analytical skills, involvement, and authority of citizens expanded (Gordon, 2017; Rosenau, 2003). These changes created an environment of turbulence and the need for international reorganization.

The battle between continuity and change, localization and globalization became evident (Ferguson & Mansbach, 2007; Rosenau, 2003). Identities were evolving while people struggled to maintain former principles. As globalization expanded, a blast of new actors, technological, educational, and economic innovations, interdependence, and sub-groupism widened the space between globalization benefactors and opponents (Rosenau, 2003; Bellamy, 2017; Rogers, 2009).

The new political terrain is a *fusion* and *fission* of authority. Fusion, a growth of networks that ties and inspires people regardless of location, and fission, a rupturing of political parties, localization, and specialization in favor of globalization and generalization (Ferguson & Mansbach, 2007; Rosenau, 1990, 2003). States are powerful and very much present, but the armies of change are rendering them vulnerable. This contradiction of integration and fragmentation has led to a range of institutions and processes that overlap and integrate to operate heterogeneously.

4. Surviving Dynamism: Redefining Authority and Legitimacy

Postinternational change is unrelenting and involves patience, indulgence, and tolerance. To survive in this dynamic system, society must make *conceptual jailbreaks* from traditional patterns to acknowledge the active global complex political dimension (Rosenau, 1990). Such intellectual jumps require conceptualizing a world that is constantly changing and defining authority in that world.

This does not mean we should ignore the hierarchies that structure social and political systems. Rather, co-action can be a step forward in exploring new modes of fragmegration within our structures (Belmonte & Cerny, 2021). For example, a recognition of the actors of inclusive politics can provide pragmatic direction for revaluation and reorganization. Actors in the postinternational system can be categorized into micro (citizens, officials, private) and macro levels (states, subgroups, transnational organizations, leaderless publics, and movements) (Rosenau, 1990). Some of these actors are NGOs, domestic labor, conscientious individuals, corporations, and multilateral institutions (Rosenau, 2003). Aggressive subgroupism and the formidable presence of these organizations is paralyzing states and implies that authority and legitimacy must be redefined.

Current political systems feature two general levels which make up multilevel governance. Level 1 is the state echelon, with clearly defined authority structures and mostly stable connections, while level 2 is a chaotic system with overlapping powers, fluid, and constantly changing relationships (Curry, 2012, 2018; Papadopoulos, 2010).

In this configuration, there is a hierarchy of actors in which some can control or influence policymaking, while others cannot. For example, actors may be allowed a certain degree of flexibility which is evidence of a level 2 dichotomy. However, this capacity may depend on other actors, essentially a level 1 system (Curry, 2012, 2018). Actors function in designated zones, which defines the current climate as a rigid/flexible structural design (Curry, 2012). In this system, authority depends on institutional processes that bound actors, diverse and complex contemporary issues, and policy constraints.

This composition reflects the differences between heterarchical and hierarchic organizations. Heterarchical actors can operate freely and autonomously, while hierarchical actors operate with selective power (Curry, 2012, 2018). In such a structure, authority and legitimacy is determined by accountability.

Accountability encompasses process and legitimacy. As more actors become involved in policymaking, the process becomes open and accountable to the broader society (Curry, 2012). With this perspective, legitimacy is not determined by the process but by the result. By contrast, a hierarchical system is inflexible; although it allows actors to be involved in policy input, there is no room for multiple actors to determine policy outcomes (Curry, 2012). A heterarchical framework proves to be desirable because it is results-oriented.

5. Solving Pinocchio's Problem

The quandary of the postinternational world is restless progression. An equipped society is a dissatisfied one (Rosenau, 1990, 2003). Society itself is undergoing a power diffusion much like Pinocchio's tale of power, choice, freedom, ability, and modernization (Strange, 1996). The *growing nose dilemma* reflects Pinocchio's decision to trust in his own conscience to make decisions as he grew older and more intelligent, instead of yielding to authority structures around him.

Pinocchio's story echoes the reality of modern politics with disappearing state allegiances and individual and philosophical identity-creation (Ansell et al., 2017; Rosenau, 1990). Pinocchio's problem was a conflicting power supply conundrum. Every puppet once guided by strings must grow up and secure its cords (Strange, 1996). In this new experience, strings are unattached, and individuals rely on personal power to guide their loyalties (Rosenau, 2003).

The world is becoming less interstate and more intrastate and trans-state (Ansell et al., 2017; Ferguson & Mansbach, 2007). The contemporary global atmosphere includes a range of actors or polities, spheres of authority, policy networks, advocacy coalitions, or scales of interaction that dictate the political pace (Ferguson & Mansbach, 2007; Rosenau, 2003; Sabatier & Weible, 2017; Prichard & Cerny, 2017). Goals and assets unite these new entities; they co-exist, cooperate, compete, clash, overlap, layer, and nest together, contributing to both stability and volatility (Ferguson & Mansbach, 2007).

Dominant identities and loyalties were reworked, and multiple selves and constancies became trendy. In this interface, the state occupies only one space among other contenders, as concepts like legitimacy and power are ascertained by influence (Bellamy, 2017; Ferguson & Mansbach, 2007; Rosenau, 2003; Karns et al., 2015). To address this assault on sovereignty and the growing discontent among populations, we need to shift our attention to consolidation and *sectoral differentiation*.

6. Networks and Coalitions: Transforming Politics through Coexistence

At the center of the heterarchical processes is the intersection between private and public entities. In this system, actors depend on each other's capacities to create new direction and build ties despite competing interests (Belmonte & Cerny, 2021). Cross-border synchronization has amassed significant influence for actors across multiple levels, enabling them to achieve political outcomes transnationally, globally, and regionally, transforming politics through coexistence and overlapping functionalism.

Networks establish multiple forms of engagement beyond traditional political involvement, focusing less on actors and more on relationships to establish roles and linkages that can shape the current political process (Belmonte & Cerny, 2021; Curry, 2012; Henning, 2009). This approach maximizes the importance of interdependence in moving the policy process beyond the state level to create opportunities for participation. For example, transnationalism involves multinational firms and global markets stepping across governments to solve problems in communities (Belmonte & Cerny, 2021).

Any attempt to define policymaking in the current turbulent environment must include the perspectives of multiple actors or advocacy coalitions who are dependent on each other to achieve their goals (Jenkins-Smith & Sabatier, 1994). One way to conceptualize the multitude of actors occupying the political space today is the Advocacy Coalition Framework (ACF), which emphasizes the value of coalitions (Jenkins-Smith & Sabatier, 1994; Weible & Sabatier, 2017).

Coalitions are naturally formed when similar interests align, and the policy process is driven by the networks that its participants create. For networks to survive, there must be cooperation. Policy change can be achieved with belief changes, such as replacing a dominant coalition with a minority one (Jenkins-Smith & Sabatier, 1994). External shocks, such as socio-economic shifts, disasters, and variations in administrations, essentially turbulence, are pushing society to make this leap (Weible & Sabatier, 2017).

Network politics explores policymaking in subsystems, containing private and public actors and active and effective communication to sustain strong bonds (Belmonte & Cerny, 2021; Weible & Sabatier, 2017). This approach is relevant today because of fading global boundaries and the escalating incompetence of the state. There is a need for a global political transformation and collaborative problem-solving.

Social and political networks explore actors and their relationships and advance actors' capabilities, perceptions, and preferences as necessary in the policy process (Weible & Sabatier, 2017). While interaction among actors can be conflictual, bargaining, or cooperative, the distribution of actors' capabilities defines the power structure of the network and the policy monopoly (Jenkins-Smith & Sabatier, 1994; Weible & Sabatier, 2017).

Previous politics have been bound by territory and nation-states, but this system is creating problems of administration and command today. Political organization that is centered on flexible power tracks is the most effective in shaping policy outcomes and contemporary politics.

7. Conclusion

The modern environment is turbulent, wobbly, volatile and challenging to prescribe. In this environment, the only constant is change, and change is always uncomfortable and upsetting but offers hope for a reshuffle, new prospects, innovative knowledge, and attitudes. Change impacts political attitudes and expectations. Over the last year, the world has experienced dramatic political shifts with the arrival of COVID-19. Many core issues were put on hold as the pandemic became the governments' top preoccupation. Citizens expressed their approval and disapproval of policy decisions and state action in areas such as paid sick leave, childcare, protection for seniors, stimulus packages and vaccine rollout plans. So, how have these adjustments impacted politics?

First, there appears to be a more significant divide among nations as they prioritize and protect their populations. A challenge lies in arriving at foreign policies suited to a multipolar world amid rising tensions among significant players. Second, the business community appears to be losing confidence in the state to secure its long-term growth, as economies are in crisis due to the pandemic. Third, topics like poverty, environmental concerns, immigration, and racism have now re-emerged, and more people are now aware of these realities and demand shifts in policy to re-think and re-address these critical issues. Fourth, differences in perspectives among generations will impact political ideologies and responses to policies. Fifth, the digitization of life as information technologies contribute to the "infodemic," and the rapid spread of information through social media may threaten states attempting to implement control.

During the COVID-19 pandemic, states presented themselves as the principal force of guidance and direction. It can be argued that their role has been more critical due to citizens' expectations of practical measures and protection against loss. Are we witnessing a reversion to nationalism, state sovereignty and the great power conundrum of the state? Do we see a more weakened state as their response to the pandemic is criticized as inadequate and unimpressive?

These political, social, and economic alterations are diagnosed as features of a postinternational world in which turbulence and distant proximities pervade. Attempts at state territoriality and prominence prove impractical and unfeasible in a constantly changing, multifaceted, and intersecting structure.

As an alternative, heterarchical structures present an approach to governance that reenergizes politics in dynamic and complex conditions. Traditional politics is confronted by layers of autonomous actors involved in responsibility and decision-making. Regulating dynamism and complexity with heterarchical arrangements can enhance stability and efficiency because it accounts for hierarchical systems still in place while also dispersed across levels and layers. This approach can improve the flexibility of governance and its overall effectiveness.

Policy networks are characterized by pluralistic, interdependent, heterogeneous actors found in complex network relations. The interdependence between governments and interest groups, and policy networks offer a new perspective of governance alongside bureaucracies and markets. This process of exchange and interaction cannot be side-lined because the policy process involves public, private, formal, and informal entities and the need to solve problems with multifocal perspectives. Policy networks offer significant potential for governance to be strengthened despite state failure and economic collapse.

Since heterarchy dispenses with notions of rigidity, validation, and domination, innovation is unearthed. Heterarchical structures typically favor values and norms consistent with an innovative, creative culture. Efficiency is achieved through adaptability, multiple channels, and numerous approaches to enabling ingenuity.

These ideas present some exciting implications. Governance can flourish in turbulent settings by adopting a heterarchical form in which authority is decentralized and specialization is advanced. The higher systems need not flatten unconventional political actors; instead, networks and coalitions offer a solution to turbulence and enable political systems to reinvent and bolster themselves. Ultimately, the introduction of heterarchy provides new opportunities to accumulate knowledge and experience and heightens the ability of diverse actors to collaborate in the policy-making process.

References

Andaya, B. (2017). Glocalization and the Marketing of Christianity in Early Modern Southeast Asia. *Religions*, 8 (1): 7. doi: 10.3390/rel8010007

Ansell, C., Trondal, J., & Ogard, M. (2017). *Governance in Turbulent Times*. Oxford: Oxford University.

Bellamy, R. (2017). A European Republic of Sovereign States: Sovereignty, Republicanism and the European Union. *European Journal of Political Theory*, 188–209. doi: 10.1177/1474885116654389

Belmonte, R., & Cerny, P. G. (2021). Heterarchy: Toward Paradigm Shift in World Politics. *Journal of Political Power*, 14 (1): 235–257. doi: 10.1080/2158379X.2021.1879574

Bubolz, M. M., & Sontag, M. S. (2009). Human Ecology Theory. In *Sourcebook of Family Theories and Methods* (pp. 419–450). Boston, MA: Springer.

Byrne, D. (1998). *Complexity Theory and the Social Sciences: An Introduction*. London: Routledge.

Cerny, Philip G. and Prichard, Alex (2017). "The NewAnarchy: Globalisation and Fragmentation in 21st Century World Politics", *Journal of International Political Theory*, vol. 13, no. 3 (October), pp. 378–394.

Crumley, C. (2015). Heterarchy. In S. Kosslyn, ed. *Emerging Trends in the Social and Behavioral Sciences* (pp. 1–14). Hoboken, NJ: John Wiley and Sons.

Curry, D. (2012). *The Structure-Agency Paradox of New Forms of Non-Binding Governance: Actor Networks, Multi-Level Governance and Canadian and EU Lessons*. Working Paper for 2012, 84th Annual Conference of the Canadian Political Science Association, 13–15 June 2012, University of Alberta.

Curry, D. (2018). *Multi-Level Governance in British Columbia*. British Columbia, Canada. Retrieved from www.researchgate.net/publication/320085647_Multilevel_Governance_of_Sustaiability_Transitions_in_Canada_Policy_Alignment_Innovation_and_Evaluation

Ferguson, Y., & Mansbach, R. (2007). Post Internationalism and IR theory. *Journal of International Studies*, 529–550. doi: 10.1177/03058298070350031001

Galaz, V., & Pierre, J. (2017). Superconnected, Complex and Ultrafast: Governance of Hyperfunctionality in Financial Markets. *Complexity Governance & Networks*, 3 (2): 12. doi: 10.20377/cgn-55

Gordon, S. (2017). *Online Communities as Agents of Change and Social Movements*. PA: IGI Global.

Guy, S. (2009). What is Global and What is Local? A Theoretical Discussion around Globalization. *Parsons Journal for Information Mapping*. Retrieved from http://piim. newschool.edu/journal/issues/2009/02/pdfs/ParsonsJournalForInformationMapping_Guy-JeanSebastian.pdf

Harvey, D., & Reed, M. (1996). Social Science as the Study of Complex Systems. In L. D. Kiel and E. Elliott, eds. *Chaos Theory in the Social Sciences: Foundations and Applications*. Ann Arbor: University of Michigan Press.

Henning, C. (2009). Networks of Power in the CAP System of the EU-15 and EU-27. *Journal of Public Policy*, 29(2): 153–177.

Hobbs, H. H. (2000). *Pondering Postinternationalism*. New York: State University of New York.

Hofstadter, D. (1979). *Godel, Escher, Bach: An Eternal Golden Braid*. New York: Basic Books.

Jenkins-Smith, H., & Sabatier, P. (1994). Evaluating the Advocacy Coalition Framework. *Journal of Public Policy*, 14 (2): 175–203. Retrieved May 5, 2021, from www.jstor.org/stable/4007571

Karns, M., Mingst, K., & Stiles, K. (2015). *International Organizations*. CO: Lynne Rienner.

Kibbler, J. (2011). Cognitive Disequilibrium. *Encyclopedia of Child Behaviour and Development*, 380. doi: 10.1007/springerreference_179877

Kontopoulos, K. (1993). *The Logics of Social Structure*. New York: Cambridge University Press.

Lipschutz, R. D. (2000). Crossing Borders: Global Civil Society and the Reconfiguration of Transnational Political Space. *GeoJournal*, 52, 17–23. https://doi.org/10.1023/A:1013162812371

Maull, H. (2011). *World Politics in Turbulence*. Retrieved from library.fes.de: http://library.fes.de/pdf-files/ipg/ipg-2011-1/2011-1__03_a_maull.pdf

McCulloch, Warren S. (1945). A Heterarchy of Values Determined by the Topology of Nervous Nets. *Bulletin of Mathematical Biophysics* 7: 89–93.

McNair, B. (2017). *An Introduction to Political Communication*, 6th ed. London; New York: Routledge.

Minsky, M., & Papert, S. (1972). *Artificial Intelligence Progress Report* (AI Memo 252). Cambridge, MA: MIT Artificial Intelligence Laboratory.

Mouzelis, N. (1995). *Sociological Theory: What Went Wrong?* London: Routledge.

Papadopoulos, Y. (2010). Accountability and Multi-Level Governance: More Accountability, Less Democracy? *West European Politics*, 33(5): 1030–1049.

Pierre, J., & Galaz, V. (2017). Superconnected, Complex and Ultrafast: Governance of Hyperfunctionality in Financial Markets. *Complexity, Governance & Networks*, 12–28. doi: 10.20377/cgn-55

Ramadan, A., & Fregonese, S. (2017). Hybrid Sovereignty and the State of Exception in the Palestinian Refugee Camps in Lebanon. *Annals of the American Association of Geographers*, 107 (4): 949–963. doi: 10.1080/24694452.2016.1270189

Rogers, D. (2009). *Postinternationalism and Small Arms Control: Theory, Politics, Security*. Burlington: Ashgate.

Rosenau, J. N. (1990). *Turbulence in World Politics: A Theory of Change and Continuity*. New Jersey: Princeton University Press.

Rosenau, J. N. (2003). *Dynamics beyond Globalization*. New Jersey: Princeton University Press. 2016.1160599.

Stark, D. (2010). Ambiguous Assets for Uncertain Environments: Heterarchy in Postsocialist Firms. *Journal of Economic Sociology*, 1 (2): 7–34. doi: 10.17323/17263247-2000-2-7-34

Strange, S. (1996). *The Retreat of the State: The Diffusion of Power in the World Economy* (Cambridge Studies in International Relations). Cambridge: Cambridge University Press. doi: 10.1017/CBO9780511559143

Tarrow, S. (2010). The Strategy of Paired Comparison: Toward a Theory of Practice. *Comparative Political Studies*, 43 (2): 230–259. https://doi.org/10.1177/0010414009350044

Trondal, J., & Bauer, M. (2017). Conceptualizing the European Multilevel Administrative Order. Capturing Variation in the European Administrative System. *European Political Science Review* vol. 1, no. 1, pp. 1–22 (Sept. 2015).

Wang, F. (2010). The Evolution of Hierarchy toward Heterarchy. *Frontiers of Business Research in China*, 515–540. doi: 10.1007/s11782-010-0109-9

Weatherby, J., Arceneaux, C., Leithner, A., Reed, I., Timms, B., & Zhang, S. (2017). *The Other World: Issues and Politics in the Developing World*, 10th ed. New York: Routledge.

Weible, M., & Sabatier, P. (2017). *Theories of the Policy Process*, 4th ed. New York: Westview.

Worth, O. (2017). *Hegemony, International Political Economy and Post-Communist Russia*. London; New York: Routledge.

3

HETERARCHY AND SOCIAL THEORY

Carole L. Crumley

Introduction

The concept of heterarchy has been widely used by anthropologists, archaeologists, and sociologists to study the complexity and unevenness of social structures and processes. As with political scientists, these theorists and analysts have been deeply invested in the study of the state and political power for more than a century. For example, there is the work of James C. Scott, who is trained in both anthropology and in political science. His several books (e.g., 1985, 1998, 2009, 2017) on the subject have been met with considerable appreciation in anthropology and archaeology, with some critique that nonetheless illuminates the potential for his ideas and closer relations among anthropologists, archaeologists, and political scientists.

For a particularly lucid overview of the evolution of anthropological and archaeological research on state-level societies, I recommend Christopher More-hart and colleagues' introduction to a volume that takes up politics in the context of heterarchy (Morehart et al. 2018) and particularly Wendy Ashmore's thoughtful overview in that volume (Ashmore 2018). Also useful is Vernon Scarborough's (2018) review of James C. Scott's *Against the Grain* (2017). Finally, if you wish to understand how the current paradigm as regards state formation will soon be replaced in many disciplines and for the general public, read *The Dawn of Everything* by David Graeber and David Wengrow (2021).

In this chapter I offer an overview of heterarchy and its essential characteristics, and some means by which heterarchy might be further employed in studying the organization of power.

1. Expanding the Study of Power Relations

My interest in heterarchy arose from my discomfort with an assumption. In the social sciences the architecture of power is routinely described as hierarchical: that

DOI: 10.4324/9781003352617-4

is, tiered and ranked. While this description may fit popular understanding, it does not capture the collective and dynamic management strategies that undergird forms of exchange in all societies. Thus, the sociopolitical structure of so-called "complex" societies (chiefdoms and states, in less recent archaeological terms; see Morehart et al. 2018) is assumed to be ranked or hierarchical, despite archaeological and ethnographic evidence that economic, political, and social power takes many complex forms that are not entirely hierarchical, even in nation-states.

Historically this assumption has provided the intellectual and moral rationale for scientific racism, colonialism, and other forms of domination, in that "complex" societies (e.g., nation-states) were considered more advanced than "simple" (e.g., pastoral) societies, the antidote being conquest and rehabilitation. In this guise, complexity refers to the number of levels in a hierarchy. Hierarchy remains a controlling model: ubiquitous, unchallenged, and all but invisible (Clarke 1972; Crumley 1987:157).

All past and present human societies are fluid, interdependent, and characterized both by levels and by richly networked nodes and links. As it happens, concepts and methods in many social sciences and in the humanities have anticipated research into complex systems; there already exist ways of gathering knowledge and recognizing patterns that are better prepared for the unexpected, and that move beyond the limitations of quantitative analysis and reductionist models. This humanist exploration of the many dimensions of human activity and thought elegantly explores the non-linear and ultimately unpredictable world in which we live.

There is considerable evidence for heterarchical social and political formations in the past. The archaeological record confirms many forms of social power (e.g., Angelbeck and Grier 2012; Becker and Juengst 2020; Crumley 2003; Ehrenreich et al. 1995; Kohring and Wynne-Jones 2007; McIntosh 1999; Ray and Fernández-Gotz 2021). Many recent interpretive advances in archaeological theory (e.g., gender, class, and ethnicity in the archaeological record) begin as a critique of the assumption of hierarchy in power relations.

It is particularly important to have language that permits description of how power relations change over time. How can system-wide change be understood holistically, without resorting to the simplistic notion of "collapse"? For example, what are the system-wide effects of the breakdown of elite dominance of trade? Perhaps an equally hierarchical "mafia" takes over, or perhaps a guild, or an association of independent shippers. Each potential arrangement has very different implications for the society as a whole. Heterarchies of power-coalitions, federations, leagues, associations, communities-are just as important in states as they are in non-state polities.

In a larger sense, the ability to trace past societies' political forms *in context* is fundamental to understanding what factors kept the society sustainable and which led to its demise. The heterarchy/hierarchy framework enables the search for these and other forms, along with their social, political, environmental, and values-based contexts. With these tools, organizational change can be studied, and its findings applied to the future.

2. An Overview of Heterarchy

Heterarchy addresses the diversity of relationships among elements in a system and offers a way to think about change in spatial, temporal, and cognitive dimensions. This section outlines the convergent origins of the idea, examines the evidence for the ubiquity of heterarchy in mathematical and biophysical contexts and in human societies, explores its application in the social sciences, and advances understanding of how heterarchical thinking can help envision the human future.

The earliest definition is by McCulloch (1945) who examined cognitive structures in the brain, the collective organization of which he terms heterarchy. He demonstrates that the human brain is not organized hierarchically but adjusts to the re-ranking of values as circumstances change. The heterarchical structure of individual and collective memory may be a chief means by which human societies address change and the inevitable conflicts that arise (Mithen 1996). McCulloch contrasts a hierarchy of (ranked) values with a heterarchy of values that defies both ranking and predictability (1945).

In artificial intelligence and computer design, Minsky and Papert (1972) refer to the organization of computer sub-routines that can call one another as heterarchical. Mathematician Hofstadter (1979:134) defines heterarchy as a program in which there is no "highest level." Sociologist Stark defines heterarchy as "an emergent organizational form with distinctive network properties . . . and multiple organizing principles" (2001; 2009). Social theorist Kontopoulos defines heterarchy as "a partially ordered level structure implicating a rampant interactional complexity" (1993:381). I offer a general-purpose definition that suits a variety of contexts: the relation of elements to one another when they are unranked, or when they possess the potential for being ranked in a number of different ways, depending on systemic requirements (Crumley 1979:144). These definitions offer an arena for examining diversity and change in systems, organizations, or structures. In general, heterarchical relations are sources of difference and dynamism, and they may be spatial, temporal, or cognitive.

For example, an individual may highly value human life in general and be against abortion rights, but be for the death penalty (or vice versa). The context of the inquiry, along with changing (and conflicting) values, mitigates this logical inconsistency; they are related to what Bateson (1972) terms a "double bind." Priorities are re-ranked relative to conditions and can result in major structural adjustment. McCulloch's "nervous nets," the source of the brain's flexibility, are structurally similar to the adaptive capacities of fluidly organized, highly communicative groups. His work reminds us that it is quintessentially human to make nimble cognitive leaps among scales.

McCulloch's insight about the autonomous nature of information and communication in the brain revolutionized its neural study; it also solved major organizational problems in the fields of artificial intelligence and computer design (Minsky and Papert 1972). McCulloch (1989) realized that information stored in bundles as values in one part of the brain may or may not be correlated with information stored elsewhere; in computer terminology, subroutine A can subsume ("call") subroutine B and vice versa, depending on the requirements of the program, in contrast with the "tree" hierarchy of the first computers. Today, all computers use an addressing (information locating) Random Access Memory (RAM) system that is heterarchical.

Heterarchy does not stand alone but is in a dialectical relationship with hierarchy (where elements are ranked). This means that both heterarchical and hierarchical forms are routinely found in the same entity, although from a mathematical standpoint heterarchy is the more general category and subsumes hierarchy as a special case (von Goldammer et al. 2003). While heterarchy may be modeled mathematically, it need not rely on mathematical or spatial representations for its application; heterarchy is equally useful as an abstract model or in a narrative. In exhibiting this flexibility, it resembles emergence or self-organization in complex systems.

Heterarchy meets three criteria upon which any social model must be judged (Byrne 1998:46; Harvey and Reed 1996; Kontopoulos 1993; Mouzelis 1995). They are: (1) How adequate is the model in relating the micro (individual) level to the macro (social) level? (2) How adequate is the model in relating the conscious agency of social actors to the social structure in which they operate? (3) Can it provide an explanation for discontinuous and fundamental changes in the social system as a whole? Heterarchy can be said to meet these requirements for a robust social theory.

3. Paradigm Shifts

The flexibility and polyvalence of heterarchy are some of its most attractive qualities and explain, at least in part, why the idea has steadily gained popularity in the biological, physical, and social science disciplines (e.g., Crumley 2005, 2007, 2015; Latour 2005). There is now clear evidence that economic, political, and social power take many forms and are never entirely hierarchical, even in the most autocratic states. In a recent volume (Ray and Fernandez-Gotz 2021) the authors argue that stable collaborative governance has a long history, that both hierarchical and heterarchical relations are demonstrably complex, and that together they enable the analysis of shifting forms of power over time.

The definition of *complexity*, not that of heterarchy, poses the greatest barrier to applications in the social sciences. For decades, social scientists have uncritically embraced a paradigm and constructed models that define social complexity in terms of *levels* (a spatial position on a vertical axis) of organization. In the biophysical sciences *complex systems* are interdependent, richly networked, and characterized by *nodes, links*, and *networks*, not levels. Except for their epistemology, biophysical complex systems are without rank. Instead, *state* (a particular combination of properties) serves the function of level in the social sciences. While analytic tools that distinguish time intervals or spatial distance are indispensable, it is a mistake to confuse the analytic architecture with that which is being analyzed, creating everywhere a tiered landscape of power (Crumley 1987, 2005; De Landa 2000).

As Ostrom (1990) and others (e.g., Lindholm et al. 2013) demonstrate, communities have found ways to organize their collective and individual tasks without central authority. They identify "design principles" of stable common-pool resource management that include local knowledge, clear rules, effective communication, monitoring, sanctions, paths for conflict resolution, internal trust, and the recognition of self-determination by other institutions.

In archaeology, the old paradigm has given way, in part due to archaeologists' realization that many of them have spent their careers digging sites full of evidence for collaborative management. A more balanced paradigm has begun to take its place, one that sees many sources of power and new implications for governance. This paradigm shift started several decades ago, but has only found acceptance in the past decade. It is important that this dynamic moment and its implications be fully examined (Graeber and Wengrow 2021).

Thomas Kuhn's *The Structure of Scientific Revolutions* (1962, 1970) has thrilled generations of young scholars with the prospect that their work would revolutionize their chosen field. For Kuhn, *paradigms* are universally recognized scientific frameworks that, for a time, provide model problems and solutions to a community of practitioners (1970:viii). Kuhn's book introduced into common usage the term *paradigm shift*, meaning a fundamental change in a widely used model or perception.

Kuhn defines *scientific revolutions* as

> when . . . the profession [adopts] a new set of commitments, a new basis for the practice of science. The extraordinary episodes in which that shift of professional commitments occurs are the ones known . . . as *scientific revolutions*. They are the tradition-shattering complements to the tradition-bound activity of normal science.
>
> *(1970:6)*

Kuhn reminds us that there are elements, levels, and dimensions of paradigmatic methods and theories, each of which must be retained, modified, or disassembled with due consideration (1970:34). So it behooves us to hold *revolutions*—scientific or otherwise—in abeyance, and take the time to proceed carefully.

Accordingly, the enormous body of work that has focused on hierarchies of power need not be jettisoned. The uncovering of alternate paths to power marks the beginning of a more complete understanding of how societal governance is achieved and what can emerge from the transtemporal examination of political forms and their fluctuating utility in environmental, social, and other contexts.

The social implications of the new paradigm could reverse understandings that have prevailed for millennia. One example is the current global shift in the understanding of sex and gender. In archaeology, despite a number of early 20th-century pioneers, the climate for women was chilly through the 1980s.

As women's presence in the field was accepted, new ways of seeing sex and gender in the archaeological record emerged (Gero and Conkey 1991; Spector 1993) and evidence was re-evaluated. Advances in methods have strengthened these new interpretations (e.g., Hedenstierna-Jonson et al. 2017).

A recent volume reports archaeological findings (Thurston and Fernández-Götz 2021) that question aggression as a central driver toward centralization. The authors argue that individual power requires social interaction and the social recognition of roles. Our findings are that collectively organized centers enjoyed longer apogees than their autocratic neighbors, which suggests that compliance built on trust makes strong communities. Tracing shifting power relations over time, the changing roles of elements in past landscapes—food storage units, enclosures, defensive structures—lead to a more robust explanation of the motivations for monumental construction. The authors question earlier characterizations of certain peoples and eras as bellicose, demonstrating that new evidence points instead to community-based defense. This approach supports a new appreciation of the importance of trust in social and political relations.

Next steps are to extract this knowledge from the archaeological, historical, and contemporary record, and to learn how to grow and integrate frameworks that include both ranked and nested structures along with those that are flatter and networked, and forms that are yet to be recognized. The balancing of social, geographical and temporal diversity with multivalent conceptual coherence points a clear way to proceed. It is in this manner that a new vision of the world order can emerge.

4. Deploying Heterarchy in the Social Sciences

There is a paucity of language to describe structures or relations that are not hierarchical. Some effort has been made to enrich the descriptive vocabulary of nonlinear (not predictable) relations among entities: sociologist Kontopoulos offers "tangled composite structures" (1993:55), philosopher De Landa suggests "meshworks" (1997), ecologists Gunderson and Holling prefer "panarchy" (2001), and there is considerable interest among anthropologists and political scientists in social forms that hold resources in common, from common pool assets (Agrawal 2003; Ostrom 1990) to anarchy (Graeber 2004; Scott 2012). Here the term anarchy does not refer to popular notions of lawlessness, but to principles of *self-organization*: individual and local autonomy, voluntary association, mutual aid, communal decision making, network organization, and the rejection of imposed power (Angelbeck and Grier 2012:551).

There are also efforts to redefine hierarchy in a way that allows for varying degrees of connectivity and control (e.g., Ahl and Allen 1996; Allen and Starr 1982; Bondarenko 2007). In a control hierarchy each higher level exerts control over the next lower level; the US court system and the army are control hierarchies. In contrast, disturbances at any level in a scalar hierarchy can affect any other scales (Crumley 1995:2), more in keeping with ecological principles that do not emphasize a ranking of species. This is because in control hierarchies, the same people and/or groups control multiple sources of power (e.g., religious, military, diplomatic, commercial): information and the means of communicating it become commodities to be hoarded (e.g., literacy). In *scalar hierarchies*, elements at all scales are in communication with one another. Scalar hierarchies are found in many types of systems, ranging from the simplest (static, mechanical) to the most complex (language, self-consciousness) and constitute a holistic world (Jantsch 1982:349). As such, scalar hierarchies combine hierarchical and heterarchical elements.

This glance into the struggle to develop a vocabulary to describe heterarchical relations suggests that the concept should be considered a placeholder awaiting the emergence of a new way of thinking, particularly as regards human organization. For example, definitions of the terms *scale, complexity,* and *system* pose the greatest barrier to wider application of complex systems in the social sciences, where many researchers recall all too well earlier uses of the terms. Definitions often confuse epistemological and ontological applications of scale: epistemological scale is a spatial or temporal tool deployed by the investigator, while ontological scale is a demonstrable characteristic of what is being studied. This confusion is important because it often exhibits unconscious hierarchical thinking. Thus, forms may be termed "complex" if they contain many levels (tiered, hierarchical) and also if they comprise many links (networked, heterarchical).

What distinguishes contemporary complex systems science from the systems theory of the 1960s is that the definition of *system* has profoundly changed. Today's complex adaptive systems are no longer tidy, closed models unperturbed by change. They are messy and dynamic, nonlinear (exhibiting behavior of limited predictability), are connected to the larger environment, and can completely change state. Complex systems have no up and down, no ranking, no steps and no stages. Instead, dimension (a non-spatial category) or state (a particular combination of properties) serves to discriminate groupings of system elements and recurrent conditions.

Thus, complex systems are interdependent, richly networked and characterized not by levels, but by nodes, links, and networks. Contemporary complex systems research is not a single theory; rather it aggregates several highly interdisciplinary strands of investigation that are widely applied in the biological, physical and social sciences, business, law, and elsewhere. Any single formal description of complexity is inadequate to capture all its properties (Mikulecky 2007).

5. A Closer Look at Authority Structures

It is both impractical and inaccurate to exclude such a fundamental adjustment mechanism from the characterization of any political form, however large or small its population. The more a society consolidates power and melds distinct hierarchies (e.g., religious, political, economic) into hyperhierarchy or hypercoherence (where the same individuals, factions, or groups hold many sources of power), the less flexibility there is in dealing with surprise (Piketty 2014).

White (1995:118) provides a useful scheme for understanding continua in the various organizational dimensions of complex societies, characterizing rules for behavior, gender relations, economy, social status, conflict resolution, ideology, the relation between leaders and followers, and temporal dynamics. To this I add an examination of the contrasting conditions of decision making and clarify the relation between administrative structure and environmental stability and change. To do this, I simplify a diverse landscape of forms that characterize societies' rules of political engagement.

Hierarchical polities. Administrators in strong hierarchies (authoritarian states, oligarchies, hyperhierarchies) have a number of advantages. Due to a clear decision-making chain, they respond well to fast-developing crises (e.g., military attack, insurrection). Because the rules and responsibilities are familiar, political interactions among decision makers are few and formalized, and political maintenance of the system is low. Administrative hierarchies are equipped with powerful security forces that can successfully defend the state perimeter and suppress internal dissent.

Hierarchical polities are at a disadvantage because data-gathering techniques, tied to the pyramidal decision-making framework, slow the arrival of some kinds of information (especially subversive activity) at the apex of the pyramid and necessitate the formalization and elaboration of internal security forces. Decisions are not necessarily popular; popular dissatisfaction is high and there must be considerable investment in coercion or propaganda. Security costs are high.

Heterarchical polities. Administrators in polities with strong heterarchical organization receive good quality information from many sources within and outside of the decision-making lattice. In general, decisions are fair and reflect popular consensus. Decision makers hear of a variety of solutions to problems. Because heterarchies are more likely to value the contributions of disparate segments of the community (e.g., ethnic groups, women), the society as a whole is better integrated, and the workforce is proud and energized.

Heterarchical polities are at a disadvantage because consensus is slow to achieve, increasing the time it takes to arrive at a decision. Decision makers must engage in dialogue with constituents; this requires considerable time and energy investment and constant maintenance. The cacophonous voices and choices a decision maker hears complicate the search for workable solutions.

Tradeoffs. The greater a group's involvement, the greater the possible response and the more inclusive the consensus, but the response time is slower and long-range planning is more difficult. Spontaneity, polyvalent individuality linked to achieved status, a counterpoised definition of state power, and flexibility are valued in heterarchies; hierarchies value rule-based authority, rigid class lines linked to ascribed as well as achieved status and rank, a control definition of state power, and the status quo. Of course, state democracies exhibit characteristics of both, which explains in part why they are more stable than authoritarian states.

6. Key Issues for Future Research

In all societies, the power of various individuals and factions fluctuates relative to changing circumstances. Today, as resources worldwide are being depleted and environmental conditions deteriorate, new ways to stabilize societies and reduce conflict must be found. One of the most important conditions for reducing conflict is to ensure inclusive and equitable conditions for everyone, particularly as regards food and water security, personal and group safety, and a satisfying quality of life.

In non-linear systems, heterarchy is related to symmetry-breaking, a key feature and source of novelty in evolution. In human societies, heterarchy is a corrective to power theories that conflate hierarchy with (civil) order, thereby creating a conundrum: will you submit and be safe or resist at your peril? To re-envision an equitable future for humankind, there must be a means to conceptualize and evaluate shifts between exclusive and inclusive power relations in diverse spatial and temporal scales and contexts, and to assess their implications for society and their suitability for the future.

Created in the process of building nation states around the globe, analytic tools that measure efficiency illuminate only hierarchical political, economic, and social forms and ignore the stabilizing power of heterarchical forms; thus, hyper-hierarchical and other inherently unstable forms of wealth distribution and political power accumulate. The controlling model of hierarchy-as-order, ubiquitous and all but invisible, exacerbates growing tensions.

New tools can produce reliable determinations of historic risk and vulnerability from the individual to large populations. Bioarchaeologists are among the leaders in the study of paleopolitics: their research can form a picture of life-as-lived, marking stressful and tranquil periods that the person or the group survived and identifying both individual and group mobility. Together with other research in public policies, systems of exchange, subsistence strategies, and social roles, this information can reveal how people obtained resources and how they experienced the result of toil and violence.

This recent work also demonstrates an impressive range in size of cooperative political bodies. While community-wide governance in smaller sized groups is no surprise, there were also cooperative states, regions, and urban agglomerations (Callejón de Huaylas/Requay, central Thailand, Mimbres, Tiawanaku, Marroquíes) and even empires (Xianbei, Genghis Khan's Mongols) that were collaboratively organized (Becker and Juengst 2020; see also Thurston and Fernández-Götz 2021). Minimally, this understanding will require a re-thinking of how states are defined, and in what circumstances large collaborative formations appear.

This is important information for the human future: the old paradigm that asserted competition and conflict as the primary motors of civilization can now be refuted with solid evidence. In the course of human history, societies engaged in cooperative activities which advanced their wellbeing, as well as periodically falling into conflict. If we begin with the premise that the tension between competition and cooperation exists in all human societies, it then behooves us to explore the ways rules and norms permit or deny each, and how both interact with history and changing conditions to forge institutions (Chapman 2003).

The political climates of the past demonstrate that human accomplishment is not on a rising staircase culminating in the State; instead, we find a long history of diverse experiments and their results, to which we now have access. In the contemporary world, how can the equity and effectiveness of coalitions, federations, leagues, unions, and communities in societies of all sizes help envision societies of the future?

References

Agrawal, Arun (2003). Sustainable Governance of Common-Pool Resources: Context, Methods, and Politics. *Annual Review of Anthropology* 32:243–262.

Ahl, V. and T. F. H. Allen (1996). *Hierarchy Theory, a Vision, Vocabulary and Epistemology*. New York: Columbia University Press.

Allen, T. F. H. and T. B. Starr (1982). *Hierarchy: Perspectives for Ecological Complexity*. Chicago: University Chicago Press.

Angelbeck, Bill and Colin Grier (2012). Anarchism and the Archaeology of Anarchic Societies: Resistance to Centralization in the Coast Salish Region of the Pacific Northwest Coast. *Current Anthropology* 53(5):547–587.

Ashmore, Wendy (2018). Why the Archaeology of Political Ecology Matters. *Archaeological Papers of the American Anthropological Association* Special Issue 29(1) *Uneven Terrain: Archaeologies of Political Ecology* 175–184.

Bateson, Gregory (1972). *Steps Toward an Ecology of Mind*. New York: Ballantine.

Becker, Sara K. and Sara L. Juengst, eds. (2020). Cooperative Bodies: Bioarchaeologists Address Nonranked Societies. Vital Topics Forum. *American Anthropologist* 122(4).

Bondarenko, D.M. (2007). What is there in a Word? Heterarchy, Homoarchy and the Difference in Understanding Complexity in the Social Sciences and Complexity Studies. In *Explorations in Complexity Thinking: Pre-Proceedings of the 3rd International Workshop on Complexity and Philosophy*, K.A. Richardson and P. Cilliers, eds., pp. 35–48. Mansfield, MA: ISCE Publishing.

Byrne, David (1998). *Complexity Theory and the Social Sciences: An Introduction*. London: Routledge.

Chapman, Robert (2003). *Archaeologies of Complexity*. London: Routledge.

Clarke, David L. (1972). Models and Paradigms in Contemporary Archaeology. In *Models in Archaeology*, David L. Clarke, ed., pp. 47–52. New York: Academic Press.

Crumley, Carole L. (1979). Three Locational Models: An Epistemological Assessment for Anthropology and Archaeology. In *Advances in Archaeological Method and Theory*, Michael B. Schiffer, ed., pp. 141–173. Amsterdam and London: Elsevier.

Crumley, Carole L. (1987). A Dialectical Critique of Hierarchy. In *Power Relations and State Formation*, Thomas C. Patterson and Christine Ward Gailey, eds., pp. 155–168. Washington: American Anthropological Association.

Crumley, Carole L. (1995). Heterarchy and the Analysis of Complex Societies. In *Heterarchy and the Analysis of Complex Societies*, Robert M. Ehrenreich, Carole L. Crumley, and Janet E. Levy, eds. Washington: American Anthropological Association.

Crumley, Carole L. (2003). Alternative Forms of Societal Order. In *Heterarchy, Political Economy, and the Ancient Maya: The Three Rivers Region of the East-Central Yucatan Peninsula*, Vernon Scarborough, Fred Valdez Jr., and Nicholas Dunning, eds., pp. 136–145. Tucson: University of Arizona Press.

Crumley, Carole L. (2005). Remember How to Organize: Heterarchy Across Disciplines. In *Nonlinear Models for Archaeology and Anthropology*, Christopher S. Beekman and William S. Baden, eds., pp. 35–50. Aldershot (Hampshire), UK: Ashgate Press.

Crumley, Carole L. (2007). Heterarchy. In *International Encyclopedia of the Social Sciences* (Second edition, volume 3), William A. Darity, ed., pp. 468–469. Detroit: Macmillan Reference USA.

Crumley, Carole L. (2015). Heterarchy. In *Emerging Trends in the Social and Behavioral Sciences*, R. Scott and S. Kosslyn, eds. New York: Wiley & Sons. doi: 10.1002/9781118900772.etrds0158

De Landa, Manuel (1997). *A Thousand Years of Non-Linear History*. New York: Zone Books.

Ehrenreich, Robert M., Carole L. Crumley, and Janet E. Levy, eds. (1995). *Heterarchy and the Analysis of Complex Societies. Archaeological Papers of the American Anthropological Association* no. 6. Washington: American Anthropological Association.

Gero, Joan and Margaret Conkey, eds. (1991). *Engendering Archaeology*. Oxford: Blackwell.

Graeber, David (2004). *Fragments of an Anarchist Anthropology*. Chicago: Prickly Paradigm Press (distributed by University of Chicago Press).

Graeber, David and David Wengrow (2021). *The Dawn of Everything: A New History of Humanity*. London: Allen Lane.

Gunderson, Lance and C. S. Holling (2001). *Panarchy: Understanding Transformations in Systems of Humans and Nature*. Washington: Island Press.

Harvey, David L. and Michael Reed (1996). Social Science as the Study of Complex Systems. In *Chaos Theory in the Social Sciences: Foundations and Applications*, L. D. Kiel and E. Elliott, eds. Ann Arbor: University of Michigan Press.

Hedenstierna-Jonson, Charlotte, Kjellström, Anna, Zachrisson, Torun, Krzewińska, Maja, Sobrado, Veronica, Price, Neil, Günther, Torsten, Jakobsson, Mattias, Götherström, Anders (2017). A Female Viking Warrior Confirmed by Genomics. *American Journal of Physical Anthropology* 164(4):853–860. doi:10.1002/ajpa.23308. ISSN 1096–8644. PMC 5724682. PMID 28884802.

Hofstadter, Douglas (1979). *Godel, Escher, Bach: An Eternal Golden Braid*. New York: Basic Books.

Jantsch, Erich (1982). From Self-Reference to Self-Transcendence: The Evolution of Self-Organization Dynamics. In *Self-Organization and Dissipative Structures: Applications in the Physical and Social Sciences*, William C. Schieve and Peter M. Allen, eds., pp. 344–361. Austin: University of Texas Press.

Kohring, Sheila and Stephanie Wynne-Jones (2007). *Socialising Complexity: Structure, Interaction and Power in Archaeological Discourse*. Oxford: Oxbow Books.

Kontopoulos, Kyriakos (1993). *The Logics of Social Structure*. New York: Cambridge University Press.

Kuhn, Thomas A. (1970). *The Structure of Scientific Revolutions* (First edition 1962). Chicago: University of Chicago Press.

Latour, Bruno (2005). *Reassembling the Social: An Introduction to Actor-Network-Theory*. Oxford: Oxford University Press.

Lindholm, Karl-Johan, Sandström, Emil, and Ekman, Ann-Kristin (2013). The Archaeology of the Commons. *Journal of Archaeology and Ancient History* 10.

McCulloch, Warren S. (1945). A Heterarchy of Values Determined by the Topology of Nervous Nets. *Bulletin of Mathematical Biophysics* 7:89–93.

McCulloch, Warren S. (1989). *Embodiments of Mind*. Cambridge: MIT Press.

McIntosh, Susan Keech (1999). *Beyond Chiefdoms: Pathways to Complexity in Africa*. Cambridge: Cambridge University Press.

Mikulecky, Donald C. (2007). Complexity Science as an Aspect of the Complexity of Science. In *Worldviews, Science, and Us: Philosophy and Complexity*, Carolos Gershenson, Diederik Aerts, and Bruce Edmonds, eds., pp. 30–52. Singapore: World Scientific Publishing Co.

Minsky, M. and S. Papert (1972). *Artificial Intelligence Progress Report* (AI Memo 252). Cambridge, MA: MIT Artificial Intelligence Laboratory.

Mithen, Steven (1996). *The Prehistory of the Mind: The Cognitive Origins of Art, Religion and Science*. London: Thames and Hudson.

Morehart, Christopher T., John T. Millhauser, and Santiago Juarez (2018). Archaeologies of Political Ecology—Genealogies, Problems, and Orientations. *Archaeological Papers of the American Anthropological Association* Special Issue 29(1) *Uneven Terrain: Archaeologies of Political Ecology*, pp. 5–29.

Mouzelis, N. (1995). *Sociological Theory: What Went Wrong?* London: Routledge.

Ostrom, Elinor (1990). *Governing the Commons: The Evolution of Institutions for Collective Action*. Cambridge: Cambridge University Press.

Piketty, Thomas (2014). *Capital in the Twenty-First Century*. Cambridge, MA: Harvard University Press.

Ray, Celeste and Manuel Fernandez-Gotz, eds. (2021). *Historical Ecologies, Heterarchies and Transtemporal Landscapes*. New York: Routledge.

Scarborough, Vernon L. (2018). Review of James C. Scott: Against the Grain: A Deep History of the Earliest States. *Human Ecology* 46(4):783–785. https://doi.org/10.1007/s10745-018-0021-z

Scott, James C. (1985). *Weapons of the Weak: Everyday Forms of Peasant Resistance*. New Haven: Yale University Press.

Scott, James C. (1998). *Seeing Like a State: How Certain Schemes to Improve the Human Condition Have Failed*. New Haven: Yale University Press.

Scott, James C. (2009). *The Art of Not Being Governed: An Anarchist History of Upland Southeast Asia*. New Haven: Yale University Press.

Scott, James C. (2012). *Two Cheers for Anarchism: Six Easy Pieces on Autonomy, Dignity, and Meaningful Work and Play*. Princeton: Princeton University Press.

Scott, James C. (2017). *Against the Grain: A Deep History of the Earliest States*. New Haven: Yale University Press.

Spector, Janet (1993). *What This Awl Means: Feminist Archaeology at a Wahpeton Dakota Village*. Minneapolis: Minnesota Historical Society Press.

Stark, David (2001). Ambiguous Assets for Uncertain Environments: Heterarchy in Post-socialist Firms. In *The Twenty-First-Century Firm: Changing Economic Organization in International Perspective*, Paul DiMaggio, ed., pp. 69–104. Princeton: Princeton University Press.

Stark, David (2009). *The Sense of Dissonance: Accounts of Worth in Economic Life*. Princeton: Princeton University Press.

Thurston, T. L. and Manuel Fernández-Götz, eds. (2021). *Power from Below in Premodern Societies: The Dynamics of Political Complexity in the Archaeological Record*. Cambridge: Cambridge University Press.

Von Goldammer, Eberhard, Joachim Paul, and Joe Newbury (2003). Heterarchy-Hierarchy: Two Complementary Categories of Description. *Vordenker: Webforum for Innovative Approaches in Sciences, Economy and Culture*. www.vordenker.de/ Accessed January 15 2022.

White, Joyce C. (1995). Incorporating Heterarchy into Theory on Socio-political Development: The Case from Southeast Asia. Heterarchy and the Analysis of Complex Societies. Robert M. Ehrenreich, Carole L. Crumley, and Janet E. Levy, eds. *Archaeological Papers of the American Anthropological Association* 6. Washington: American Anthropological Association.

4

NEW MEDIEVALISM (RE)APPRAISED

Framing Heterarchy in World Politics

Aleksandra Spalińska

Introduction: Revisiting the International[1]

This chapter investigates how new medievalism—formulated as "a system of overlapping authority and multiple loyalty" (Bull 2002: 245), emerging due to neoliberal globalization and technological unification of the world—and its research *problématique* contribute to understanding and framing heterarchy. Namely, similarly to heterarchy, new medievalism is often seen as a challenge to the dominant methodological nationalism as well as state-centrism, given that it questions the status of the nation-state as the one and only structural category of political actors.[2] Therefore, the dialogue between both ideas can be substantial for their development. The paper is organized as follows. First, I outline the assumptions and applications of new medievalism in order to lay out and specify the conceptualization, given that it originates from different intellectual traditions and its meanings can be confusing for the wider audience. Then I consider the eponymous concept of heterarchy and its conceptual ingredients as a depiction of world order as well as its conditions as an observed phenomenon. Following this, I revise the wider understandings of politics, security and order in the context of new medievalism and its links to heterarchy. Finally, I discuss how the ideas involved in new medievalism are crucial for developing heterarchy as a concept.

In sum, I argue that the contribution of new medievalism to heterarchy is threefold. First, new medievalism offers heterarchy a range of civilizational and conceptual backgrounds that include reframing the international as the central concept of international relations and world politics. Within new medievalism the nation-state is not the main unit of analysis, so the international requires a different conceptualization, even if the means generally employed to conduct politics, for example diplomatic relations, often remain the same. Secondly, I reconsider approaching territoriality, which in the neomedieval frames acquires new

DOI: 10.4324/9781003352617-5

non-statist meanings, especially in context of plurality of political actors which (still) operate in different spatial contexts. Thirdly, new medievalism indicates the necessity of acknowledging issues of loyalty and identity which are almost absent in the framework of heterarchy.

1. New Medievalism as a Conceptualization of Order and Heuristics

New medievalism is one of many ideas that aim at improving our understanding of the contemporary world. It describes the world order in the globalized era (Bull 2002: 225–247) as a system of "overlapping authority and multiple loyalty" that would emerge as a consequence of globalization and internationalization of power (ibidem: 245). It frames the globalized world order as "neomedieval" due to the supposed transformation of the modern state system towards more heterogenous and flexible socio-political environment; the analogy is, however, used only because our imagination is limited by experience and hence it is difficult to describe the future without a reference to the past (ibidem: 247).[3] Simultaneously, a reference to the European Middle Ages does not mean here that we will return to the past or that the transformation should be stopped to save the modern order (or, otherwise, endorsed to make the most of globalization). Bull's standpoint is descriptive, not normative.

In Bull's words, the thing is just to imagine "modern and secular counterpart of it that embodies its central characteristic: *the system of overlapping authority and multiple loyalty*" (ibidem), so the order within which no government or ruler can be sovereign like it was in medieval Western Europe, so "in the sense of being supreme over a given territory" (ibidem) which resulted in sharing authority "with vassals beneath, and with the Pope and (in Germany and Italy) the Holy Roman Emperor above" (ibidem). Ultimately, it refers to the organization of the world order, mechanisms of ordering, and features of involved actor (Kobrin 1998: 365–366) Simultaneously, the conception was proposed separately in cultural studies by Umberto Eco (1996), however for similar reasons—to frame the outcomes of globalization and (post)modern transformation of Western societies.[4]

In particular, for Bull neo-medieval could only be that order in which sovereignty would be uncertain both in theory and practice (ibidem: 256). Indeed, new medievalism in IR is related to qualitative changes in world politics, resulting from globalization, deregulation of economies and technological progress. Interestingly, Arnold Wolfers (1962: 242), noted a trend of blurring of the differences between the international and the domestic issues during the Cold War. He believed it was the outcome of the rivalry between world-wide ideologies (communism and capitalism) and the nation-state, resulting in conflicts that were difficult to recognize as exclusively foreign or domestic, and which exposed the vulnerability of the state (ibidem). Wolfers described this trend as "new medievalism" (ibidem).

Following the first theoretical considerations, new medievalism has started to be considered a heuristic device and analytical framework (Friedrichs 2001: 19). Also, it serves as a conceptual redescription of world politics (Cerny and Prichard

2018) and can be employed for crafting "the thick description of global order" (ibidem: 2). Indeed, for Ronald Deibert, new medievalism can be used for "therapeutic re-description" (as proposed by Richard Rorty) of the world order to trigger new forms of its framing, "and thus better accommodate new actors and processes emerging in world politics" (Deibert 1997: 184). The purpose of redescription is to provide a more insightful (but not decisive) depiction of the contemporary world and, simultaneously, to liberate us from the state-centric conceptual prison in which our minds are locked and which makes re-organizing the world impossible (ibidem: 185). Thus, employing new medievalism can impact both the research framing and the (re-)construction of world order in practice because it highlights issues which are not sufficiently seen in the present debates or have been considered insignificant.

The content of the conception was also developed further. A definition similar to Bull's was proposed by Philip G. Cerny who described new medievalism as a system of "competing institutions with overlapping jurisdictions" (Cerny 1998). Furthermore, Jörg Friedrichs has contributed to the content of the neo-medieval analogy, analyzing not only the shifts in order architecture, but also the impact of rival universal and superior forces of neoliberal capitalism and the nation-state (Friedrichs 2001: 475–502). This led him to re-formulate new medievalism as "a system of overlapping authority and multiple loyalty, held together with the duality of competing universalistic claims" (ibidem). In the Middle Ages, there were the papacy and the empire; today we have the global economy and the nation-state (given that it is politically a universal body) (Friedrichs 2001: 486); or transnational business and international politics (Friedrichs 2004: 17). "Nowe Średniowiecze" jest zaś metaforą przyszłości tego systemu i kierunku jego przemian w zakresie sposobu jego organizacji i funkcjonowania oraz tworzących go podmiotów, a także symbolem znaczenia samej zmiany, która może mieć ogromny wpływ na polityczną działalność człowieka i jego miejsce jako jednostki w strukturze władzy.[34] Next, new medievalism is employed for conceptualizing and examining European integration (Zielonka 2006), given the developing process of supranational polity formation—the European Union (ibidem). Furthermore, new medievalism is used to depict the "period of transition" associated with the turbulent onset of the third millennium (Hassner 2002).

New medievalism thus has become a framework to analyze the consequences of globalization and neoliberalism (Rapley 2006), non-state actors (Télo 2012; Brütsch 2013), the role and capabilities of paramilitaries and gangs for enforcing territorial control (Norell 2003; Kan 2019), geopolitical conditions of the post-Westphalian world (Doboš 2020), etc. Moreover, new medievalism encourages us to investigate units other than nation-states: city-states, metropolitan areas, empires (Brütsch 2013; Godehardt 2014), those aspiring for autonomy or independence (Kennedy 2017) as well as regional and supranational formations (Zielonka 2006). Consequently, employing new medievalism enables us to embrace both universality and plurality, order and chaos, the local and the global—contradictory qualities—within one framework.

2. New Medievalism and Heterarchy Intertwined: Framing World Politics

Heterarchy and new medievalism have a lot in common, given that they both describe and frame political order in the globalized world, pointing to the same qualities: plurality, heterogeneity, and de-centeredness (Belmonte and Cerny 2021). Moreover, both can be applied as analytical/conceptual frameworks. However, heterarchy is a concept of specific order construction, whereas new medievalism widely describes the "state of the world" and—given Bull's original formulation—logics of ordering (similarly to Rosenau's [1990] concept of "frag-megration"; see Dana-Marie Ramjit's chapter). In the following section I revise the understandings of politics, security and order in the frames of new medievalism and its links to heterarchy.

2.1. Politics and Actors

The neo-medieval order(s) is usually recognized as the opposite of the "Westphalian" ideals of a world structured around hierarchically organized and interacting nation-states (Falk 2002). In context of politics, new medievalism reminds us that the true difference in political organization existed before the modern era; naturally, later it also appeared but not so explicitly, limited by "fixed" categories of "the national" and "the foreign," "inside" and "outside." In the neomedieval scenario, political and social differences are implied by "multiple loyalties" which are uneven and complex, while in politics it is suggested by functional differentiation of "overlapping authorities" that (re)produces ties between authorities of different sectors (political, legal, economic, etc.), levels (local, regional, etc.), and competences.

That, in turn, translates into the differentiation of political agency and to the growing number of those willing to claim political recognition as well as money and influence. Parag Khanna (2016: 45) outlined five categories of such actors: "territorial *countries*, networked *cities*, regional *commonwealths*, cloud *communities*, and stateless *companies*."[5] The "networked cities" actually create the "diagonal" category, reproduced at the intersection of overlapping spatial and functional dimensions—the megacity (ibidem). Furthermore, there are international organizations/institutions which operate "between" or "among" states, including UN agencies. Also, there are "alt-state" or "anti-state" actors (Gardner 2019: 145), whose actions are against the states (terrorists, criminal networks, warlords, hackers) (Manwaring 2007). They constitute "asymmetrical threats" that include private and dispersed violence. Moreover, terrorists are the subject of the "global war on terror" the declaration of which actually meant recognition of violent non-state actors in practice, assuming that they should be treated like criminals, not combatants (O'Connell 2005). In the framework of new medievalism, political agency is not only quantitative but also qualitative—meaning that it is not only plural but also *heterogeneous*.

2.2. Security and Violence

The issue especially affecting public authority is terrorism as a politic(ized) violence that acts across the spatial and functional dimensions of the world order. Terrorists are "free riders" (Jackson 2011: 171) that act inside and against the state system, trying to enforce their power and spread the fear; the same applies to pirates (Bueger 2018). Moreover, terrorism, like organized crime, is a danger for other non-state actors as well. Actually, there are governments which benefit from these non-state violent entities, given the growing interest in the private mercenaries, employed particularly for operations in Africa (McFate 2014) and for proxy wars (Marshall 2016). The result is increasing privatization of warfare and growing number of paramilitaries and militias (Kan 2019). Simultaneously, we need to keep in mind the role of private killing firms that are used by intelligence and internal security agencies (Peterson 2021).

Thus, we have the "unsovereign" security (Spalińska 2019), enforced by informal groups for "political control of ungoverned territory and/or areas governed by corrupt politicians and functionaries" (Manwaring 2007: 4). This relates to, e.g., warlords, insurgents, and gangs which "are more interested in commercial profit and controlling territory to allow maximum freedom of movement and action to achieve their longer-range objectives" (ibidem: 1). Consequently, we have different patterns of hybrid warfare, such as unconventional non-state or inter-state war in which non-state actors participate (ibidem: 7). Also, self-defense groups are established where the public authority is too weak (Curry and de Vries 2020). It especially relates to big cities, among which many are spaces of violence and discrimination. This makes urban planning increasingly politicized (Enright and Rossi 2017).

2.3. Order Architecture and Structural Dependencies

Then, we need to consider how the components of new medievalism translate into specific order architecture. As mentioned, the competing logics in this model are the global economy and nation-states (Friedrichs 2001: 486) or transnational business and international politics (Friedrichs 2004: 17). They provide structure and rules, including normative justification for or against recognition of involved subjects. The position of business is strengthened by transnational trade law (Cutler 2003). Consequently, the public/private divide is transcended, and endless interactions between countless actors can occur (including the individual). Informal groups exercise control over their members beyond or against public authority (Cerny 1998: 58). This leads to the "new paternalism" (Williams 2008). Moreover, regional and global inequalities as well as dependencies affect the sovereignty of weaker countries—in the wake of the financial crisis, Greece and Cyprus became "half-protectorates governed by a consortium of creditor countries represented by the IMF and the Euro-group" (Zielonka 2018: 121).

Thus, we have the layout of a heterarchical order. Interestingly, it is also called "asymmetrical governance" (Shouten and Miklian 2020: 414), given its uneven nature. Growing differentiation results from particular levels and mechanisms of "imperial" authority of neoliberal capitalism; according to Friedrichs, it actually constitutes the universalistic power of the global economy, while for John Ruggie (1986) it is the consequence of co-existence of territorial and functional logics, however in different terms than in modern era. Moreover, it is worth recalling the definition of order as "systemic configurations of political authority" (Reus-Smit 2013: 1059) which, when affected by the power of neoliberal capitalism, are constantly questioned (Hardt and Negri 2000).

In practice, the interconnections between involved actors take heterarchical form, so quasi-institutionalized multi-layered and multi-nodal structural patterns emerge that shape the aggregated power over the differentiated social structures and public/private units across the states (Cerny 2009); it is both vertical and horizontal with diagonal links (Belmonte and Cerny 2021). Another layer is the formal/informal divide, and its scope for the advantage of informality which simultaneously contributes to blurring the foreign/domestic dichotomy. Consequently, distribution of power is also affected, taking the shape of non-polarity (Haas 2008), according to which there will be numerous centers of power with no distinct hegemon; importantly, these centers can be constituted not only by states but also by corporations, NGOs, terrorist networks, and other non-state actors (ibidem).[6] Consequently, logics of ordering (e.g. global interdependence), "traditionally" centered in the dominating state (like the US) are not supposed to overlap. In context of new medievalism, it is even more relevant to consider the "polarity" in regard to these logics rather than to the states.

3. New Medievalism and the International: Contributing to Heterarchy

Therefore, there is the chance of a new order based on "new" forms of postmodern entanglement and plurality, decentered from the nation-state. That order would be embedded in "actors" or "subjects," not only "states." Consequently, we would have to see the international as it is understood within neo-medieval frames. In fact, neo-medieval logic co-exists with the modern one; it can be even stated that there are two competing logics that create the core of contemporary world society—the "pluralist" which is based in the states system and the "solidarist" which endorses the agency of non-state actors, global markets and cosmopolitan networks which advocate for universalistic values (Buzan 2004). Simultaneously, the rivalry of these logics is implicitly expressed by the persistent role of states and inter-state relations in a globalized world (Ferguson and Mansbach 2007). That creates the basis for growing heterarchical order.

3.1. Civilizational Background and Re-Framing the International

For Pierre Hassner (2002: 46–48), the contemporary world is indeed determined by the "new dialectics" as the boundaries and distinctions, established by culture, religion and law have been abandoned or their delimitation has changed.

Consequently, social reality is reproduced through contradictory and all-embracing qualities like universalism and anarchy, civilization and barbarism, deviating warfare and (un)secured peace; these dialects actually depict the beginning of the third millennium (ibidem). The supposed neomedieval order is therefore a "product" of never-ending dialectical changes. Simultaneously, when referring to the dialectics as the key feature of the modern order, the neo-medieval framework seems to be "post-dialectical" (and in this sense postmodern) as born out of the contradictions of modernity. Thus, new medievalism situates heterarchy within the postmodern ways of approaching world order.

That translates into the ways of conceptualizing the international. New medievalism is helpful in this case because it indicates the uncertainty and fluidity of existing boundaries (physical and metaphorical) and distinctions (Hassner 2002; Belmonte and Cerny 2021). It acknowledges the anarchy in a non-realist way—through recognizing the multitude of actors which are supposed to have the capacity of making political account and influence. Moreover, Bull's idea points to universality as well as to the plurality of involved actors/subjects. Then, when put into neomedieval frames, the international becomes "inter-actoral."[7]

Regarding the inspirations provoked by historical analogy (e.g., medieval suzerainty of monarchs), "subject" seems to be more relevant; however, "actor" is more neutral (as it does not indicate subordination and does not presume hierarchical relations). Thus, the inter-actoral is actually an extension of well-known hierarchical relations, both horizontally and diagonally, not only vertically. That corresponds with postmodern discursive deconstruction of polities and responds to the "post-international" theorizing that most often is limited to analyzing the contemporary world in terms of growing complexity, fuzziness and disorder (Corry 2010: 161–162). As a result, we are better equipped to re-image the world politics after globalization.

Moreover, emphasis put on "actors" is due also to fully grasp the picture which already exists in the legally based political relations: the picture of both formal and informal relations between state and non-state units which, however, are recognized as sovereign entities (like the Sovereign Order of Malta) or just have their actorness formally recognized (as it is in the case of international organizations) or have diplomatic missions in spite of being a non-sovereign entity (like Scotland to the EU).

Thanks to those assumptions not only would supposed neo-medieval qualities be more visible in the academic discourse but also indeed the medieval ones—like the formal recognition of the Sovereign Order of Malta which, as an exception from territorial principle, has persisted despite all modern changes applied to regulate international order. On the other hand, there are states for which sovereignty is only a *façade*—as in the case of Nauru (its economy depends on Australia) or Marshall Islands (its defense policy is maintained by the US). However, despite this, those insular states are still recognized as sovereign entities while Guernsey, Jersey and Isle of Man are not, even if the scope of their autonomy as Crown Dependencies is broader (they depend on the UK only in foreign affairs and defense). Similarly, *de facto* states, which are not recognized, still function in practice (e.g., Kosovo).

3.2. Agency and Territoriality

New medievalism, just like heterarchy, offers a functionalist account as complementary to the spatial dimension (Zielonka 2014) indicating that, when the power is dispersed, the "added value" of the "inter-actoral" is created by differentiated subjects, not only "traditional" units like societies or nations. However, in opposition to heterarchy, new medievalism relates also to territoriality—yet approached differently than in state-centrism. The examples of this qualitatively different approach to territoriality actually were presented above—when emphasis is put on entities like Sovereign Order of Malta, Scotland, Nauru, Marshall Islands or Crown Dependencies, our perspective dramatically changes, with the same concerns as focusing on terrorists, pirates and corporations. Firstly, small entities show up instead of "normal" states. The same concerns actors on a higher level of analysis, e.g., the EU.

Secondly, economic and technological ties—that were the main inspiration for the idea of "overlapping authority and multiple loyalty"—make the world smaller and closer, discarding the "exceptionalist" claims submitted by national governments to the global agenda. To the contrary, we can actually see and experience the exceptional nature of non-state entities and, also, how they operate within the logics of contemporary world politics. Some of them have agency defined territorially (like sub-state regions or cities) whereas others do not—or, at least, they do not depend on territorial dynamics so strongly because they are not responsible for delivering public authority (like corporations). On the other hand, unrecognized states and violent non-state actors equip themselves with the means of power sufficient to enforce recognition and authority (even only temporally) but only on a factual basis, not legal. These interplays demonstrate the scope of informal arrangements permitted in the practice of international order; simultaneously, we can see that, even if the logic of interests seems to dominate, formal recognition still is desirable, especially for territorial actors who claim to be capable of establishing public authority.

Regarding the foregoing considerations, one might say that new medievalism actually liberates territoriality from statism, indicating its new meanings and ways of approaching and imagining it. For instance, one might say that Khanna's concept of "connectography" (actually drawing on functional geography) was invented based on the heterogeneous "inter-actoral."[8] Moreover, given the historical analogy, new medievalism makes a link to the pre-modern entities where ways of relating to territoriality were also different from those within the modern West. As mentioned, new medievalism is rooted in the observation that, due to the Cold War rivalry and globalization processes, the differences between "the foreign" and "the domestic" are blurred (Wolfers 1962; Zielonka 2006). Actually, within the neo-medieval frames, it is more relevant to discuss "boundaries" or "frontiers" (ibidem). In neomedieval polity, unlike the modern sovereign state, the borders are semi-open, fuzzy and permeable, and the territorial reach of the public authority does not overlap with particular legal or economic jurisdictions (ibidem). These remarks prompted employing the neomedieval understanding of polity formation as a viable alternative to territorialism as an ordering principle within the EU's spatial planning (Faludi 2018).

3.3. Loyalty and Identity

If borders are weakened, there is a question what can be stated about identities and loyalties that were formed within them. They are essential for the new medievalism but within the framework of heterarchy they are not addressed directly despite that they constitute the actual content of the order architecture, outlined in the previous section. Nevertheless, even if their contents change, collective and individual identities still exist, given that "although ethnic identity levels are lower in the more globalized than the less globalized countries, globalization has no differential effect on the strong and positive link between patriotism and ethnic identity" (Ariely 2019: 763).

National imaginaries are also affected "by a path-dependency process rooted in their historical experience" (ibidem: 777; Brubaker 1992). Thus, even in the configurations that transcend the internal-external dialectics, mechanisms of reproducing identity exist but simply are different from these adopted in the modern era, as has been the case for a long time in territories that were excluded from state-building—like the Crown Dependencies, where medieval construction of authority and loyalty has remained almost unchanged (Spalińska 2020). This is due because national "moods" are inaccurate when seeking the ingredients of identities which are shattered and multi-layered (Cerny 1998: 55–56). In response to the increasing fragmentation, new medievalism literature points to both universality and plurality (in organizational and civilizational terms). Universality is maintained as complementary to plurality. It can be considered in at least two dimensions—organizational (as in the EU or global capitalism) and ideational (like liberal democracy). In both cases, it constitutes an "arch" as Catholic Church and Christianity did in medieval Europe (Jackson 2011).

4. Conclusions: Framing World Politics Differently

This paper aimed to analyze how new medievalism contributes to understanding and framing heterarchy. As indicated, new medievalism informs this concept variously and, especially in the context of 1) civilizational background, inclusive of re-framing the international; 2) approaching territoriality; and 3) embracing loyalty and identity. That is not surprising, given that new medievalism has a plethora of conceptual layers. Actually, it is already applied as a heuristic device or analytical framework, capable to embrace wide scope of contradictory qualities which also are described by heterarchy. Moreover, just like heterarchy, new medievalism responds to the challenge of insufficient academic vocabulary, given that it provides categories and phrases necessary in describing the contemporary world. Simultaneously, it makes a link between heterarchy and "traditional" IR due to the fact that new medievalism is rooted in the English school and relates to general considerations on defining world order. That in turn enables us to think differently about the core IR concepts, so the international, which, within the neo-medieval outlook, takes the shape of "the inter-actoral" as happening between and among different actors, not only nation-states. Thanks to this, we are equipped to avoid the simplistic state-centrism that dominates in IR literature and to frame world politics more accurately.

Notes

1 Parts of research used in this chapter were presented and discussed during the European Workshops in International Studies (2020), ISA Annual Convention (2021), BISA Annual Conference (2021), and Millennium Journal Conference (2020; 2021). I would like to thank chairs, discussants and other participants for their comments and questions.
2 The standpoint towards historical analogies, employed in this chapter, is pragmatic: new medievalism is understood as a conception of order and heuristic tool, used to approach and frame the world order architecture. Discussion of the particular meanings and layers of as well as controversies around neo-medieval analogy is beyond the scope of this chapter.
3 As Bull noted himself: "Of course, any future form of universal political organisation will be different from previous historical experience, in the sense that it will have certain features that are unique and will not exactly resemble any previous system. . .. But our view of possible alternatives to the states system should take into account the limitations of our own imagination and our own inability to transcend past experience" (Bull 2002: 247).
4 In cultural studies, the meaning of "neo-medieval" is wider and relates to postmodern ideas in the theory of literature and art, including contemporary readings of medieval motifs in popular culture (Lukes 2014).
5 "Cloud communities" are ethnical diasporas and Internet groups (Khanna 2016: 54–56).
6 Amitai Etzioni argues that "the change seems to be toward more regional autonomy, or increased devolution, and greater variety in the relationships between the United States and regional powers" (Etzioni 2012).
7 It is worth noting that in medieval political thought, the state is just one of the "other associations" (Bull 2002: 245).
8 That refers to the infrastructure, trade, transportation corridors, digital connections and telecommunication For Khanna the factors that enhance worldwide connectivity are: devolution, urbanization, dilution, mega-infrastructures, and digital ties (Khanna 2016: 19).

References

Ariely, G. (2019). The Nexus between Globalization and Ethnic Identity: A View from Below. *Ethnicities*, 19(5): 763–783. https://doi.org/10.1177/1468796819834951.
Belmonte, R. and Cerny, P. G. (2021). Heterarchy: Toward Paradigm Shift in World Politics. The Changing Faces of Power. *Journal of Political Power*, Special Issue ed. by G. Gallarotti.
Brubaker, R. (1992). *Citizenship & Nationhood in France & Germany*. Cambridge, MA: Harvard University Press.

Brütsch, Ch. M. (2013). From Sovereign Prerogatives to Metropolitan Rule? The Anarchical Society in the Urban Age, Source. *International Studies Perspectives*, 14(3): 307–324.

Bueger, C. (2019). Performing Piracy: A Note on the Multiplicity of Agency. *Journal of International Relations and Development*, 22: 832–852. https://doi.org/10.1057/s4126 8-017-0122-0.

Bull, H. (2002). *The Anarchical Society. A Study of Order in World Politics*. New York: Palgrave Macmillan.

Buzan, B. (2004). *From International to World Society?: English School Theory and the Social Structure of Globalisation*. Cambridge: Cambridge University Press.

Cerny, P. G. (1998). Neomedievalism, Civil War and the New Security Dilemma: Globalisation as Durable Disorder. *Civil Wars*, 1(1): 36–64. doi: 10.1080/13698249808402366

Cerny, P. G. (2009). Multi-Nodal Politics: Globalisation is What Actors Make of It. *Review of International Studies*, 35: 421–449. doi: 10.1017/S0260210509008584.

Cerny, P. G. and Prichard, A. (2018). *Neomedievalism Revisited: Uneven Heterarchy in 21st Century World Politics*. Paper presented at ISA Annual Convention, San Francisco.

Deibert, R. D. (1997). "Exorcismus Theoriae": Pragmatism, Metaphors and the Return of the Medieval in IR Theory. *European Journal of International Relations*, 3(2): 167–192.

Doboš, B. (2020). *New Middle Ages. Geopolitics of Post-Westphalian World*. Springer Nature. doi: 10.1007/978-3-030-58681-2_3.

Eco, U. (1996). *Semiology of Everyday Life*. Polish Edition. Warsaw: Czytelnik.

Enright, T. and Rossi, U. (eds.) (2017). *The Urban Political. Ambivalent Spaces of Late Neoliberalism*. Palgrave Macmillan.

Etzioni, A. (2012). The Devolution of American Power. *The Fletcher Forum of World Affairs*, 37(1): 13–14.

Falk, R. (2002). Revisiting Westphalia, Discovering Post-Westphalia. *The Journal of Ethics*, 6(4): 311–352.

Faludi, A. (2018). *The Poverty of Territorialism. A Neo-Medieval View of Europe and European Planning*. Edward Elgar Publishing.

Ferguson, Y. H. and Mansbach, R. W. (2007). Post-Internationalism and IR Theory. *Millennium*, 35(3): 529–549. doi: 10.1177/03058298070350031001.

Friedrichs, J. (2001). The Meaning of New Medievalism. *European Journal of International Relations*, 7(4): 475–501. doi: 10.1177/1354066101007004004.

Friedrichs, J. (2004). The Neomedieval Renaissance: Global Governance and International Law in the New Middle Ages. In: Dekker, I. F. and Werner, W. G. (eds.) *Governance and International Legal Theory* (vol. 23). Springer: Dordrecht.

Gardner, H. (2019). *IR Theory, Historical Analogy, and Major Political War*. Palgrave Macmillan.

Godehardt, N. (2014). *The Chinese Constitution of Central Asia: Regions and Intertwined Actors in International Relations*. Palgrave Macmillan.

Haas, R. (2008). The Age of Nonpolarity: What Will Follow US Dominance? *Foreign Affairs*, 87(3).

Hardt, M. and Negri, A. (2000). *Empire*. Cambridge, MA; London: Harvard University Press.

Hassner, P. (2002). *Koniec pewników. Eseje o wojnie, pokoju i przemocy* [The End of Axioms: Essays on War, Peace and Violence]. Ed. by K. Szotkowska, M. Ofierska. Translated by M. Ochab. Warsaw: Sic!.

Jackson, R. (2011). *Sovereignty. Evolution of an Idea*. Polish Edition. Transl. by J. Majmurek. Warsaw: Sic!.

Kan, P. R. (2019). *The Global Challenge of Militias and Paramilitary Violence*. Springer International Publishing; Palgrave.

Kennedy, L. (2017). *Supranational Union and New Medievalism: Forging a New Scottish State*. Arktos Media Limited.

Khanna, P. (2016). *Connectography. Mapping the Future of Global Civilization*. New York: Random House.

Kobrin, S. (1998). Back to the Future: Neomedievalism and the Postmodern Digital World Economy. *Journal of International Affairs*, 51(2).

Lukes, D. (2014). Comparative Neomedievalisms: A Little Bit Medieval. *Postmedieval*, 5: 1–9. doi: 10.1057/pmed.2013.41.

Manwaring, M. G. (2007). *A Contemporary Challenge to State Sovereignty: Gangs and Other Illicit Transnational Criminal Organization in Central America, El Salvador, Mexico, Jamaica, and Brazil*. Carlisle: Strategic Studies Institute.

Marshall, A. (2016). From Civil War to Proxy War: Past History and Current Dilemmas. *Small Wars & Insurgencies*, 27(2):183–195.

McFate, S. (2014). *The Modern Mercenary: Private Armies and What They Mean for World Order*. Oxford University Press.

Norell, M. (2003). A New Medievalism? The Case of Sri Lanka. *Civil Wars*, 6(2): 121–137.

O'Connell, M. E. (2004–2005). Enhancing the Status of Non-State Actors Through a Global War on Terror? *Columbia Journal of Transnational Law*, 43: 435. https://scholarship.law. nd.edu/law_faculty_scholarship/94.

Peterson, U. (2021). Onset of New Business? Private Military and Security Companies and Conflict Onset in Latin America, Africa, and Southeast Asia from 1990 to 2011. *Small Wars & Insurgencies*. doi: 10.1080/09592318.2020.1866404.

Reus-Smit, C. (2013). The Concept of Intervention. *Review of International Studies*, 39(5): 1057–1076.

Rosenau, J. N. (1990). *Turbulence in World Politics. A Theory of Change and Continuity*. Princeton: Princeton University Press.

Ruggie, J. (1986). Continuity and Transformation in the World Polity: Toward a Neorealist Synthesis. In: *Neorealism and its Critics*. New York: Columbia University Press.

Spalińska, A. (2019). The Insecure Sovereignty and Unsovereign Security in the XXI Century and the Role of Non-State Actors. In *SESCO 2018. Security & Sovereignty in the 21st Century. Conference Proceedings*. Budapest: Institute for Cultural Relations Policy.

Spalińska, A. (2020). *Beyond Methodological Nationalism and Negativity in Researching Culture-Politics Nexus: The Case of Political and Cultural Identity of the Inhabitants of Guernsey*. Paper Presented at ISA-Midwest Annual Conference.

Télo, M. (2012). *State, Globalization and Multilateralism: The Challenges of Institutionalizing Regionalism*. Netherlands: Springer.

Williams, P. (2008). *From The New Middle Ages to a New Dark Age: The Decline of The State and U.S. Strategy*. Carlisle: Strategic Studies Institute.

Wolfers, A. (1962). *Discord and Collaboration. Essays on International Politics*. Baltimore: The John Hopkins University Press.

Zielonka, J. (2006). *Europe as Empire. The Nature of the Enlarged European Union*. Oxford: Oxford University Press.

Zielonka, J. (2014). *Is the EU doomed?* Cambridge: Polity Press.

Zielonka, J. (2018). *Counter-Revolution. Liberal Europe in Retreat*. Polish Edition. Translated by J. Bednarek. Warsaw: PWN.

5

FROM EMPIRE TO HETERARCHY

Gita Subrahmanyam

Introduction

Acknowledging the existence of global empires prior to and during the 20th century shows that "heterarchy" is not a new development in world politics, but reflects secular trends going back to earlier centuries. Empires and imperialism tend to be neglected in mainstream International Relations (IR) accounts, which focus instead on hierarchically organized sovereign nation-states interacting on an equal standing in an anarchical "inter-national" system (Waltz, 1979; Wendt, 1992). Yet, as some authors have pointed out, factoring global empires into our thinking about states and the world system highlights certain "established myths" that underlie much IR scholarship (de Carvalho et al., 2011). Most states in existence today lacked sovereignty at the time that the IR discipline came into being, "nation-states" have been a rarity throughout history, and the interstate system has been characterized by hierarchy and unfair competition since the mid-19th century (Lawson, 2018: 84), and also—as I argue in this chapter—by heterarchy. The neglect of empires and imperialism in IR seems deliberate in a field of study that emerged just after the First World War. As Barkawi (2010: 1361) has noted: "IR was founded amidst empire, but discovered instead only a world of sovereign states and their collective action problems."

Authors calling for a paradigmatic shift in IR to replace the concept of "hierarchy" with that of "heterarchy" view heterarchy as a recent phenomenon, beginning around the mid-20th century, when the dialectic of globalization and fragmentation began to undermine the nation-state system, leading to the emergence of powerful transnational non-state actors able to compete and/or collude with states to determine political outcomes using their economic power, social or intellectual capital, and/or networks (Belmonte and Cerny, 2021, Cerny, this book). While I agree with their critique that the three mainstream IR "competing

DOI: 10.4324/9781003352617-6

paradigms," which regard sovereign nation-states as the main components (or nodes) of the international system, should be replaced by a paradigm that views world politics as "*multi-nodal* and characterized by *heterarchy*" (Cerny, this book), I argue that the concept of heterarchy must be applied to the past, as well as the present, to accurately reflect global trends. After all, historical evidence suggests that heterarchy—characterized by "great organizational diversity" as well as non-hierarchical forms of order and collaboration (Crumley, 2015)—was a feature in European "empire-states," as well as in other political units prior to the development of states and the international states system.

Reassessing IR theories from an empire-state, rather than a nation-state, perspective demonstrates that current examples of heterarchy are not new developments but instead continuations of systems and processes that took place during the age of empire. To draw out these themes, this chapter is structured as follows. The first section makes the case for adopting a more dynamic view of world politics, which for the purposes of this paper means shifting the IR focus from nation-states to empire-states. The second section adopts an empire-state analytical lens to demonstrate the existence of heterarchy within and among European empire-states during and prior to the 20th century. Examples of heterarchy presented in this section focus on the British empire-state during the New Imperialism period beginning in the late 19th century. The final section summarizes the main findings and shows how systems and processes taking place during the age of empire have influenced contemporary world politics.

1. Shifting the IR Focus to Empire-States

The mainstream IR vision of a world populated by consensually-constructed "nation-states" with legitimate rulers serving a "guardianship" role is questionable when assessing the historical facts, even those pertaining to the period when the modern nation-state is said to have developed. Two foundational myths have been continually repeated in IR, despite the existence of historical and historiographical works to the contrary: the "myth of 1648," which views the Peace of Westphalia as having brought about the end to empires and given birth to the territorially-bounded sovereign state and the anarchic states system; and the "myth of 1919,"[1] which promotes a Eurocentric "nation-state" metanarrative through an ahistorical backwards extrapolation that elides the role of empire in the theory and practice of IR (de Carvalho et al., 2011). These myths obscure the fact that the period following 1648 was characterized by a proliferation of global empires, in which a small number of European "nation-states" controlled large numbers of non-sovereign overseas dependencies, and that from 1919 until the late 20th century there were more colonized regions than sovereign states across the globe.

Factoring empires into our thinking about states and state development calls into question certain "key traits" associated with the modern nation-state. Most states in existence today did not evolve through natural social processes, but were instead artificially or forcibly created. European "great powers" did not rule over a single concentrated region comprising a single society, but instead controlled multiple far-flung territories comprising diverse communities. While colonies that gained independence in the post-World War II period could be described as states, most could not be termed "nation-states," since their arbitrarily-drawn territorial boundaries cut across cultural communities that lack a shared history (Tripathi and Chaturvedi, 2020; Griffiths, 1986), and/or because colonial administrative practices produced deep social divisions which prevented the populations of the new states from identifying as single societies (Subrahmanyam, 2006). In other words, consensually-constructed "nation-states" have been a rarity throughout history.

IR's neglect of empires and imperialism is surprising when considering the origins of the discipline. Brian Schmidt (1998: 72) has noted that the IR discipline "had its real beginning in studies of imperialism, not world order," while Robert Vitalis (2005: 161–162) has argued that IR's intellectual foundations are rooted in racism and white supremacism, pointing out that the *Foreign Affairs* journal began its life as *The Journal of Race Development*, which "was a forum for the discussion of the problems which relate to the progress of races and states generally considered backward in their standards of civilization" (Blakeslee, 1910: 1). George Lawson (2018: 77) is far kinder, attributing the neglect of empires and imperialism in most mainstream IR accounts to an absence of historicism and tendency towards "presentism":

> "By taking a static picture of the structure of world politics (the anarchical states system), structural realism occludes differences between polities (such as empires and nation-states), fails to distinguish between types of international order (such as imperial and sovereign orders), ignores social structural forces (such as capitalism, patriarchy and racism), and reduces agency to the actions of state managers, generals and financiers. In this way, historically specific social categories—the balance of power, sovereignty, anarchy, and so on—are seen as stable, fixed entities that can be deployed without regard for time and space specificity."

To analyze world politics in a historically accurate manner, an alternative analytical framework is needed—one that does not involve ahistorical backwards mapping (Subrahmanyam, 2003). Given that colonies by definition lack sovereignty, which is the key trait required to be considered a "state" (Vincent, 1992), and that European powers were the ultimate sources of authority for the domestic and the overseas portions of their empires, it stands to reason that the focus of IR during the period from 1648 to the late 20th century should have been on "empire-states" rather than "nation-states." To conceive of a world populated by empire-states requires rejecting ingrained notions of states as static constructs operating within a "geographically identifiable territory" (Vincent, 1992: 44), and instead adopting a dynamic view of state formation and development that takes into account the growth and shrinkage of states over time. After all, as European empire-states amassed colonies, their territorial boundaries expanded, and as they decolonized, their boundaries contracted.

Adopting an empire-state focus also allows for state development processes in former colonies to be taken into account. Prior to gaining independence in the post-World War II period, most European colonies experienced extensive institutional growth processes, which were essential precursors to their eventual recognition as "states" (Subrahmanyam, 2003: 12). Legal sovereignty alone would not have sufficed; they also needed to possess a capacity for unitary action. When India gained independence from Britain in 1947, it already possessed a developed government structure—including a professionalized salaried bureaucracy, a centralized taxation system, and a standing army—which British administrators had installed and modernized over many years. Similar state-building processes took place in most of the new states that joined the international system after 1945. However, institutional modernization processes were not evenly distributed across colonies, leading to social and political instabilities that persist today.

2. Heterarchy, Hierarchy, and Anarchy within the British Empire-State and the International Empire-States System

Applying an empire-state lens to examine theories concerning the characteristics of states and the international system at different points in time suggests that heterarchy is not a new phenomenon in world politics, but was a feature of European empire-states, as well as of polities prior to the development of states and the international states system. Carole L. Crumley—one of the first authors to apply the term "heterarchy" to power relations within and between states (Crumley, 1987) and, earlier still, to systems of social organization in archaeology (Crumley, 1979)—has pointed to archaeological and ethnographic evidence of heterarchical political and social relations in empires dating as far back as the 2nd century (Crumley, this book). According to Crumley (this book), the tendency of the social sciences to regard societies as hierarchically organized, rather than to acknowledge the presence of non-hierarchical forms of order and collaboration, "has provided the intellectual and moral rationale for scientific racism, colonialism, and other forms of domination, in that 'complex' societies (e.g., nation-states) were considered more advanced than 'simple' (e.g., pastoral) societies, the antidote being conquest and rehabilitation."

Similar issues have been raised regarding the mainstream IR assumption that the international system is anarchic, which has two parallel meanings in IR: (1) the absence of a common superior, such as a world government, to police interactions among states, or (2) horizontal order between formally equal sovereign states, as opposed to hierarchical order between subordinate and superordinate polities (Lechner, 2017; Helal, 2019). The assumption of international anarchy has been criticized on the basis that it is supremacist, since "realism, liberalism and constructivism derive their notions of anarchy from social contract theses that are based in a racist dualism that dichotomizes humanity and the relations of states," with "one set of assumptions for whites and another for nonwhites" (Henderson, 2013: 1–10). Lawson (2018: 84) argues that the international system is in fact hierarchical and has been characterized by a "core-periphery" order and unfair competition since the mid-19th century. Meanwhile, David Lake (1996) argues that there is "a variety of international relations," which can be mapped along a continuum from anarchy to hierarchy (see Figure 5.1), depending on whether polities voluntarily enter into alliances (anarchy) or one polity has been forced to relinquish its sovereignty to another, as during empire formation (hierarchy).

Providing evidence of heterarchy within the British empire-state and the international empire-states system during and prior to the 20th century is one means of challenging ahistorical and Eurocentric assumptions of state-level hierarchy and international anarchy, so the remainder of this section is dedicated to this aim. The decision to focus on the British empire-state has been made on two grounds: first, that Britain was the greatest empire-builder during this time period and, second, that a developed body of research already exists which documents growth and development patterns within the British empire-state (Subrahmanyam, 2003, 2004, 2006). The examples presented in this section mainly relate to the New Imperialism period beginning in the late 19th century and to Britain's non-white colonies in India and Africa. However, similar trends may be identified for other colonies and time periods. The exposition below is not intended to provide a comprehensive or balanced picture of how Britain ran its empire-state, but simply to provide examples of heterarchy within the British empire-state.

Figure 5.2 illustrates the structure of power relationships that challenged Britain's ability to claim unrivalled authority over its empire-state during the period from the late 19th to the late 20th century. As Figure 5.2 shows, a variety of state as well as non-state authorities operating at different levels—above, below and at the same level as central empire-state authorities—were able to influence how Britain amassed and ran its global empire, as well as the speed at which it decolonized. This in turn had implications for the overall size, structure and scope of the British empire-state. The architecture of power within the British empire-state was complex and multi-nodal—that is, heterarchical—as well as hierarchical and anarchical, while the international system was characterized by hierarchy and heterarchy, as well as anarchy. Further details are provided in the paragraphs below.

FIGURE 5.1 Continuum of international relations.

Source: Lake (1996: 7).

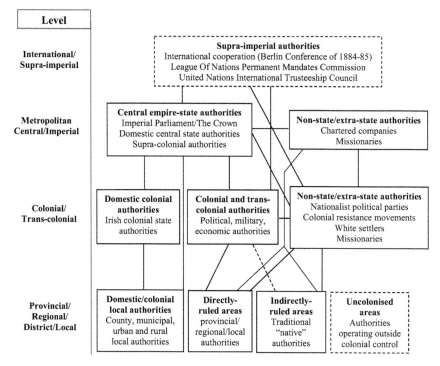

FIGURE 5.2   Power relationships in the British empire-state (late 19th to late 20th century).
Source: Created by author based on information from Subrahmanyam (2003).

During the period from the late 19th to the late 20th century, the international system was characterized by anarchy—in the sense that two world wars took place, which may not have occurred had there been a superior authority to resolve disputes among European empire-states—but also by hierarchy, since there were internationally established rules and supra-imperial institutions that constrained European powers' abilities to freely acquire and administer colonies. International agreements—such as the General Act ratified by all major powers, including the US, during the Berlin Conference of 1884–85—set out the conditions under which colonies could be acquired and trade could be conducted in Africa (Craven, 2015). After the First World War, the newly-established League of Nations was vested with the authority to transfer colonies from one imperial power (e.g., Germany) to another (e.g., Britain), which resulted in the shrinkage of the former empire-state and the expansion of the latter. The European powers that were awarded "mandated territories" by the League of Nations were directly answerable to its Permanent Mandates Commission (and later to the United Nations International Trusteeship Commission) for how they administered these colonies (Bentwich, 1946). Thus, they did not retain full sovereignty over the overseas portions of their empire-states (Louis, 1969: 74).

Evidence of international-level heterarchy was also present during this period, in that colonial-level non-state actors could lobby supra-imperial authorities to mobilize for their interests, taking advantage of the latter's superordinate position compared to European empire-states in the hierarchical chain of command. For example, after the Second World War, the UN created channels for "direct native consultation," allowing different segments of colonial society within mandated territories to petition the Trusteeship Council and raise concerns. According to one account, these consultations resulted in the Trusteeship Council exerting pressure on British officials to meet African demands for greater political representation, as well as to move African territories on a swifter pace towards responsible government and independence (Taylor, 1963).

Internally, the British empire-state was hierarchically organized, with domestic as well as imperial/supra-colonial authorities located in the metropolitan center controlling and coordinating activities at home and abroad through different forms of tiered administration (Subrahmanyam, 2003). However, state development patterns diverged between the UK and its non-white colonies. Whereas UK local government institutions became increasingly uniform and tightly controlled during the period, with centrally established standards upheld by domestic central state authorities (Abramovitz and Eliasberg, 1957: 10), local government institutions in Britain's non-white colonies were organizationally diverse, with some areas "directly ruled" by British officials, others "indirectly ruled" by traditional native authorities (princes, emirs, chiefs, etc.), and still others—as in the case of "uncontacted" or "isolated" indigenous groups—avoiding colonial control entirely (Hailey, 1957; Rapporteurship on the Rights of Indigenous Peoples, 2013). In other words, the British empire-state system was characterized by *globalization*, with the homogenization and modernization of administrative arrangements in directly-ruled areas, as well as by *fragmentation*, with differentiated localized governing arrangements applied in indirectly-ruled areas. *Anarchy* was also in evidence, since uncolonized areas fell outside the empire-state hierarchy.

Linked to these divergent institutional arrangements was British empire-state "schizophrenia" in terms of developmental goals pertaining to the domestic state versus the non-white colonies (Subrahmanyam, 2004). Although both supra-colonial agencies and the agencies responsible for UK domestic administration were based (mainly) in London and answerable to the Westminster Parliament, the two sets of institutions did not pursue the same goals, meaning that the British empire-state was not "unitary" and only partially served a "guardianship" role. For example, while UK domestic spending on welfare increased substantially between 1890 and 1960, in Britain's Indian and African colonies public outlays on social development were scant and non-growing during the same period (ibid). From 1830 to 1920, when trade unions were being progressively decriminalized and workers' rights being embedded in law in the UK, a "new system of slavery" involving low-wage migrant "coolie" laborers was being introduced in Britain's overseas colonies, with empire-state authorities often turning a blind eye to abuses being committed against these workers by plantation owners (Tinker, 1974). As

Elliott Young (2015: 132) put it: "Britain . . . was both the leader of the anti-coolie trade movement and at the forefront of establishing indentured labor as a replacement for African slaves in their Caribbean colonies."

Inequalities between the core and periphery of the British empire-state were often the focus and/or the outcome of heterarchical processes taking place during the period, as non-state economic, political and/or social actors operating at different levels sought to influence how the empire-state was run and/or to challenge empire-state authorities' abilities to unilaterally determine political outcomes. The most important "extra-state authorities"[2] at the start of the New Imperialism period were the chartered companies that European empire-states used to amass and run their colonies in Africa and, during earlier periods, in Asia and the Americas (Staley, 1935). These "company-states" were hybrid entities, combining the features of a sovereign state and a private corporation, and played a strong role in state-building in Britain's overseas dependencies by building bureaucracies, taxation systems, infrastructure and military/policing systems (Phillips and Sharman, 2020).

Chartered companies could use their wealth and influence to subvert empire-state authority. For example, the British East India Company, which operated from 1600 until 1874, was able to persuade British MPs—nearly a quarter of whom held its company stock—to render decisions in its favor (Dalrymple, 2019). Some returning staff of the Company went further and purchased parliamentary seats. By 1772/3, the East India Company became so powerful that, when it ran into financial difficulties, it was considered "too big to fail" and benefited from history's first "mega-bailout." However, in exchange it had to submit to greater parliamentary scrutiny and regulation, which it had previously evaded.

A range of other extra-state authorities operating at colonial or trans-colonial level also challenged British empire-state sovereignty at different times and from different locations. For example:

- *Nationalist political parties* emerged in most British colonies to mobilize for self-government and independence. Groups such as the Indian National Congress, the Tanganyika African National Union and the Kenya African National Union challenged empire-state authority and questioned its legitimacy, transforming British policy from being proactive to reactive. In some cases, they grew very powerful; for example, British metropolitan authorities were forced to negotiate with Indian National Congress leaders to secure their cooperation in the run-up to the Second World War, which culminated in Britain owing a sizeable debt balance to India following the war (Hughes, 1958). Some nationalist political parties formed transcolonial or international networks to coordinate their efforts and increase pressures for self-government and independence.[3]
- *Colonial resistance movements*, whose aims were not chiefly political but instead economic, cultural and/or religious, occasionally formed to oppose colonial policies or legislation. In some cases, British government reactions

to their protests or rebellions eroded empire-state capacity and/or legitimacy. For example, British officials in Kenya spent an estimated £50 million in current revenues between 1952 and 1960—amounting to nearly one-third of total ordinary public expenditures in 1954/5 alone—to put down the Mau Mau uprising, which was a reaction to discriminatory colonial land policies and labor laws (Subrahmanyam, 2003: 268). While Gandhi's Salt Satyagraha in India did not lead to the repeal of the 1882 Salt Act—which gave the British government a monopoly on the manufacture and sale of salt, and allowed it to levy hefty salt taxes—it nevertheless undermined the legitimacy of British rule by drawing international media attention to the brutality with which the colonial government put down the (generally) non-violent protests (Sellars and Oltvai, 2016).

- *White settlers* constituted a small minority in non-white colonies such as Kenya, but were able to mold state policies through concerted actions, which could include threatening government officials or plotting to seize control of the colonial administrative apparatus (Best, 1979: 67; Good, 1976: 611). Settlers with substantial economic resources—such as plantation owners and their merchant associates—could successfully negotiate policy reversals on issues as emotive as the reenactment of indentured labor (Green, 1983). During the early stages of colonial rule, British authorities tended to align government policies to the interests of white settlers, but during the later stages—particularly in the wake of popular uprisings such as the Mau Mau rebellion—they tended to balance African interests against settler interests (Nissimi, 2006).

- *Christian missionaries* supported British imperialism by preparing the ground for formal occupation and/or providing social services on behalf of the Crown, but sometimes challenged empire-state authority. For example, missionaries in Nairobi formed a powerful political lobby with religious and humanitarian groups in Britain to raise public awareness of the poor treatment of Africans in Kenya, which precipitated shifts in policy, such as the 1923 Devonshire Declaration proclaiming the "paramountcy" of African interests (Allen, 2013).

As the above examples show, power relations within the British empire-state and the international empire-states system could be described as heterarchical, hierarchical and/or anarchical at different time periods and in different locations. The groups that challenged British empire-state authority also shifted over time, with some groups exhausting their social and/or economic capital by becoming steeped in corruption and scandal (e.g., East India Company), while others gained political influence by exploiting social/mass media to shift public opinion (e.g., Gandhi, Nairobi missionaries). What seems clear is that the mass decolonizations that took place following the Second World War, which led to a dwindling of the British empire-state until it approximated a "nation-state," were the result of heterarchical forces subverting empire-state hierarchies.

3. Conclusion: From Empire to Heterarchy

This chapter has shown that heterarchical power relations are not new, just as globalization and "fragmegration" are not processes that emerged in the late 20th century. Furthermore, examining the "plurality of new orders" that are said to be subverting or overcoming state authority today (see Belmonte, this book) suggests that many of the extra-state authorities regarded as having recently emerged have their origins in systems and processes that took place during the age of empire. Nevertheless, opportunities for strategically situated actors to engage in state capture or evade state regulation are far greater today than during previous epochs due to the speed of technological change and extent of global interconnectedness.

Most multinational corporations (MNCs) operating today are organized using the joint-stock company model pioneered by European governments in the late 16th century to pursue overseas trade and expansion via chartered companies (Phillips and Sharman, 2020: 1250). Analyses of the British East India Company— termed the "world's first aggressive multinational corporation" (Dalrymple, 2019: xxxvii)—note that its funding model encouraged it to act in the interests of its shareholders and to maximize profits, which was contradictory to its role as a political actor ruling a substantial portion of the Indian subcontinent. These institutional anomalies led the Company to loot rather than develop the territories and populations under its control. As Robins (2008) has remarked: "The political, economic and human consequences [of these arrangements] were profound, with a share price bubble in London's markets and famine and de-industrialization in Bengal." One lesson to be learned from the British East India Company experience is the danger of putting too much political power in the hands of a commercial enterprise without requisite checks—which in today's complex globalized environment, where MNCs can easily evade regulation by national states, means some form of global governance (Cerny, 2021).

Divisive and/or non-developmental British colonial policies and practices have produced fragile states that face challenges from a range of extra-state authorities. For example, the system of indirect rule, combined with policies such as preserving conservative forms of Islamic law and permitting unregulated and unreformed Quranic education to be applied, are said to explain the emergence of Boko Haram terrorism in Northern Nigeria (Afzal, 2020; Ukwandu, 2016; Robinson, 1999). European governments' arbitrary determination of territorial boundaries and imposition of secular nation-states in areas containing ethno-religiously fragmented populations have been identified as factors explaining the rise of ISIS in the Middle East (Masoom, 2016; Matin, 2018). Uneven political modernization, use of divide-and-rule strategies, rushed transitions to independence, lack of political training for non-white elites, and handovers of governing systems not fitting the pattern of social cleavages in given territories are said to explain political and social instability—including coups, civil wars and secessionist movements— in some of Britain's former colonies (Subrahmanyam, 2006). Understanding the causes of these developments is necessary for finding lasting solutions and ensuring that heterarchy does not lead to greater inequality.

Russia's invasion of Ukraine, taking place at the time of writing, signals the importance of adopting a dynamic and historically accurate view of states when analyzing world politics. After all, some European leaders (e.g., Germany's Olaf Scholz) have attributed the conflict to Russia's desire to rebuild its lost empire, while others (Russia's Mikhail Gorbachev) argue that it is instead America that seeks to build an empire. It is notable that the only academic article connecting the concept of heterarchy to contemporary empires focuses on the post-Cold War international system and argues that the world order is moving towards both hierarchy, since military power is increasingly concentrated in US hands, *and* heterarchy, since power otherwise is dispersed across many actors (Baumann and Dingwerth, 2015). Time will tell whether this analysis still applies in a year's time, given that the balance of power could be shifting.[4]

Notes

1 1919 refers to the year that the IR discipline is widely regarded as having come into being
2 Belmonte (this book) refers to these actors as "extra-state authorities," since despite their non-state nature, these agencies "compete with the state's ability to establish rules, control borders, formulate and implement public policies autonomously, and [also] go beyond states' boundaries [to] create their own sovereign system".
3 Examples of such networks include the National Congress of British West Africa, the Pan-African Freedom Movement for East and Central Africa, and the International League Against Imperialism.
4 Richard Sakwa (this book) provides a useful perspective on this dynamic.

References

Abramovitz, M. and Eliasberg, V.F. (1957) *The Growth of Public Employment in Great Britain.* Princeton: Princeton University Press.

Afzal, M. (2020) *From "Western Education is Forbidden" to the World's Deadliest Terrorist Group.* Washington, DC: Brookings Institute.

Allen, C. (2013) 'Missions and the Mediation of Modernity in Colonial Kenya.' *Penn History Review* 20(1): 9–43.

Barkawi, T. (2010) 'Empire and Order in International Relations and Security Studies', pp. 1360–1379. In Denemark, R. and Marlin-Bennett, R. (ed.) *The International Studies Encyclopaedia*, Vol. 3. London: Blackwell-Wiley.

Baumann, R. and Dingwerth, K. (2015) 'Global Governance vs Empire: Why World Order Moves Towards Heterarchy and Hierarchy.' *Journal of International Relations and Development* 18(1): 104–128.

Belmonte, R. and Cerny, P.G. (2021) 'Heterarchy: Toward Paradigm Shift in World Politics.' *Journal of Political Power* 14(1): 235–257.

Bentwich, N. (1946) 'Colonial Mandates and Trusteeships.' *Transactions of the Grotius Society* 32: 121–134.

Best, N. (1979) *Happy Valley: The Story of the English in Kenya.* London: Secker & Warburg.

Blakeslee, G.H. (1910) 'Introduction.' *The Journal of Race Development* 1(1): 1–4.

Cerny, P.G. (2021) 'Business and Politics in an Age of Intangibles and Financialization', Chapter 12. In Kellow, A., Porter, T. and Ronit, K. (eds.) *Handbook of Business and Public Policy.* Cheltenham: Edward Elgar.

Craven, M. (2015) 'Between Law and History: The Berlin Conference of 1884–1885 and the Logic of Free Trade.' *London Review of International Law* 3(1): 31–59.

Crumley, C.L. (1979) 'Three Locational Models: An Epistemological Assessment for Anthropology and Archaeology', pp. 141–173. In Schiffer, M.B. (ed.) *Advances in Archaeological Method and Theory*. New York: Academic Press.

Crumley, C.L. (1987) 'A Dialectical Critique of Hierarchy', pp. 155–169. In Patterson, T.C. and Gailey, C.W. (eds.) *Power Relations and State Formation*. Washington, DC: American Anthropological Association.

Crumley, C.L. (2015) 'Heterarchy'. In Scott, R.A., Kosslyn, S.M. and Buchmann, M. (eds.) *Emerging Trends in the Social and Behavioral Sciences*. Hoboken, NJ: John Wiley & Sons.

Dalrymple, W. (2019) *The Anarchy: The Relentless Rise of the East India Company*. London: Bloomsbury Publishing.

de Carvalho, B., Leira, H. and Hobson, J.M. (2011) 'The Big Bangs of IR: The Myths That Your Teachers Still Tell You about 1648 and 1919.' *Millennium* 39(3): 735–758.

Good, K. (1976) 'Settler Colonialism: Economic Development and Class Formation.' *The Journal of Modern African Studies* 14(4): 597–620.

Green, W.A. (1983) 'Emancipation to Indenture: A Question of Imperial Morality.' *Journal of British Studies* 22(2): 98–121.

Griffiths, I. (1986) 'The Scramble for Africa: Inherited Political Boundaries.' *The Geographical Journal* 152(2): 204–216.

Hailey, Lord (1957) *An African Survey: Revised 1956*. London: Oxford University Press and Royal Institute of International Affairs.

Helal, M.S. (2019) 'Anarchy, Ordering Principles and the Constitutive Regime of the International System.' *Global Constitutionalism* 8(3): 470–505.

Henderson, E. (2013) 'Hidden in Plain Sight: Racism in International Relations Theory.' *Cambridge Review of International Affairs* 26(1): 1–22.

Hughes, J.R.T. (1958) 'Financing the British War Effort.' *The Journal of Economic History* 18(2): 193–199.

Lake, D.A. (1996) 'Anarchy, Hierarchy and the Variety of International Relations.' *International Organization* 50(1): 1–33.

Lawson, G. (2018) 'International Relations as a Historical Social Science', Chapter 6. In Gofas, A., Hamati-Ataya, I. and Onuf, N. (eds.) *The Sage Handbook of the History, Philosophy and Sociology of International Relations*. London: Sage Publications.

Lechner, S. (2017) 'Why Anarchy Still Matters for International Relations: On Theories and Things.' *Journal of International Political Theory* 13(3): 341–359.

Louis, W.R. (1969) 'The United Kingdom and the Beginning of the Mandates System, 1919–1922.' *International Organization* 23(1): 73–96.

Masoom, S.N. (2016) 'A Colonial Catalyst: Reverberations of the Sykes-Picot Agreement in the Rise of ISIS.' *Inquiries Journal* [online] 8(11). www.inquiriesjournal.com/a?id=1494.

Matin, K. (2018) 'Lineages of the Islamic State: An International Historical Sociology of State (De)formation in Iraq.' *Journal of Historical Sociology* 31(1): 6–24.

Nissimi, H. (2006) 'Mau Mau and the Decolonisation of Kenya.' *Journal of Military and Strategic Studies* 8(3): 1–35.

Phillips, A. and Sharman, J.C. (2020) 'Company-States and the Creation of the Global International System.' *European Journal of International Relations* 26(4): 1249–1272.

Rapporteurship on the Rights of Indigenous Peoples (2013) *Indigenous Peoples in Voluntary Isolation and Initial Contact in the Americas: Recommendations for the Full Respect of Their Human Rights*. San José, Costa Rica: Inter-American Commission on Human Rights.

Robins, N. (2008) 'This Imperious Company: The East India Company and the Modern Multinational.' Lecture given at Gresham College, Friday, 27 June, 12:00am.

Robinson, F. (1999) 'The British Empire and the Muslim World', pp. 398–420. In Brown, J. and Louis, R. (eds.) *Oxford History of the British Empire: Volume IV: The Twentieth Century*. Oxford: Oxford University Press.

Schmidt, B. (1998) *The Political Discourse of Anarchy: A Disciplinary History of International Relations*. Albany, NY: SUNY Press.

Sellars, M. and Oltvai, K. (2016) 'The Salt March Today: Gandhian Lessons for Social Media Activism.' *Denison Journal of Religion* 15, article 6.

Staley, E. (1935) *War and the Private Investor: A Study in the Relations of International Politics and International Private Investment*. New York: Doubleday, Doran and Company.

Subrahmanyam, G. (2003) 'Bringing the Empire Back in: Patterns of Growth in the British Imperial State, 1890–1960 (with Special Reference to India and Africa).' Unpublished PhD thesis, London School of Economics and Political Science.

Subrahmanyam, G. (2004) 'Schizophrenic Governance and Fostering Global Inequalities in the British Empire: The UK Domestic State versus the Indian and African Colonies, 1890–1960.' Paper Presented to the 'Victory, Occupation, and Identity in International History' Panel at the American Political Science Association Annual Meeting in September.

Subrahmanyam, G. (2006) 'Ruling Continuities: Colonial Rule, Social Forces and Path Dependence in British India and Africa.' *Commonwealth & Comparative Politics* 44(1): 84–117.

Taylor, J.C. (1963) *The Political Development of Tanganyika*. Stanford, CA: Stanford University Press.

Tinker, H. (1974) *A New System of Slavery: The Export of Indian Labour Overseas 1830–1920*. London: Oxford University Press.

Tripathi, D. and Chaturvedi, S. (2020) 'South Asia: Boundaries, Borders and Beyond.' *Journal of Borderlands Studies* 35(2): 173–181.

Ukwandu, D. (2016) 'The Relationship between Indirect Rule and Quranic Education: Considerations for the Emergence of Boko Haram Terrorism in Northern Nigeria.' *African Journal of Public Affairs* 9(4): 174–192.

Vincent, A. (1992) 'Conceptions of the State', pp. 43–55. In Hawkesworth, M. and Kogan, M. (eds.) *Encyclopaedia of Government and Politics*, Vol. 1. London: Routledge.

Vitalis, R. (2005) 'Birth of a Discipline', Chapter 7. In Long, D. and Schmidt, B. (eds.) *Imperialism and Internationalism in the Discipline of International Relations*. Albany, NY: SUNY Press.

Waltz, K. (1979) *Theory of International Politics*. New York: McGraw-Hill.

Wendt, A. (1992) 'Anarchy is What States Make of It.' *International Organization* 46: 391–425.

Young, E. (2015) 'Chinese Coolies, Universal Rights and the Limits of Liberalism in an Age of Empire.' *Past & Present* 227(1): 121–149.

6

HETERARCHY AND STATE TRANSFORMATION

Lee Jones and Shahar Hameiri

Introduction: Things Fall Apart?

Most fair-minded readers of this volume's introduction will easily recognize the many fissiparous processes described therein. The age of nationally-cohesive societies being robustly governed exclusively by nation-states that then interact with each other as "unitary actors" is long gone—if it ever really existed. The question, however, is how to obtain theoretical traction in this more confusing era. Clearly, one can observe a host of disintegrative, cross-cutting processes and develop a wide variety of concepts to describe them. But how are we supposed to actually study and explain specific real-world outcomes?

This chapter outlines one possible approach focused on the dynamics of state transformation, which we have explored extensively in previous research. By "state transformation," we mean (a) the uneven and contested fragmentation, decentralization, and internationalization of state apparatuses, and (b) the reworking of state apparatuses into new, functionally-specific modes of governance operating at multiple territorial scales. Of course, the concept of heterarchy goes well beyond the state, acknowledging the emergence of hybrid or even entirely private governance regimes. Nonetheless, the concept is also premised on the dissolution of the traditional, Westphalian, Weberian state as a unitary, territorially bounded, and hierarchically organized system. New, experimental forms of governance cannot emerge until and unless this traditional approach to social, economic, and political management is "relativized" rather than seen as primary or absolute (Jessop 2009). State transformation is therefore the *necessary precondition* for heterarchy to emerge. Moreover, states are *transformed further* by the processes described by the label of heterarchy, as state apparatuses are reworked into new governance frameworks. They may be connected with international organizations, private authorities, civil society actors, overseas counterparts, and

DOI: 10.4324/9781003352617-7

so on, with their functions reconfigured to serve transnational agendas rather than domestic ones. State transformation is thus a crucial aspect of heterarchy. It is not necessarily involved in every form of heterarchy, but in many of the most important cases it will provide an important focus for analysis, theoretical development, and empirical analysis. Without such a focal point, heterarchy risks remaining a purely descriptive, overly broad, and potentially confusing concept.

Notwithstanding the fact that heterarchy can encompass non-state actors, there are good reasons to retain a focus on state power, even under contemporary conditions. Although states' "capacity" and ability to govern authoritatively certainly appears weaker today than at their postwar zenith, in our view, it is misleading to claim that states are "vulnerable and impotent," or to analytically "*decentre* . . . the state . . . by placing it *alongside* other social and economic groups," as if they are simply one actor among many, thereby "flattening the social" (Belmonte and Cerny 2021, 241, 242, original emphasis). To accept claims of "impotence" is to distort reality and let state managers—and the social groups whose interests they advance—off the hook. It is state managers who have promoted and enabled globalization and thus connive in their own transformation. "Impotence" is in many cases performative: elites claim, in the words of Margaret Thatcher, that "there is no alternative" to subordination to global market forces because this clothes their particularistic strategies and agendas in an aura of inevitability and helps to disable contestation—or simply legitimizes a lack of political vision and leadership. Moreover, even transformed states retain important capacities absent in other actors. Even where their authority is weak or contested, they typically exercise powers of legislation, regulation, taxation, and coercive enforcement that few or no non-state actors enjoy. This is precisely why so many new forms of governance emerging under heterarchy only rarely involve attempts to establish "their own sovereign system," rivalling that of states (cf. Belmonte and Cerny 2021, 246). Far more commonly, they seek to transform how state power is organized and exercised, further reconfiguring state apparatuses so that they serve transnational agendas (Hameiri and Jones 2016).

Moreover, the question of how effective these new regimes are and what interests they serve in practice is still determined by the structural power of social forces, which shape how far, in what ways, and for what purposes state power is actually transformed (Hameiri and Jones 2015). As Belmonte and Cerny (2021, 242) rightly but somewhat self-contradictorily note, many heterarchical regimes "embed 'the privileged position of business.'" But why should business have a "privileged position" relative to any other group? This cannot be understood through a "neo-pluralist" approach that understands states or heterarchical regimes as "flat." Instead, we need to foreground the "strategic selectivity" of institutions—the way that they reflect and entrench social power relations by being more open to certain forces and agendas than others (Jessop 2008). This Marxist insight is more consistent with Belmonte and Cerny's (2021, 245–246) observation that heterarchical governance is shaped more powerfully by special interest groups able to organize transnationally and typically operates to the disadvantage of those limited to national political action, enabling transnational regulatory capture. But it also focuses attention, more appropriately, on the contestation of state transformation "on the ground" in specific locales—because, after all, "global" regulations must still be implemented "locally," amid concrete relations of social, political, and economic power.

1. State Transformation as a Precondition for Heterarchy

The tendency in mainstream IR theory is to see states as transhistorical actors: ancient Athens was as much "a state" as, say, contemporary North Korea. In reality, states are a relatively recent innovation, emerging only through a prolonged struggle against a host of competing authorities. The state form fetishized in mainstream IR theory—unitary, territorially bounded, exercising exclusive sovereign power—only really emerged in the late 19th century, consolidating worldwide only for just a few decades after World War II. Since the late 1970s, this state form has been transformed by processes of fragmentation, decentralization, and internationalization associated with the promotion of neoliberal globalization. This transformation was a necessary condition for the processes characterized as heterarchy to emerge.

As international historians have emphasized, the modern nation-state emerged only quite recently and slowly. Contrary to those who see the states system emerging fully formed with the 1648 Treaty of Westphalia, through the medieval and early modern periods, state authority had to compete with other modes of governance. These included cross-cutting feudal relations, in which the ostensible ruler of one "state" might actually be the vassal of the ruler of another; sub-"national" units like city-states; and transnational suzerains like the Holy Roman Emperor and the Papacy (Spruyt 1994; Teschke 2003). It took centuries of struggle, religious wars, experiments with absolutism, and revolution for "nation-states" to emerge in Europe, with most consolidating only in the late 1800s. Even then, many of them were imperial formations, and it was not until well after World War II that the sovereign state form beloved of IR theory became the default "unit" of world politics.

The period from the 1940s to the late 1970s represents the high-tide of this form of political organization. This was underpinned domestically by new class compacts and internationally by mechanisms designed to support the consolidation of national power. In the advanced capitalist states, the experiences of depression, fascism, and war, and the rapid onset of the Cold War, drove the capitalist class into a new compromise with organized labor. In exchange for industrial peace and the containment of left-wing radicalism, capitalists conceded rising wages and state welfare. Corporatist institutions brought these forces together with state bureaucrats to collaboratively manage the national economy in the interests of this social compact. This Fordist–Keynesian arrangement was supported internationally by the United Nations framework, which emphasized state sovereignty and non-intervention, and the Bretton Woods institutions, which were designed to support the national management of domestic economies by, for example, regulating international exchange rates (Ruggie 1982). Notwithstanding continued neo-imperialist practices and superpower interventions, emerging post-colonial "quasi-states" also benefited from this regime, which normally presumed incumbent regimes' formal sovereignty (even in the absence of practical control), with development assistance provided to support the government's national development objectives (Jackson 1990).

Thus, as Jessop (2009, 99) observes, the post-war order

> rested on the primacy of *national* money over international currency and of the individual and social wage as a source of domestic demand rather than as a cost of international production, and these twin priorities were reflected in the primacy of *national* economies, *national* welfare states, and *national* societies managed by *national* states concerned to unify *national* territories and reduce uneven development.
>
> *(emphasis added)*

One should neither romanticize this era nor imagine that states were unchallenged authorities. Even as national states increasingly "caged" social relations from the late 19th century, they simultaneously gave rise to transnational forces and movements, with capitalism and socialism alike knowing no borders (Lacher 2003, 529). Revolutionary influences continued to cut across national borders, prompting interventions to contain them (Jones 2013). Nonetheless, compared to what preceded and followed it, this was a period characterized by the marked centralization of power in the form of the national state. It is hardly surprising that this profoundly shaped the main theories of modern IR, which all developed during this period.

Equally, the fact that the IR literature on international "regimes"—and, later, global governance—only emerged from the 1970s onwards is not coincidental but tracks the gradual transformation of this state form. This was triggered by successive crises of global capitalism: the collapse of the gold standard and thus the global arrangements supporting autonomous economic management by states; the oil crises; and a crisis of profitability that caused capitalists to withdraw from the post-war settlement with organized labor, prompting widespread industrial conflict. Through prolonged and sometimes violent struggle, this conflict was eventually settled in favor of capital, most prominently by the forces of the "new right"—Reagan, Thatcher, Pinochet—but also by ostensibly social democratic governments—such as those led by Hawke in Australia, Mitterrand in France, and Schröder in Germany (Harvey 2005). Trade unions were restricted or quashed, corporatist institutions dismantled, and the purposes of state power and policy fundamentally reconfigured, from managing and developing the national economy to promoting national competitiveness within a global marketplace (Cerny 1997). Global capital, never "euthanized," as Keynes had hoped for, but merely anaesthetized, was freed of its national shackles, unleashing what we now call "globalization" (Glyn 2007).

State apparatuses were reconfigured to enable this process, which can be described through three analytically distinct but related dynamics:

1. *Fragmentation.* This denotes the horizontal dispersion of authority and control over resources from powerful executive agencies to a host of public, private, and hybrid actors. For example, authority over the economy shifted from central planning units to a host of privatized enterprises, arms-length sectoral regulators, independent central banks, private standard-setting bodies, etc. (Leys 2003).
2. *Decentralization.* This denotes the devolution of authority and responsibility (though not necessarily control over the requisite resources) from national to subnational levels, such as provinces, regions, and cities. This involves the "rescaling" of state power from the national to the "meso" level (Keating 2013).
3. *Internationalization.* This involves state apparatuses, previously confined to purely domestic affairs, acquiring an international role and function. This could involve, for example, subnational governments engaging in "paradiplomacy" to attract foreign investment (Kuznetsov 2015); the networking of sectoral regulators, judicial authorities, etc., across state borders to harmonize policies and support greater foreign trade and investment (Slaughter 2004); and the extension of powerful states' domestic authorities beyond their borders to help manage problems like crime and disorder (Hameiri 2009).

Although initially originating through processes in the Global North, these dynamics have been spread worldwide through a series of more-or-less coercive interventions. These include: International Monetary Fund conditionality after the 1980s debt crisis and subsequent financial crises; post-conflict state-building interventions; the World Bank's promotion of decentralization; and "good governance" programs pushed by powerful northern donors (Harrison 2004; Hameiri 2010).

As the description of internationalization suggests, it is this transformation of the state that has given rise to heterarchy. In the peak era of the nation-state, foreign relations were dominated by heads of government, ministries of foreign affairs, and military organizations. Subsequently, the horizontal and vertical dispersal of power and authority has empowered a much wider range of actors to engage in international relations, breaking this traditional monopoly (Jayasuriya 2012). Governance has become more functionally specific as policy becomes delinked from a cohesive social compact and responsibilities are hived off to sectoral regulators and nongovernmental authorities. And it has become more transnational as these agencies seek to develop shared regulatory frameworks to ease the flow of goods, services, and capital, and to tackle the "dark side" of globalization: nontraditional security threats that arise from, or exploit the same infrastructure as, transboundary economic flows (Hameiri and Jones 2015). As Jessop (2009, 100) argues, with the transformation of the national state and the merging of national economies into a globalizing world market, the national scale of governance has become "relativized," as just one possibility among many, giving rise to

> significant experimentation with network forms of organization that might contribute to the development of a stable, post-national state better able to steer the integration of changing economic and political spaces into a globalizing knowledge-based economy marked by increased uneven development.

2. State Transformation as the Product of Heterarchy

However, these new modes of governance are not merely enabled by the transformation of statehood; they also operate through promoting further state transformation in the service of transnational agendas. Arguably, this is the main way in which "global governance" actually operates today (Hameiri and Jones 2016). Precisely because of the legacy of the era of peak nation-statehood, states remain formally legally sovereign, and they retain important capacities relating to regulation, resource mobilization, and enforcement. So far, no extant international organization—whether intergovernmental, private, or hybrid—can really hope to rival states in terms of these capacities. Consequently, the focus of most governance projects under heterarchy is not on generating rival "sovereignties," but rather on changing the way in which states govern their societies domestically. This focus is doubly important because the nature, form, and extent of state transformation remains conditioned by structural forces and socio-political conflicts operating around particular states. This allows us to explain the relative success or failure of governance projects but also in whose interests they actually operate.

Rather than understanding the transformed state as "weak" or "impotent," it is important to recall two conceptual points. First, contrary to Weberian state theory, which implicitly underpins both mainstream IR theory and much of the emerging literature on heterarchy, it is never accurate to describe a state as "strong" or "weak" *in general*. A state might simultaneously be very "weak" at regulating capital in the interests of the majority or providing public healthcare, for example, but exceedingly "strong" at incarcerating vast numbers of people, operating a highly intrusive global surveillance regime, and projecting military force around the world. This is a fair characterization of the contemporary United States, which in some respects appears to be a "failed state," while in other respects retains unparalleled power.

The correct question, then, is: in what ways are state apparatuses strong and weak, and—most importantly—whose interests are being served by this particular institutional configuration and use of resources? As Jessop (2008) rightly argues, no states are neutral; they all exhibit "strategic selectivity," being more open to certain forces and agendas than to others. As the preceding section showed, neither the consolidation of the post-WWII state nor its subsequent transformation was accidental. Rather, it corresponded to distinct moments in an evolving social conflict, rooted in dynamic political economy contexts. State transformation has, above all, corresponded to the needs of globalizing fractions of capital to pursue new modes of capital accumulation. As Belmonte and Cerny (2021, 245) rightly note, it has occurred at the expense of all those whose power and interests relied on a national scale of governance, especially the working class and organized labor. This is not a remotely "flat" social ontology. Heterarchy is emerging in the shadow of a social—especially class—hierarchy that is more acute than at any time since the late 19th century.

Second, reflecting the legacy of the "Westphalian" era, even ostensibly "weak" states retain important residual capacities that must be harnessed (or at least, not wielded in opposition) for many forms of heterarchical governance to emerge. International organizations, whether public, private, or hybrid, rarely (if ever) try to develop independent legislative, taxation, or enforcement powers. Certainly, they may try to develop action plans, codes of practice, standards, regulatory frameworks, targets, and other sorts of international agreements, and they may also monitor these and, in a smaller number of cases, settle disputes and identify appropriate sanctions for rule-breakers. However, typically, they rely upon states to actually enact the rules in their domestic contexts. This is true regardless of the issue area—from human rights to climate change and from trade to money laundering.

In human rights, for example, the UN and regional bodies may propagate rules, monitor compliance, produce reports, and so on, but the main bodies tasked with improving human rights in a given jurisdiction remain states. To be sure, international bodies may try to engage other actors, including civil society, media, and business groups, to improve monitoring and compliance. But ultimately, if a government is either recalcitrantly committed to continuing to abuse human rights, or unable to take necessary action to improve the situation, these actors will not be able to do much. This is because even supposedly "weak" states still possess considerable power: to legislate (to promote or prevent this or that form of human rights abuse); to extract and allocate resources (to fund or not fund bodies responsible for human rights protection); and to coercively enforce rules (to punish perpetrators or to enable impunity). To be sure, other actors could respond by punishing this state, such as by withdrawing investment or imposing sanctions. But in cases where regimes see conceding as excessively costly, and where they are sufficiently well-entrenched relative to domestic opposition, they are likely to withstand such punishment (Jones 2015).

By virtue of their formal sovereignty, states also retain an important "scale management" function (Peck 2002). That is, they have a powerful influence over whether the governance of an issue in their domain is *substantively* (rather than merely *formally*) rescaled to a subnational, regional, or global level. A government targeted for UN scrutiny on human rights can always use its sovereign authority to deny entry to the UN's special rapporteur, and invoke the non-interference principle at the UN Human Rights Council. A government can consent to the rules of the World Trade Organization, yet not implement them domestically, retaining important domestic limitations on the liberalization of trade and investment—as, for example, China does. Even very poor, "weak," and post-conflict states can and do reject development assistance projects that seek to rescale governance in market-promoting ways where this might undermine the interests of dominant social forces (Hameiri and Jones 2017). Again, such behavior may be externally punished, but more often it is recognized that securing the cooperation of an incumbent government is a *sine qua non* for governance projects to succeed.

Consequently, the dominant form that governance projects take under heterarchy is to promote the further transformation of state apparatuses, in line with international agreements. The classic form this takes is to identify a focal point within the state that will be responsible for governing a particular issue area, then seeking to reconfigure it such that it will impose international disciplines on the rest of its state and society. This may involve building new forms of state capacity (and/or reducing other forms), altering how a state apparatus relates to the rest of the state and society (e.g., through procedural, regulatory and/or legal changes), and potentially networking the transformed state apparatus across borders to facilitate ongoing policy diffusion, capacity building, and monitoring. Reflecting the fragmentation of state power, these efforts are typically functionally specific and so involve very different assemblages of actors in different issue areas. Where the cooperation of subnational governments is seen as important, governance projects may also reach deeply within states to engage decentralized actors. These efforts also spur the further internationalization of state apparatuses, as they ostensibly become less responsive to domestic interests and agendas, acting more on the basis of international rules, norms, or agreements, and also develop international relations of their own through transnational networking.

A good example of this approach is the governance of money laundering and terrorist financing. Anti-money laundering (AML) and countering the financing of terrorism (CFT) efforts are led globally by the Financial Action Task Force (FATF), an international organization created in 1989 by the Group of 7. FATF's basic purpose is to globalize the AML/CFT rules and priorities of the US. However, it does not do this by establishing a new "sovereignty" to rival that of states. Instead, FATF has developed a rule book—the so-called "40 Recommendations"—containing detailed prescriptions for the laws, regulations, and institutional arrangements that states should adopt. The 40 Recommendations designate a focal point within states for AML/CFT efforts—the Financial Intelligence Unit (FIUs)—and specify how it should relate to other state and non-state actors. FIUs are to receive and investigate suspicious transaction reports from financial institutions (in banking, gambling, real estate, etc.), and coordinate the activity of other law-enforcement agencies. They are thus the key node through which international disciplines are to be imposed on the rest of the state and society. FIUs are also internationalized. They are networked through the Egmont Group, a club of FIUs devoted to policy diffusion and capacity-building. And they belong to "FATF-style regional bodies," responsible for monitoring one another's implementation of the 40 Recommendations through periodic inspections. The IMF and World Bank also include AML/CFT criteria in their evaluations of developing countries. Importantly, FATF has no supranational enforcement or sanctioning powers. The force of its 40 Recommendations instead comes from the willingness of private financial institutions to use FATF evaluations in their estimations of country risk profiles. A jurisdiction that is "blacklisted" or "grey-listed" by FATF thus risks isolation from or considerably higher costs within global financial markets. FATF is thus a good example of heterarchy: a functionally specific governance network that links state apparatuses, international organizations and private institutions across multiple scales, cutting across traditional boundaries of states and regional organizations alike.

As noted above, state managers could theoretically use their scale management functions to reject the rescaling of AML/CFT governance. However, this is an unusual case of heterarchical governance insofar as the costs of outright rejection are extremely high, given the link to financial market access. Consequently, only Iran and North Korea have simply refused to adopt the 40 Recommendations.

More important in this case are the wider structural constraints that determine how far state apparatuses are transformed and operate according to FATF's rules. Here, even apparently "weak" and marginal states actually exhibit considerable noncompliance. Myanmar, for example, which is widely seen as a sort of "rogue" state, is identified as a major AML/CFT risk, given its central place in regional narcotics production and trafficking, and has effectively been grey-listed by FATF. Myanmar formally adopted FATF's 40 Recommendations in 2005, under its then military regime. The Myanmar state has been transformed along the lines of FATF's blueprint, with money laundering criminalized, an FIU established, and so on.

However, the system's practical capacity to prevent money laundering and tackle predicate crimes is clearly constrained by the interests of dominant social forces, rooted within Myanmar's political economy context. Myanmar's banking system, and the country's main conglomerates, were founded in the 1990s on money laundered from smuggling and drug trafficking, as the military regime sought to bring former rebel and criminal groups into the legal fold (Turnell 2009). Even with Myanmar's transition to a constrained electoral regime in 2010, the army maintains complex relations with ethnic-minority armed groups (EAGs) in the country's borderlands, ranging from outright warfare to ceasefires to the ostensible incorporation of militias into the state as "border guard forces." Although the government and some allied ceasefire groups have formally sought to suppress drug-trafficking, they are frequently forced to tolerate it in order to secure cooperation from local power brokers (Meehan 2011). In addition, EAGs frequently operate casinos in their areas, catering to wealthy "tourists," mostly from China, which have become hives of money-laundering and gangsterism. The country's booming real estate market is also seen as an easy route for money-laundering as buyers are not required to show the origins of their funds. Furthermore, much of Myanmar's economy is informal and dollarized, with lucrative trade often occurring outside of official channels. For example, Global Witness (2015) estimates that 50–80% of jade is smuggled directly across the Chinese border, netting the powerful groups involved US\$31 billion in 2014 alone, equivalent to half of Myanmar's formal gross domestic product (GDP). Proceeds from such activities must either be laundered domestically or internationally. The US-based NGO Global Financial Integrity estimates that almost US$120 billion in illicit income has been funneled through Myanmar from 1960–2013 (Spanjers and Kar 2015).

Given these circumstances it is easy to understand why the practical operation of Myanmar's AML/CFT is highly constrained. It is simply not in the interests of most private-sector institutions to report suspicious transactions, which in some cases are the foundation of their business model. It would also be exceedingly dangerous—indeed, potentially life-threatening—for FIU officers to investigate many cases too closely, as very powerful actors could be involved in some way. Consequently, as peer reviews from the Asia/Pacific Group, the FATF-style regional body covering Myanmar, have repeatedly found, practical enforcement is very limited. As we have shown elsewhere, high-profile AML cases are limited to those considered disloyal to the government—i.e. the whole regime is used to bolster political control over key economic actors, in a sort of society-wide protection racket (Hameiri and Jones 2015, 190–203). This is very far from a "flat" social ontology: powerful social forces determine how heterarchy works in practice.

Lest this dynamic be thought peculiar to "weak" states like Myanmar, let us consider the heartlands of global capitalism, home to supposed "strong" states. Experimental research has shown that it is actually easier to violate FATF rules in the US and Britain than anywhere else on Earth (Findley et al. 2014). This is because the state-facilitated financialization of the US and British economies has fostered large, powerful financial centers operating as *de facto* tax havens (Shaxson 2011). State power in these jurisdictions is now firmly subordinated to financial sector interests, as demonstrated in the post-2008 banking bailouts (Tooze 2018). This is achieved both agentially—through a "revolving door" between regulators and banks, large-scale donations to leading political parties, etc.—but also structurally, with banks becoming so central to the wider economy that they are "too big to fail."

Consequently, these countries' FIUs are kept weak and underpowered relative to the industry they ostensibly regulate. Britain's FIU's budget in 2017/18 was just £3.49 million, with 109 staff, while the country's financial sector employed 2.3 million people managing $10.8 trillion assets (Wallace 2018a, 2018b; TheCityUK 2018). As of 2019, the US FIU, FinCEN, employed just 332 people with a budget of US$115 million, while the financial sector employed 6.3 million people managing over $70 trillion of assets (FinCEN 2019, 4; United States Department of Commerce n.d.). Leaks show that the financial sector overwhelms FinCEN with reports, filing over 12 million from 2011 to 2017, covering over $2 trillion in transactions. Since FinCEN lacks the capacity to investigate even a tiny minority of these, banks can thus demonstrate "compliance" while continuing to launder money (International Consortium of Investigative Journalists 2020). Again, there is nothing "flat" about social ontology here: the most powerful sections of capital are determining how heterarchical governance actually works in practice.

3. Conclusion

This chapter has argued that state transformation is implicated in the emergence of heterarchy in two ways. First, the fragmentation, decentralization and internationalization of the state is a necessary precondition for the emergence of heterarchy. Second, heterarchical governance projects predominantly operate through the further transformation of state apparatuses, seeking to network them transnationally so that they impose international disciplines on the rest of their states and societies. We have only been able to sketch broad outlines and quick illustrations here. But elsewhere we have developed detailed analytical frameworks for studying these processes, allowing us to explain exactly how heterarchical governance projects are pursued, implemented, and operate in practice—and, crucially, to whose benefit (Hameiri 2010; Hameiri and Jones 2015; Hameiri et al. 2017; Jones and Hameiri 2021). As our introduction pointed out, focusing on state transformation will not capture or be useful for studying every form of heterarchical governance. Purely private forms of governance, for example, may not involve or rely directly upon state power in any way. However, in many instances, focusing on state transformation is a crucial way to gain analytical traction on the slippery concept of heterarchy.

This focus also entails several theoretical insights that should shape the empirical study and normative evaluation of heterarchy.

1. Although the state has been fragmented, decentralized, internationalized, and relativized, it still remains extremely important to explaining social, political and economic outcomes. Because states retain important and unique capacities, they should not simply be downgraded to one actor among many. They still require careful study as specific kinds of social organization. Consequently, state theory should be central to the development of work on heterarchy.

2. Social power relations are hierarchical, not "flat." A paradigmatic shift from anarchy to heterarchy should not lose sight of the fact that power and resources remain distributed in a highly uneven manner. Heterarchy scholars need to use frameworks that do not simply describe a host of confusing processes, but are sensitive to the ways in which these processes are patterned, reflecting these underlying power relations. The fact that heterarchical governance often seems to privilege business, for example, is not accidental; it is a product of the structural power of capital. Rather than straining to avoid full recognition of this fact—and the perhaps uncomfortable acceptance of Marxist insights that this may entail—heterarchy scholars need to confront this fact openly.

3. "Regulatory capture" is not simply a transnational phenomenon but also occurs "locally," reflecting the multiscalar nature of many heterarchical regimes. It is correct to foreground the strategic selectivity of transnational governance regimes: they are indeed open to only a limited range of societal actors, capable of mobilizing at regional or global levels. However, insofar as these regimes seek to transform domestic governance, internationally-networked regulators must still, at some point, go back home and seek to

implement these projects. Here, they will generally encounter structural limitations, opposition and contestation—possibly entailing forms of regulatory capture. The practical effects of heterarchical governance are therefore determined by struggles occurring at multiple territorial scales.

References

Belmonte, Rosalba, and Philip G. Cerny. 2021. "Heterarchy: Towards Paradigm Shift in World Politics." *Journal of Political Power* 14 (1): 235–257.

Cerny, Philip G. 1997. "Paradoxes of the Competition State: The Dynamics of Political Globalization." *Government and Opposition* 32 (2): 251–274.

FinCEN. 2019. *Department of the Treasury Financial Crimes Enforcement Network, Congressional Budget Justification and Annual Performance Report and Plan*. Washington, DC: FinCen. https://home.treasury.gov/system/files/266/12.-FINCEN-FY-2020-CJ.pdf.

Findley, Michael G., Daniel L. Nielson, and J. C. Sharman. 2014. *Global Shell Games: Experiments in Transnational Relations, Crime, and Terrorism*. Cambridge: Cambridge University Press.

Global Witness. 2015. *Jade: Myanmar's "Big State Secret."* London: Global Witness.

Glyn, Andrew. 2007. *Capitalism Unleashed*. Oxford: Oxford University Press.

Hameiri, Shahar. 2009. "Governing Disorder: The Australian Federal Police and Australia's New Regional Frontier." *Pacific Review* 22 (5): 549–574.

Hameiri, Shahar. 2010. *Regulating Statehood: State Building and the Transformation of the Global Order*. Basingstoke: Palgrave Macmillan.

Hameiri, Shahar, Caroline Hughes, and Fabio Scarpello. 2017. *International Intervention and Local Politics: Fragmented States and the Politics of Scale*. Cambridge: Cambridge University Press.

Hameiri, Shahar, and Lee Jones. 2015. *Governing Borderless Threats: Non-Traditional Security and the Politics of State Transformation*. Cambridge: Cambridge University Press.

Hameiri, Shahar, and Lee Jones. 2016. "Global Governance as State Transformation." *Political Studies* 64 (4): 793–810.

Hameiri, Shahar, and Lee Jones. 2017. "Beyond Hybridity to the Politics of Scale: International Intervention and 'Local' Politics." *Development and Change* 48 (1): 54–77.

Harrison, Graham. 2004. *The World Bank and Africa: The Construction of Governance States*. London: Routledge.

Harvey, David. 2005. *A Brief History of Neoliberalism*. Oxford: Oxford University Press.

International Consortium of Investigative Journalists. 2020. "Global Banks Defy US Crackdowns by Serving Oligarchs, Criminals and Terrorists." www.icij.org/investigations/fincen-files/global-banks-defy-u-s-crackdowns-by-serving-oligarchs-criminals-and-terrorists/.

Jackson, Robert H. 1990. *Quasi-States: Sovereignty, International Relations, and the Third World*. Cambridge: Cambridge University Press.

Jayasuriya, Kanishka. 2012. "Breaking the 'Westphalian' Frame: Regulatory State, Fragmentation and Diplomacy." In *Diplomacy and Developing Nations: Post-Cold War Foreign Policy-Making Structures and Processes*, edited by Justin Robertson and Maurice A. East, 39–54. Abingdon: Routledge.

Jessop, Bob. 2008. *State Power: A Strategic-Relational Approach*. Cambridge: Polity.

Jessop, Bob. 2009. "Avoiding Traps, Rescaling States, Governing Europe." In *Leviathan Undone? Towards a Political Economy of Scale*, edited by Roger Keil and Rianne Mahon, 87–104. Vancouver: UBC Press.

Jones, Lee. 2013. "Sovereignty, Intervention, and Social Order in Revolutionary Times." *Review of International Studies* 39 (5): 1149–1167.

Jones, Lee. 2015. *Societies Under Siege: Exploring How International Economic Sanctions (Do Not) Work*. Oxford: Oxford University Press.

Jones, Lee, and Shahar Hameiri. 2021. *Fractured China: How State Transformation in Shaping China's Rise*. Cambridge: Cambridge University Press.

Keating, Michael. 2013. *Rescaling the European State: The Making of Territory and the Rise of the Meso*. Oxford: Oxford University Press.

Kuznetsov, Alexander S. 2015. *Theory and Practice of Paradiplomacy: Subnational Governments in International Affairs*. Abingdon: Routledge.

Lacher, Hannes. 2003. "Putting the State in Its Place: The Critique of State-Centrism and Its Limits." *Review of International Studies* 29 (4): 521–541.

Leys, Colin. 2003. *Market-Driven Politics: Neoliberal Democracy and the Public Interest*. London: Verso.

Meehan, Patrick. 2011. "Drugs, Insurgency and State-Building in Burma: Why the Drugs Trade is Central to Burma's Changing Political Order." *Journal of Southeast Asian Studies* 42 (3): 376–404.

Peck, Jamie. 2002. "Political Economies of Scale: Fast Policy, Interscalar Relations, and Neoliberal Workfare." *Economic Geography* 78 (3): 331–360.

Ruggie, John Gerard. 1982. "International Regimes, Transactions, and Change: Embedded Liberalism in the Postwar Economic Order." *International Organization* 36 (2): 379–415.

Shaxson, Nicholas. 2011. *Treasure Islands: Tax Havens and the Men Who Stole the World*. London: Vintage Books.

Slaughter, Anne-Marie. 2004. *A New World Order*. Princeton: Princeton University Press.

Spanjers, Joseph, and Dev Kar. 2015. *Flight Capital and Illicit Financial Flows to and from Myanmar: 1960–2013*. Washington, DC: Global Financial Integrity. https://gfintegrity.org/report/flight-capital-and-illicit-financial-flows-to-and-from-myanmar-1960–2013/.

Spruyt, Hendrik. 1994. *The Sovereign State and Its Competitors: An Analysis of Systems Change*. Princeton: Princeton University Press.

Teschke, Benno. 2003. *The Myth of 1648: Class, Geopolitics, and the Making of Modern International Relations*. London: Verso.

TheCityUK. 2018. *Key Facts about the UK as an International Financial Centre 2018*. London: TheCityUK. www.export.org.uk/resource/resmgr/media/news/key-facts-about-the-uk-as-an.pdf.

Tooze, Adam. 2018. *Crashed: How a Decade of Financial Crises Changed the World*. London: Allen Lane.

Turnell, Sean. 2009. *Fiery Dragons: Banks, Moneylenders and Microfinance in Burma*. Copenhagen: NIAS Press.

United States Department of Commerce. n.d. "Financial Services Spotlight: The Financial Services Industry in the United State." *SelectUSA*. www.selectusa.gov/financial-services-industry-united-states#:~:text=The%20financial%20services%20and%20insurance%20sectors%20employed%20more%20than%206.3,significant%20advantages%20for%20financial%20firms.

Wallace, Ben. 2018a. "UK Financial Intelligence Unit: Expenditure." *TheyWorkForYou*. www.theyworkforyou.com/wrans/?id=2018-10-18.181273.h.

Wallace, Ben. 2018b. "UK Financial Intelligence Unit: Staff." *TheyWorkForYou*. www.theyworkforyou.com/wrans/?id=2018-11-27.196263.h.

7

POLITICAL POWER IN A HETERARCHICAL WORLD

A Categorization of Extra-state Authorities

Rosalba Belmonte

1. Political Authority in XXI Century

Since the transnational flows of knowledge systems, business practices, economic bodies and the forms of social organizations produced by globalization determined an increasing erosion of nation-state sovereignty, the state-centric system has been starting to be overcome by a plurality of new orders: territories without government; governments without territory; mobile borders; mobile people; supra-national powers; private authorities; non-state public authorities (Habermas, 1999; Cassese, 2016; Cerny & Prichard, 2017).

The result of these transformations is a heterarchical world (Belmonte & Cerny, 2021) in which territorial boundaries of states no longer coincide with those of political authority. In other words, globalization disperses political power among an increasingly complex structure of socioeconomic forces and levels of governance that transform the traditional world politics in a "polycentric or multi-nucleated global political system" (Cerny, 2010, p. 12) in which domestic politics and international relations intersect.

In this new global political scenario—characterized by fluid boundaries, growing inequalities and social marginalities, the proliferation of non-national identities and the emergence of *no-go areas* that states action cannot reach anymore – complex structures of actors and jurisdictions (states, non-state authorities, private interest groups) coexist and interact or collide with each other (*ibid*). Based on their hierarchical position with respect to the states, those actors can be divided in four sets lying on three different levels of power (Figure 7.1).

At the upper level there are the supranational authorities: regional political organizations and multilateral economic actors. At the intermediate ends, there are states and the extra-state authorities, namely a large number of non-state actors that, because of their heterogeneity, compose a particularly complex set of

DOI: 10.4324/9781003352617-8

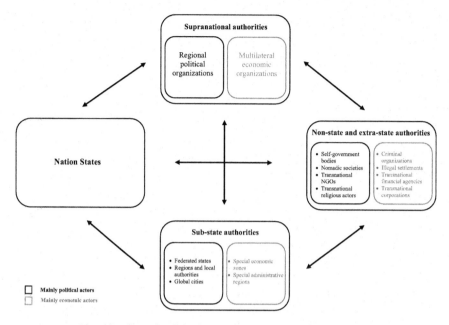

FIGURE 7.1 Classification of political authorities into four sets of actors and composition of the sets.

Source: Author's own elaboration based on the research carried out (see References).

actors that will be analyzed in the following pages. Finally, at the lower level, we find the sub-state (or local) authorities: local governments that are "able to allow large populations grouped in villages, cities or entire regions to self-govern totally or partially their communities" (Damiani, 2010, p. 15).

The set of the extra-state authorities is the most complex especially because of the variety of actors that compose it. It includes those forms of political authorities that, despite their non-state nature, self-regulate and hold the power to influence the activity of states and to take part in public decision-making processes. Indeed, in the last decades, these actors have significantly increased their role in global politics coming to compete with states' capacity to establish rules, control borders, formulate and implement public policies (Strange, 1996; Stringham, 2015; Belmonte & Cerny, 2021). This set is composed by both actors that pursue mainly political goals and actors that pursue mainly economic-financial goals. The firsts are *de facto* self-government bodies (i.e., the *Rebel Zapatista Autonomous Municipalities of Chiapas* and the *Democratic Federation of Rojava*), that do not enjoy any formal recognition; *de jure* self-government bodies (i.e., the Palestinian National Authority) that are recognized as public authorities but not as States; nomadic societies; transnational NGOs; transnational (political) religious movements. The seconds are transnational corporations; transnational financial agencies; and transnational criminal organizations.

2. Extra-State Authorities in a Globalizing World

It follows an overview of the extra-state authorities.

Transnational corporations (TNCs). TNCs are generally organizations that control the production of goods and services in more than one country (Meier & Schier, 2001). Besides being the largest economic institutions in today's world (Marchetti, 2016), TNCs are also political actors in global governance: they practice lobbying activities, create transnational networks with political aims, self-regulate and produce public regulations, and implement public policies such as development aids, disaster relief, and so on (Braithwaite & Draho, 2000; Haufler, 2001; Marchetti, 2016). TNCs operate in strategic and productive sectors that were controlled nearly exclusively by states until the mid-20th century. Moreover, they pursue a foreign policy and deal with the governments directly. Indeed, in an era when states compete to attract FDI, TNCs hold the power to make strategic actions and decisions independently of the interests of the countries in which they operate, and to influence the states regarding environmental and use of land policies. Furthermore, in the last decades we witnessed the emergence of private regulation systems for e-commerce, private police forces, private forms of dispute settlement, risk management agencies and so on (Stringham, 2015). Finally, the transnational nature of these corporations allows them to transcend the states' borders, thus bypassing the limits imposed by territorial sovereignty of states. TNCs also represent real communities that produce a sense of belonging among their members, identity cultures and consumer lifestyles (Martinelli, 2004).

Insurance, rating, risk management agencies and accountants. These actors operate in several economic-financial fields and play an increasing role in the world economy—and thus in world politics –, affecting the allocation of resources between social groups, national economies, and commercial enterprises. Their authority originates from their power to affect other actors' activities through incentives and/or deterrents aimed at determining their decisions. Their legitimacy comes from people's trust in their capacity to guarantee the long-term stability of the capitalist system by ensuring trust among participants in economic–financial transactions (Pizzorno, 2001). Consequently, through the control of huge movements of capital, the big corporations working in the field of insurances, accountants, brokers and so on, are able to determine the industrial development paths by exerting an increasing political authority. Indeed, their activity does not influence only private investors but also the behavior of rulers, who recur to transnational financial agencies to assess the security and solidity of private and public institutions, thus limiting the national government's autonomy.

Transnational political–religious movements. Shani (2009, p. 308) defines a transnational religious actor as "any non-governmental actor which claims to represent a specific religious tradition which has relations with an actor in another state or with an international organization." Through several forms of soft power such as proselytism, organization of a religious diaspora's interests and welfare services, transnational religious actors become increasingly important in the international political scenario, and today they hold the power and the legitimation to be considered political authorities and to affect the public decision-making processes.

In some cases, they constitute real global extended networks involving billions of people—especially Muslims (i.e., the Muslim Brotherhood or the Islamic Cooperation Organization), Jews (i.e., the Jewish National Fund) and Christians (i.e., the Roman Catholic Church)—whose main goal is to organize the interests and provide facilities and services to their communities (Haynes, 2001). Their influence directly affects devotees, and, in the last decades, its diffusion has been facilitated by the impetuous development of mass media, which allows religious-political messages to reach public opinion all over the world immediately (Ozzano, 2012). In this regard, Shani (2009) claims that globalization has significantly favored the development of transnational religious movements, allowing them to create a transnational identity able to question the traditional territorial world order.

These actors receive economic contributions from states and other non-state actors, donations from the devotees, and control many economic activities. All of this allows them to provide infrastructures and services to their communities, exerting both a relational power—that is legitimated by the people's faith—and structural power—that is legitimated by their ability to concretely modify the people's and environment's conditions.[1]

Transnational non-governmental organizations. According to the UN General Secretariat: "An NGO is a non-profit entity whose members are citizens or associations of citizens of one or more countries and whose activities are determined by the collective will of its members in response to the needs of the members or of one or more countries and whose activities are determined by the collective will of its members in response to the needs of the members or of one or more communities with which the NGO cooperates."[2]

By interacting with state institutions and with the global regulatory regimes, taking part in the negotiation of multilateral treaties, lobbying the states and directing public opinion, NGOs represent specific interests and collective needs. Their transnational character makes them independent from the states and able to give voice to a new type of public interest, which is interpreted by the so-called global civil society (Cassese, 2016; Ferrarese, 2000). Furthermore, they are capable of carrying out and providing facilities, services and protection whenever such tasks are included in their own policy agenda, and they are also able to obtain large funds and deploy significant resources (Martinelli, 2004; Marchetti, 2016). Consequently, states cannot do without considering the crucial role played by NGOs in world politics.

Transnational criminal cartels and mafias. They are solid power structures whose origins in many cases precede the formation of nation-states. They evolved in time, reaching such levels of complexity that made them represent a counterweight to the state power. Although engaged in activities explicitly illegal, transnational criminal cartels and mafias present many characteristics typical of the state authority: a complex power structure through which disobedience is punished by coercion; the control of economic sectors, also through the ownership of firms; forms of taxation (even if in the form of extortion); and so on (Ciconte et al., 2013). Furthermore, beyond their capacity to control territories, these kinds of criminal associations can establish transnational networks that sometimes involve states and public authorities (Strange, 1996; Ciconte et al., 2015).

Illegal settlements. This expression refers to every community based on land that belongs to other (public and legitimate) authorities. Currently, this phenomenon occurs only in the Palestinian Territory[3] and in Syria[4] where settlements are inhabited by Jewish civilians (Allegra, 2013; Petti, 2007). Their creation has been allowed over the years by various Israeli governments and, in some cases, settlements ("outposts") were also established without the permission of Israeli authorities. Settlements' administration is under the control of the Israeli government, which was condemned several times by the UN Security Council and by the UN General Assembly for their construction and extension. Indeed, their construction represents a violation of article 49.6 of the Fourth Geneva Convention: "The Occupying Power shall not deport or transfer parts of its own civilian population into the territory it occupies."[5] According to Amnesty International,[6] almost 621,000 people live in more than 120 settlements approved by Israeli governments and in as many outposts. Illegal settlements exercise power that allows them to modify the environment and the life conditions of people living in the area.

Nomadic societies. Nomadic people are "persons without a fixed place of usual residence who move from one site to another, usually according to well-established patterns of geographical mobility."[7] These societies—whose origin precedes the existence of nation-states—are ruled by systems of institutions, laws and rules that change according to the groups but are united by the common goal of efficiency (Moretti, 2012). These organizations resist the attempts of states to assimilate and make them sedentary. Although nomadism contrasts with the traditional concept of territorial nation-state, many nomadic societies are strongly linked to their territories, which are fundamental for their subsistence (*ibid.*). Nomadic people are included in the international protection systems of indigenous, tribal people and of minorities,[8] aiming at protecting their fundamental rights to non-discrimination, cultural identity, land and political autonomy.

Uncontacted tribes. These are tribal societies that have not been reached for centuries by people of dominant cultures. This form of isolation made these groups the most vulnerable on the planet, both because they did not develop any kind of immunity from diseases that are very common in the rest of the world and because of the threat represented by the foreign people interested in taking possession of their land and their territories. Nowadays, in the world there are roughly one hundred uncontacted tribes, seventy-seven of which live in the Amazon Forest.[9] Generally, state governments decide to preserve their isolation, although sometimes these decisions are violated by missionaries, tourists and criminals.

Self-government bodies. This expression refers to all those forms of non-state and extra-state authorities governing territories not subjected to another state sovereignty, thus representing an alternative model to the Westphalian system of government. Two examples of self-government bodies are the *Rebel Zapatista*

Autonomous Municipalities of Chiapas and the *Democratic Federation of Rojava* that, despite some different features, have in common the fact of originating in contexts characterized by opposition between a state that claims sovereignty on a territory and the people refusing to be subjected to this state. In addition, both of these political authorities rule territories and are legitimized by the approval of the population governed.

Because of their capacity to govern some territories, the recognition of their authority by the population and their (informal) transnational subjectivity, those examples of self-government are interlocutors that global actors should necessarily take into consideration.

Other cases of political organisms are represented by those political entities that, despite autonomously governing some territories whose populations claim their independence, are not recognized as states by many UN member-states. Those forms of authorities are called *de facto states* (Pegg, 1998; Bachelli et al., 2004; Berg & Toomla, 2009; Caspersen & Stansfield, 2011), *pseudo-States* (Kolossov & O'Loughlin, 1998; Cohen, 2003) or *unrecognized quasi-States* (Kolsto, 2006). Other authors (Papadimitriou & Petrov, 2012; Bouris & Fernández-Molina, 2018), instead, refer to political entities that suffer from a lack of international legitimacy using the expression *contested States*, in virtue of the fact that many governments and international organisms question their state nature. According to Krasner (2001), Papadimitriou & Petrov (2012), "contested statehood" is a situation where one or more of the following characteristics hold true:

- An internationally recognized state authority (as expressed by full membership of the UN) cannot maintain effective control over its respective territory (or parts of it), either because of an ongoing conflict or its profound disconnection with the local population.
- The de facto governing authority of a contested territory has declared independence, but it does not command full diplomatic recognition by the international community as expressed by full membership of the UN.
- The capacity of an internationally recognized or a de facto government to exercise authority is severely compromised due to the weakness of its state apparatus, either because of poor resources or complications in the constitutional arrangement underpinning its operation.

3. A Categorization of the Extra-State Authorities

Since extra-state authorities are constantly evolving and are so different among each other in terms of economic capability, political influence, claims, interests pursued, legitimacy and territorial configuration, it appears much complicated to approach them together in a classification based on their nature and organizational structure. Instead, an easier path to follow would be a classification having as a standard of comparison the state and considering as variables the nature of the interests pursued by these authorities and their "territoriality."

All the authorities reviewed in the previous paragraph are very different between each other in terms of shape, structure and extension but, as already mentioned, they are united by the fact that—through their existence—they question the state-centric system. Also, due to a growing participation in public decisions, an increasingly bigger availability of resources, and a larger involvement in the realization of public policies they have in common an increasing role in the world political arena.

Starting from this premise, this work proposes an ideal-typical classification of the aforementioned extra-state authorities based on the nature of the interests pursued (public- or private-oriented authorities) and the territorial extension of their power (territorial or non-territorial authorities).

3.1 Territory

Over the centuries, the relation between political authority and territory has been indissoluble. Territory, borders, public powers and juridical systems used to constitute, as a whole, a unitary phenomenon that could be summarized in the nation-state.

With the intensification of globalization, we witness a growing fragmentation of spaces, the transformation of the global political scenario and also the emergence of new universal principles that are valid regardless of the will of states. This scission between territories and power determines a loss of stability of the borders that originate new forms of construction of spaces and an increase of the flows crossing those spaces. All this produces territories without governments, authorities without states, shifting boundaries, regulatory systems transcending the borders and increasingly powerful supranational authorities (Cassese, 2016).

In this context of loss of relevance of the link between territory and authority, territoriality becomes a very important element of distinction among the several existing forms of political authority. The aspects that have been considered in order to define if an authority can be considered territorial or not are: the exclusive control of a specific territory, the use of force to defend the territory, a system of rules valid on a specific territory, sanctions imposed against any violation of rules, a system of rights and duties for people living in the territory, and, finally, historical events, foundation myths, traditions, symbols that witness the link between the authority and a specific territory.

3.2 Interest

From the second half of the 20th century—when politics has been starting to lose its supremacy on economics—many sectors traditionally dominated by state monopolies became shared between both public and private authorities. Since nowadays the border between "private" and "public" is becoming increasingly fluid, an aspect that allows differentiation between private and public authorities consists in the nature of the aim pursued (private or public/general) (Ferrarese, 2000). From this specific perspective, public/general interest consists in the purposes that individuals pursue as members of a community, from which all (or almost all) will benefit. Instead, private interest is the aim that leads people to pursue particular goals, which are not related to being a member of the society, but to other forms of belonging both legal (e.g., families, religious communities) and illegal (e.g., criminal cartels, illegal settlements). In order to establish if an authority should be considered as public- or private-oriented, the aspects to consider are related to the origin (*input*) and the destination (*output*) of the authorities' resources and consist in: legitimate forms of taxation, resources coming from public institutions to provide goods and services for the purpose of the whole community welfare, public legitimation, public and legitimate decision-making processes for what concerns the use of public resources, use of the community resources to produce goods and services accessible by everybody, equitable provision of resources and services to the community (principles of equity and solidarity).

3.3 Four Categories of Extra-State Authorities

Taking into account the *territoriality* and the *nature of the interest pursued*, it has been possible to divide the extra-state authorities in four ideal-typical categories (Table 7.1): territorial public authorities; territorial private authorities; non-territorial public authorities; non-territorial private authorities.

By observing the similarities and the elements of distinction between the components of each category, it emerges that the aspect that best qualifies them is the original source of the authority, according to which the four categories have been renamed: territorial public authorities become *self-government authorities*; territorial private authorities become *(mainly) illegal authorities*; non-territorial public authorities become *civil society authorities*; non-territorial private authorities become *economic-financial authorities*.

"*Self-government authorities*" category includes uncontacted societies,[10] nomadic societies and self-government bodies.[11] It is a widely heterogeneous category because of the different origins and structures of its components. The latter have in common the fact of being organized in communities and administering territories on which they do not recognize any other authority. Self-government authorities claim through diverse means (formal declarations, requests addressed

TABLE 7.1 Categorization of the Extra-State Authorities.

	Public-oriented	*Private-oriented*
Territorial	Nomadic societies Uncontacted societies Self-government bodies	Criminal cartels Illegal settlements
Non-territorial	Transnational religious movements Transnational NGOs	Transnational Corporations Transnational financial agencies

Source: Author.

to supranational institutions, conflicts and armed resistance against states claiming the control of the same territory) the monopolistic control of a specific territory— fundamental for the existence of the authority—due to an historical and cultural tie.

On their territories, "self-government authorities" established bureaucracies, hierarchies and systems of rules aiming to guarantee law and order and to protect the land and the people living there. Also, through standard systems of taxations, they gather economic resources that, according to the public and legitimate decisions, are employed to provide—in a non-discriminatory manner—good and services to their communities.

The *"illegal authorities"* category includes criminal organizations[12] and illegal settlements. This denomination is due to the fact that its components have in common their illegal status under the legislations of states and supranational authorities. Criminal organizations and illegal settlements are considered territorial forms of authority because they claim, especially through the use of violence, the control of specific territories to which they are linked by group identity, historical presence or religious narratives. These types of authorities impose systems of preceptive and sanctioning rules on the territories they control, regardless of the laws established by the legitimate authorities. The respect of their systems of rules is guaranteed through forces in charge of maintaining the established order. Despite they present some of the aspects characterizing state governments (e.g. solid structures of power and the threat of the use of force), those authorities do not pursue public-oriented interests because they are not considered legitimate by external public authorities and they do not establish legitimate forms of taxation,[13] their decision-making processes related to the use of resources take place in private and illegitimate contexts, and they do not provide good and services according to the principles of equity and solidarity.

The *"civil society authorities"* category includes political-religious transnational movements and the transnational NGOs. These authorities do not claim exclusive control of any territory and do not establish any rules and laws to be imposed through the threat of the use of force. For what concerns the nature of the interests they pursue, although they are private organizations, their aims can be considered public-oriented. For example, NGOs are engaged in fields such as environmental protection, consumer protection, human rights, fighting weapons trafficking, and so on. Likewise, although political-religious movements are not public organizations, among their main goals there is the wealth and the progress of their faith communities (Rudolph & Piscatori, 1997). Thus, we can say that, whereas "civil society authorities" are private authorities, they are mainly driven by social and human development aims. Furthermore, their public-oriented character is demonstrated both by the capacity of these authorities to collect resources from people's voluntary contributions and from public institutions that—on the basis of legitimate decision-making processes—are employed to produce goods and services for the members of the communities. They do not question the authority and sovereignty of states. On the contrary, they tend to have cooperative relations with states that support them.

Finally, the "*economic-financial authorities*" category includes transnational corporations and transnational financial agencies. Like "civil society authorities," these organizations do not claim any control of the territory. Rather, they are characterized by a high capacity of displacement that allows them to affect states' decisions (Strange, 1996; Bauman, 1998; Ferrarese, 2000; Martinelli, 2004;). They do not have armed forces, but they often decide to entrust the protection of their properties to private security services instead of relying on public forces. Indeed, while Public Service's priority is collective security, the aim of private security forces is the protection of private property (Stringham, 2015). "Economic-financial authorities" try to influence law-making processes and decision-making processes through lobbying activities, and more often they rely on self-regulation, private governance, risk-management and alternative dispute resolution (Stringham, 2015). However, this does not exclude that they should respect the laws and the rules imposed by the states in which they operate. Their resources come from private sources—even if governments very often support TNCs through public investments and favorable tax conditions (Mazzucato, 2013)—and are generally used to earn profits for a restricted circle of actors involved in the private decision-making processes. In summary, economic-financial authorities, although having the power to influence and shape the environment in which they operate, as well as the "civil society authorities," do not exercise a sovereign power and are not interested in it. Indeed, they are profit-oriented, and they compete with states only for economic-financial issues.

4. Conclusion

This work aims to contribute to reducing the complexity of the fragmented current global political scenario, through a categorization of the extra-state authorities that focused on two main aspects: the nature of the interests pursued by these authorities and their relations with the territory. The product of this categorization are four types of extra-state authorities: *self-government authorities*; *illegal authorities*; *civil society authorities* and *economic-financial authorities*.

Each of these categories has a different kind of relationship with the states. *Economic-financial authorities* compete with states only for economic-financial issues. *Civil society authorities* use to establish and maintain cooperative relations with states that support them. Instead, *illegal authorities* represent a counterpower to the states, since they control territories on which they impose rules regardless of the laws established by the legitimate authorities. Finally, *self-government authorities* are in opposition against those states they do not recognize as legitimate sovereign on their land (and vice versa).

The current global political scenario is thus very complex, fragmented and characterized by the interaction of a huge number of political authorities that differ between each other in terms of origins, organizational structures, interests pursued, relations with the territories and so on. Those authorities increasingly compete with the state's ability to establish rules, control borders, formulate and implement public policies autonomously, and go beyond states' boundaries and create their own sovereign system (Belmonte & Cerny, 2021).

The consequence is the necessity of reconsidering the role of states that, although remaining the predominant form of political and social organization, cannot act without taking due account of these forms of authorities that are likely to increase and evolve over the time.

Notes

1 For the definitions of structural and relational power see Strange (1988).
2 General Review of Arrangements for Consultations with Non-Governmental Organizations: Report of the Secretary-General, U.N. ESCOR, U.N. Doc. E/AC.70/1994.
3 West Bank (including East Jerusalem).
4 In the occupied Golan.
5 www.un.org/en/genocideprevention/documents/atrocity-crimes/Doc.33_GC-IV-EN.pdf
6 www.amnesty.org/en/latest/news/2017/09/reports-israeli-government-plans-to-retaliate-against-amnesty-international-over-settlements-campaign/
7 https://stats.oecd.org/glossary/detail.asp?ID=1790
8 The Convention No. 169 concerning Indigenous and Tribal Peoples in Independent Countries, adopted on 27 June 1989 by the International Labor Organization; the "Draft United Nation declaration on the rights of indigenous peoples" (1994/45); the Operational Directive (OD 4.20) on "Indigenous Peoples" adopted by World Bank in 1991; the chapter 26 of the "Rio Declaration of Environment and Development" produced on 1992 by UN; the "Declaration on the rights of Persons belonging to national or ethnic, religious and linguistic minorities" produced by UN in 1992; the "Framework convention for the protection of national minorities" adopted by the Council of Europe in 1995.
9 www.survivalinternational.org
10 Because of the absence of interactions with the uncontacted tribes, there are not enough documents to analyze them. However, in virtue of their presence on specific territories and of their community life, they can be placed in the category of self-government authorities. For more information: www.survivalinternational.org
11 The case studies analyzed are the Autonomous Communities of Chiapas (cf: Castellani, 2010; Marceau, 2010) and the Rojava region (cf: Cemgil, 2016; Hosseini, 2016; Dirik et al., 2017).
12 To analyze illegal authorities we referred in particular to the phenomenon of Italian Mafia (cf. Strange, 1996; Ciconte et al., 2013, 2015).
13 With regards to the criminal organizations, resources come mainly from racket and illegal trade; while the resources of illegal settlements come from the economic activities on their territories and from external funding.

References

Allegra, M. (2013), The politics of Suburbia: Israel's settlement policy and the production of space in the metropolitan area of Jerusalem. *Environment and Planning*, vol. 45, pp. 497–516.
Armao, F. (2020), *L'età dell'oikocrazia*, Meltemi, Sesto San Giovanni.
Bachelli, T. et al. (2004), *De Facto States: The Quest for Sovereignty*, Routledge, Abingdon.
Bauman, Z. (1998), *Globalization: the human consequences*, Columbia University Press, New York.
Belmonte, R.; Cerny, P.G. (2021), Heterarchism: towards paradigm shift in world politics. *Journal of Political Power*, vol. 14, pp. 235–257.

Berg, E.; Toomla, A. (2009), Forms of normalization in the quest for De Facto statehood. *The International Spectator*, vol. 44, n. 4, pp. 27–45.

Bouris, D.; Fernández-Molina, I. (2018), Contested states, hybrid diplomatic practices, and the everyday quest for recognition. *International Political Sociology*, vol. 0, pp. 1–19.

Braithwaite, J.; Draho, P. (2000), *Global business regulation*, Cambridge University Press, Cambridge.

Caspersen, N.; Stansfield, G. (2011), *Unrecognized states in the international system*, Routledge, London.

Cassese, S. (2016), *Territori e potere*, Il Mulino, Bologna.

Castellani, G. M. (2010), *Il caracol zapatista: lo spazio della dignità indigena*, paper presented at the Conference "Lo spazio della differenza," Università di Milano—Bicocca 20/21 ottobre 2010.

Cemgil, C. (2016), The Republican ideal of freedom as non-domination and the Rojava experiment: "states as they are" or a new socio-political imagination? *Philosophy and Social Criticism*, Vol. 42, n. 4–5, pp. 419–428.

Cerny, P. G. (2010), *Rethinking world politics*, Oxford University Press, Oxford.

Cerny, P. G.; Prichard, A. (2017), "The New Anarchy: Globalisation and Fragmentation in 21st Century World Politics", *Journal of International Political Theory*, vol. 13, no. 3 (October), pp. 378–394.

Ciconte, E.; Forgione, F.; Sales, I. (2013), *Atlante delle mafie Vol. 1*, Rubbettino, Soveria Mannelli.

Ciconte, E.; Forgione, F.; Sales, I. (2015), *Atlante delle mafie Vol. 3*, Rubbettino, Soveria Mannelli.

Cohen, S. (2003), *The resilience of the State: Democracy and the challenge of globalization*, Hurst, London.

Damiani, M. (2010), *Classe politica locale e reti di potere*, Francoangeli, Milano.

Dirik, D. et al. (2017), *Rojava. Una democrazia senza Stato*, Elèuthera, Milano.

Ferrarese, M. R. (2000), *Le istituzioni della globalizzazione. Diritto e diritti nella società transnazionale*, Il Mulino, Bologna.

Habermas, J. (1999), *La costellazione post-nazionale*, Feltrinelli, Milano.

Haufler, V. (2001), *Public role for the private sector: industry self-regulation in a global economy*, Carnegie Endowment for International Peace, Washington.

Haynes, J. (2001), Transnational religious actors and international politics. *Third World Quarterly*, vol. 22, pp. 143–158.

Hosseini, A. (2016), The spirit of the spiritless situation: the significance of Rojava as an alternative model of political development in the context of the Middle East. *Critique*, vol. 44, n. 3, pp. 253–265.

Kolossov, V.; O'Loughlin, J. (1998), *Pseudo-states as Harbingers of a new geopolitics: the example of the trans-dniester Moldovan republic. Geopolitics*, vol. 3, n. 1, pp. 151–176.

Kolsto, P. (2006), The sustainability and future of unrecognized quasi-states. *Journal of Peace Research*, vol. 43, n. 6, pp. 723–740.

Krasner, S. (2001), *Problematic sovereignty*, Columbia University Press, New York.

Marceau, S. G. (2010), *Autonomie et developpement territorial au Mexique Zapatiste*, Univ. Européenne, Strasbourg.

Marchetti, R. (2016), *Global strategic engagement: state and non-state actors in global governance*, Lexington Books, Lanham.

Martinelli, A. (2004), *La democrazia globale*, Università Bocconi Editore, Mi.

Mazzucato, M. (2013), *The entrepreneurial state: debunking public vs. private sector myths*, Anthem Press, London.

Meier, O.; Schier, G. (2001), *Enterprises multinationales. Stratégie, restructuration, gouvernance*, Dunod, Paris.

Moretti, M. (2012), *International law and nomadic people*, AuthorHouse, Bloomington.

Ozzano, L. (2012), Gli attori religiosi transnazionali e il caso del Vaticano, in Coralluzzo, W.; Ozzano, L. (eds.), *Religioni tra pace e guerra*, Utet, Torino.

Papadimitriou, D.; Petrov, P. (2012), Whose rule, whose law? Contested statehood, external leverage and the European Union's rule of law mission in Kosovo. *Journal of Common Market Studies*, vol. 50, n. 5, pp. 746–763.

Pegg, S. (1998), *International society and the facto state*, Ashgate, Farnham.

Petti, A. (2007), *Arcipelaghi ed enclave*, Bruno Mondadori, Milano.

Pizzorno, A. (2001), Natura della disuguaglianza, potere politico e potere privato nella società in via di globalizzazione, *Stato e Mercato*, n. 2, pp. 201–236.

Rudolph, S. H.; Piscatori, J. (1997), *Transnational religions and fading states*, Westview Press, Boulder.

Shani, G. (2009), Transnational religious actors and international relations, in Haynes, J. (ed.), *Routledge handbook of religions and politics*, Routledge, London.

Strange, S. (1988), *States and markets*, Pinter, London.

Strange, S. (1996), *The retreat of the state. The diffusion of power in the world economy*, Cambridge University Press, Cambridge.

Stringham, E. P. (2015), *Private governance*, Oxford University Press, Oxford.

8

GLOBALIZATION, HETERARCHY, AND THE PERSISTENCE OF ANOMIE

Alexandre Bohas and Michael J. Morley

Introduction

Introduced by McCulloch (1945) as part of a body of cognitive research, the notion of heterarchy has subsequently expanded across the social, political and information sciences, and gave rise, in particular, to several insightful and enlightening analyses of various complex systems interdependently organized around networks, nodes, and links (Crumley 1995, 2015). In this chapter we return, in part at least, to the roots of the idea of heterarchy and we explore the effects of the rising heterarchical world on the mindset, ideas, and perceptions that people hold. In particular, we concern ourselves with the manifestly negative reactions that the new world order or disorder, resulting from what has been referred to as the "dialectic of globalization and fragmentation" (Cerny & Prichard 2017; Rosenau 1990), often triggers within individuals. We suggest that this tension between integration and disintegration creates an anomic disjuncture between people's prevailing state of mind and the reshaped world with which they are confronted. This anomic disjuncture may in fact represent a more enduring divergence between the ideational and material spheres and one which results in an inherent desire among individuals, elites as laymen to return to, and entrench themselves, in an outdated, largely idealized world view, rather than adjusting to and engaging with the ramifications of widespread global transformations (Bohas et al. 2021).

Combining the notion of anomie, as a disconnection between agents' ideational matrix and their environment, with the concept of heterarchy holds the prospect of yielding new insights on the state of the current world order. We argue that the growth of heterarchy may, in no small way, account for the rise of these anomic ideas and mindsets. In other words, anomie appears to be a result and a part of the transition from a nation-state-centered world politics to a heterarchical (dis)order. After rapidly presenting the theoretical elements of this study, we will reflect on

DOI: 10.4324/9781003352617-9

the manifestations of anomie at the subnational, state, and transnational levels through individual profiles and short case studies, which shows how increasingly present and widespread this phenomenon is.

The chapter is structured as follows. In the first section, we will draw attention to the close relationship between the pluralizing globalization and the rise of heterarchy. In the next section, we will consider the enduring anomic reactions which accompany this type of change in world order. In the following section, more substance will be given to these latter by sketching out illustrative corresponding profiles and case studies at subnational, state, and transnational levels. Following on from this, we will postulate key elements of what the relationship between heterarchy and anomie reveals about globalization.

1. Pluralizing Globalization as a Driving Force of Heterarchy

While globalization has, as Robertson (1992) points out, been proceeding with occasional interruptions for some centuries, it has more recently come to be theorized as a wide re-spatialization of social and economic life (Jessop 2013; Scholte 2005) which consists of a deep pluralization. Different people are brought closer together, and fluxes of ideas, goods and values are spread throughout the world. Moreover, this process increases the level of cross-border and supra-territorial relations which implies an increase in interconnections and interactions across borders. It also qualitatively transforms how people live in their daily routines, as well as how they consume and work, because it compresses parts of the social world and disperses others. This process has provoked complex changes in people's minds, existence, and designs for living. The inherent complexity which globalization has thrown up has also been captured through the promulgation and popularization of various oxymorons such as Rosenau's notions of "fragmegration" (Rosenau 1990), "distant proximities" (Rosenau 2003), and the movement of "fusion and fission" (Ferguson & Mansbach 2008, 61–62, 156–157), ideas which have been further developed under the notion of "dialectic of globalization and fragmentation" (Cerny & Prichard 2017). In addition, the concepts of "hybridization" (Pieterse 2009, 54) and "new anarchy" (Cerny & Prichard 2017) have been advanced to emphasize the uneven, heterogeneous, and incomplete character of globalization.

Irrespective of how they are characterized, the deep transformations that lie at the heart of globalization have resulted in various characterizations of those engaged in bringing about these profound reconfigurations of social, economic, and political spaces. Two main profiles have emerged, namely the *transnational capitalist* and the *cosmopolitanist*. The first profile has been coined by world-system thinkers. Indeed, in the neo-Marxist doxa, a new capitalist class should come out of a new mode of production that is now established at the global level. The members of the Transnational Capitalist Class (TCC) implement this new mode of global production, not only by their way of living, but also by having "outward-oriented global rather than inward-oriented local perspectives" (Sklair 2001: 20, 98; Cox 1981, Robinson & Sprague 2018). They are "in the process of denationalizing, redefining [their] ties to [their] place of birth and forging new ties with global markets and partners" (Sklair 2001, 256). The other profile is that of the cosmopolitanist. Cosmopolitanism is a model which has been successfully introduced across most social sciences. Described as a way of being which embraces globalization based on tolerance and difference recognition (Beck 2006), the cosmopolitan disposition has also been characterized by a reflexive and agile identity, coupled with an attitude of openness, engagement, and moral commitment to the world (Szerszynski & Urry 2002).

Although these two archetypes, cosmopolitanist and global capitalist, adopt postures which stand in contrast to each other, they both portray people seeking to, and as they see it, successfully reorienting their way of living, albeit in opposing ways, in order to adapt to globalization and to conform to its complex demands. To extend our focus beyond the mere assembling of oxymoronic theoretical *bricolages*, which of course have served as useful heuristic devices, we cast our net wider in order to capture the actual dynamics of these global transformations among different people.

2. The Enduring Nature of the Ideational and Material Mismatch

Based on a focus on the concept of anomie, we postulate that a reconsideration of these divergences as more persistent and enduring states, as opposed to temporary ones, may offer stronger explanatory power in accounting for the reaction to globalization. The divergence between people's minds and the prevailing conditions which they experience in their proximal and distal environments has long been observed in the social sciences via the distinction between material and ideational spheres. However, this gap is commonly conceived as a temporary mismatch coming from inert minds which are expected eventually to adjust to and catch up with the prevailing conditions in their environment.

The practice literature makes it possible to capture these phenomena of divergence between the material and the ideational spheres by observing systematically individuals' understandings and behaviors and their environment. Observing this lag, Bourdieu went on to conceptualize "hysteresis" as "the persistence of the effects of primary conditioning which accounts equally well for the cases in which dispositions function out of phase and when practices are objectively non-adapted to present conditions because they are objectively adjusted to conditions that no longer obtain" (Bourdieu 1980, 104–105, our translation). He argues that it is this hysteresis which explains "the structural lag between opportunities and the dispositions to grasp them" (Bourdieu 1990, 59). As an idea, it is especially illuminating in generating insights into fields that are subject to change. It has been used, for example, in international relations referring to the case of Russian diplomacy lacking compatibility with the field of diplomacy where such terms are employed (Neumann & Pouliot 2011). Importantly, in terms of our argument here, this divergence between people's mindsets, the habitus, and their environment has been seen as a temporary lag which eventually culminates in the individual adapting to the altered prevailing conditions.

In the late 19th century, Durkheim used the term to designate the pathologies inherent in modern social regulation coming from the division of labor in society and the rise of organic solidarity (Durkheim 1967/1893; Besnard 1987; Orrù 1998). According to Durkheim, these disorders occur in a context of rapid social transformation which leave people ill-adjusted to the prevailing conditions in their new environment. Consequently, disorder emerges when new values and norms encounter and/or disrupt older social patterns, weakening formal as well as informal social control. Society and its institutions fail to effectively place normative limits upon individual desires and their efficacious pursuits (Durkheim 1930/1897). In times of radical change, traditional behavioral rules experience a loss of authority and collective representations start to break down. Merton (1964) and others have focused on the idea of a perceived lack of fit between goals and values, on the one hand, and the means and tools to achieve them on the other, as the fundamental wellspring for anomie. In Merton's conception, anomie as a notion can be drawn upon to explain different levels of deviance among and inside societies and can be considered a normal phenomenon in contemporary societies (Orrù 1998). While Durkheim also considered it a widespread phenomenon, he was broadly optimistic that actor-situation interactions would eventually culminate in a resolution of the mismatch.

The disconnection resulting from globalization as we advance it here should be distinguished from the hysteresis effect or the temporary mismatch signaled in the earlier literature. The distinction lies in the notion of the temporary, as postulated in sociological thinking, versus the more durable and persistent nature of the disconnect as we see it. In fact, there is a strong case to be made that an enduring and growing disconnection between the entrenched nation-oriented habitus of agents, and the "fragmegrated" (Rosenau 1990) environment in which they live, is indeed underway. What needs to be underlined is that anomic disconnection is not a temporary epiphenomenon of globalization, but rather is one of its key features. Its origins lie in the heterarchical elements thrown up by globalization and the incomplete and heterogeneous features resulting from deep and chronic changes.

3. The Multiple Levels of Anomie

Earlier we called attention to the profiles of the *transnational capitalist* and the *cosmopolitanist* as archetypes who initiate, participate, and embrace globalization. Concomitantly, there are others, of course, who experience the same or similar forces for globalization, but who adopt a different posture towards what they regard as the arcane changes that these forces throw up. One will refer to revealing cases of the relationship between heterarchy and anomie at the subnational, state, and transnational levels.

At the subnational level, nationalist movements have risen across Europe these last years. They take a defensive stand against globalization which questions national identity by introducing complexity, ambiguity, and uncertainty in the clear view of a world ordained by nations. It also entails the disbanding of traditional hierarchies with the flattening of the world which remodels them in a horizontal manner. The rise of plurality which comes with the mobility of people and the emergence of mixed identity brings heterogeneity which can confound many people born and raised with the certainties of nation-state and a traditional western society. Consequently, in the face of such changes and in need of familiar and common references, people—elites as ordinary individuals—can be tempted to retreat to old and idealized visions rather than pursuing the demanding path of adaptation to the new situation. In this respect, aspects of Brexit have been likened to a desire to go back to a clear, simple, and parsimonious vision of the world and to stick with it irrespective of any associated costs, economically and politically. So, while the decision to leave the European Union may be read with reference to earlier 19th century glories, the United Kingdom remains deeply engaged with and involved in contemporary globalization, most notably with its City of London Financial Centre. In the same manner, although the Trump phenomenon in the United States remains to be fully analyzed, Trump's America-first, national-exclusive and gender-biased discourse may have appealed to a number of ordinary voters in the United States because it referred to an idealized and pre-globalized time of seemingly clear-cut and ordained societies and world order and because they feel threatened by social and economic transformations caused by globalization. It is worth noting that these two emblematic examples of anomie took place in countries, the United Kingdom and the United States, which have been deeply reshaped by globalization since the early 1980s with the arrival in office of neo-liberal governments.

In the radically different context of Jihadist militants, one can also identify this search for certainty in a return to an idealized past through their quest for a pristine and pure Islam. Through their elimination of non-Muslim traditions, but also of non-fundamentalist Islam, they manifest an intent to deny the same movements of some of the ambiguities, uncertainties and complexities which surround heterarchy. The effort at suppressing any form of Islam different from their rather restrictive Salafi interpretation can be read as a case in point. In Syria, 90% of the destruction focused on Muslim artefacts such as shrines, altars and mosques, the latter dating from the 13th and 14th centuries (Bohas 2016, 23). Modeled after the image of the iconoclastic controversy (8th century) and English Puritanism (17th century) in Christianity, jihadists invoke the idolatrous character of all devotion and of each place of worship, current or past, which is not directly addressed to God.

In this perspective, only Salafi principles can be an appropriate religious practice. The sacking of Nimrod and Hatra resulted precisely from application of this fundamental principal of Islam, which features on ISIL's emblem: "لا إله إلا الله" ("There is no god but God"). This inferred that Shi'a, Sufi and other kinds of syncretism were to be abolished since they diverged from the direct and non-mediated relationship with God. Consequently, any worship of other characters than God is viewed as polytheism. All remains, shrines, altars, and tombs of the prophets Jonah, Jirjis, Seth, Daniel, and Humu-al-Qadu were destroyed in the city of Mosul because they gave way to a particular devotion and integrated non-Sunni components.

A similar analysis has been made of the destruction of the mausoleums of Timbuktu, "city of the 333 saints." Bohas (2013) has argued that these destructions can be read both as an attempt to eliminate key elements of the rising heterogeneity of the contemporary world in favor of a purer Islam, as well as a desire to inculcate a unique, simple, and singular religious form. It involves both a repudiation of enfolding complexity, ambiguity and uncertainty characteristic of a globalizing world and a desire to return to an idealized and glorious time of the beginning vested in the recreating a Caliphate. It is worth noting that globalization as a movement of space and time compression have made this heterogeneity more glaring than in the past.

At the transnational level, one has unearthed manifestations of anomie within the daily routines and the expansion strategy of multinational corporations. We have shown Western senior managers in charge of international affairs in a multinational corporation entrenching in an outmoded worldview centered on nations, reluctant to embrace heterogeneity and attached to an archaic style of management (Bohas et al. 2021). Although they could be regarded as belonging to the transnational capitalist class by their professional career, their stand against the transnational, complex and heterogeneous dimensions of the contemporary world appeared in stark contradiction with transnational capitalists' view. Furthermore, their opposition against globalization and their return to a certain, clear, and idealized past differs from unchanged ethnocentric mindsets of past managers. Hence the idea of a growing disjuncture between their prevailing mindset and their globalized environment has been encapsulated within the notion of anomic mindset.

Multinational corporations' brands and identities can be regarded as anomic. The Volkswagen Company has established a discourse on the "Made in Germany" label even if it has developed manufacturing worldwide. Indeed, of a total of 66 car production sites, 16 were located in Germany and 18 in China (Volkswagen 2016, 14–29). The remaining factories are located in 20 countries. All types of production sites can be identified outside Germany, whether they manufacture parts (component site) or assemble vehicles (vehicle site). This global presence has conditioned its development and its worldwide success. As a result, the iconic model of the group, the Golf, appears as a genuine global product. It is assembled with components coming from over 20 countries present on four continents (Head 1992, 70)—and this number doesn't take into account the countries where the parts of the components are actually manufactured.

Nevertheless, it has built a real cultural competitive advantage which draws upon a specific discourse on national identity to global audiences. By its association with Germany, the Volkswagen Company benefited from a label which was well-established (Head 1992, 10). In other words, since it rose with the internationalization and then the globalization of economies in the second half of the 20th century, it has successfully associated its name with a dominant discourse on nationality coming from late 19th century Europe. The Volkswagen Company has focused on embodying the "Made in Germany" automobile through its marketing and advertising campaigns. First, the language is part and parcel of the Germanness claim. Constituting the ultimate mark of authenticity to refer to the narrative and imageries of nationality, it clearly includes a performative effect on identities and worldviews which give them legitimacy.

The flagship brand of the Volkswagen group is the Volkswagen brand whose global slogan was "Das Auto" between 2007 and 2015. Through this motto pronounced with a male German voice, the company makes the claim that its products are the quintessence of what every car should be. The use of the national language is emblematic of what a company wants to convey. It symbolizes the certificate of authenticity of Germanness. The article "Das" makes the strong claim of Germanness for any good car, while the word "Auto" is German, yet understood by non-German-speaking people. In the domain of advertising, there is strong evidence that Volkswagen tried to stick to the doxic caricature of supposedly German behavior such as the German accent in English, their obsession with detail, and their ordered and well-organized way of life (Marcantonio et al. 2014). In this regard, Martin Winterkorn, the former CEO of the Volkswagen Group, followed the very behavior that consumers would expect from the caricature of a typical German manager (Verdevoye 2015). In addition, Volkswagen cars are said to be "made in" or "engineered in" Germany, like other automotive and industrial German goods. This label conveys the intrinsically positive aspect that German products are supposed to have. The *Deutsche Qualität* is renowned worldwide and exerts a major impact on the success of German products themselves. Besides, the "Made in Germany" label corresponds to the misleading image of a unified and national industry located within German borders. Volkswagen aimed at making their car models the reference point of the sector In terms of reliability, robustness, and rigor. To this end, a rather conservative policy has been implemented in design and assigning names by keeping the same name for decades. As previously mentioned, the bulk of its production is still named Polo, Golf and Passat.

At state level, anomie can also be identified by a disjuncture of mindsets from their external environment in a search for old certainties and a return to an idealized past especially in contexts of heightened uncertainty and complexity. For instance, the way most statesmen have first reacted to the covid-19 crisis by drawing on repertoires of war reveals all the trappings of a world consisting of well-ordained and clear-cut nation-states where military power and nations are the ordering principles. It has led some politicians to preach nationalism, attributing a foreign nationality to the virus and appearing xenophobic towards foreigners. It also neglects all the complex interdependencies that link societies with one another, constitute as many ways for the virus to spread and ignore that curbing the virus depended less on national-level policies than on micro-level individual behavior. More recently, the sort of legal fundamentalism that constitutes the originalist interpretation defended by several Judges of the U.S. Supreme Court presents characteristics of a search for clearness and certainty in the past without adaptation to current times (Talbot 2022).

4. Heterarchical World Politics and its Anomic Reactions

4.1 Anomic Reactions to a Heterarchical World

This desire to return to an outdated reality and the manifest opposition to changes provoked by globalization, while at the same time being immersed in it, come from an heterarchical world deeply reshaped by the overlapping dynamics of integration and fragmentation. The idiosyncrasies of heterarchy with a "predominance of cross-cutting sectoral mini- and meso-hierarchies above, below and cutting across states" (Belmonte & Cerny 2021, 235) serve to explain these anomic reactions from people experiencing these deep changes in their daily conditions.

First, the world is still transitioning from a world order ordained by states to one in which the destination and ultimate outcome remains unclear. The incomplete and complex process of globalization makes the external environment puzzling for individuals, elites as ordinary people, who have difficulty understanding and making sense of the waves of ongoing transformations. Although individuals see a weakening of nation-states, an increase in transnational fluxes and a rise in non-state actors, they remain essentially entrenched in statocentrism. This entrenchment creates a disjuncture between their prevailing mindset, focused on the preservation of divergence, and their environment laced with forces for convergence.

Second, these uncertain and highly complex situations made of overlapping authorities and transnational interests make the idealized certainties of states' world politics attractive. Its external facing machinery comprises clear-cut borders, economic competition, and predictable diplomatic and military relationships. Its internal functioning is governed by key reference points including a comforting hierarchical social order and integrated political regimes.

Third, people engaged in their daily routines increasingly inhabit an environment imbued with uncertainty, along with encountering events which can engender a feeling of cultural and economic vulnerability, and a perceived undermining of the heretofore taken for granted material and ideational stability characterizing their lives. This state is often reinforced in situations where space-time compression results in individuals feeling threatened by, rather than being able to embrace, those with unrelated identities and with different designs for living.

Fourth, remaining state institutions whose power comes from the inertia of pre-globalization mindsets and machinery serve to boost national identity in an effort to retain legitimacy, which can further contribute to confusing people. When confronted with paradoxical situations, people may fall back on protective, pre-established perceptions rather than adapting or changing substantially their worldviews to deal with the paradox. This sheds light on the enduring nature of national knowledge as a deeply rooted reference point for understanding the world.

4.2 Anomie and the Heterarchization Process

Linked to the previous point, people's ideational matrix appears ill-equipped to face such a changed world. Although they are already all involved and for many engaged in globalization processes, their cognition remains poorly endowed to endure such uncertainty, heterogeneity, and diversity of heterarchical world politics. Dominant worldviews, the doxa, depend on combinations of economic and social forces which impose a constructed vision of the world with specific concepts and meanings. The reproduction of the national tropism in collective representations favors the storytelling of nations and, as a result, the national level of governance through early socialization, education (Gellner 1983), and mass media (Anderson 2006; Sobe 2012; Mihelj 2011). Governments also exert an impact on their own image which results from the choice of policies they decide to put into place. Their diplomacy and their economic and cultural policies influence, domestically and internationally, people's reference points, ending up with each nation distinguishing itself from other neighboring ones. Indeed, as Bohas (2019) suggests, most of them reinforce national worldviews and practices in people's habitus through their communication policies and their and their offerings.

Ultimately, anomie appears to be not only a reaction to heterarchical world politics but also, by this very response, a part of the heterarchization process in the ideational world. It serves to entrench the coexistence and conflict of many unranked identities and values which overlap and cut across each other.

5. Conclusion

Anomie, characterized as a disjuncture between people's ideational matrix and the prevailing circumstances of their environment, can be viewed as a phenomenon which directly results from the rise of heterarchy in world affairs. This heterarchical unranked world order made up of multiple and overlapping hierarchies and fragmented governance complexes can trigger an idealization of things past in which individuals galvanize their opposition to globalization and seek a return to an indefectible, if outdated, world. While global transformations have reshaped world politics, people's worldviews and practices have not changed accordingly. Not only have national imagined communities proven to be enduring, they have also in many ways been reinforced, while concomitantly the pluralization of the world has not been integrated into collective representations.

Far from being a phenomenon of the mind which recedes as the transition from a nation-state world order to a heterarchical order proceeds, it may be the very heterarchy itself that has served as the wellspring for the rise of anomie. Current anomie should not be reduced to inert minds since it constitutes a reaction to transformational changes. This failure in correspondence between individual mindsets and the global environment in which they operate generates perceptions, understandings and explanations which yield little by way of resolution. The more effective management of rising global issues and transnational dynamics may, by their very nature, demand a more cosmopolitan, a more inclusive, and a more state-free mind.

References

Beck, U. (2006) *The Cosmopolitan Vision*. Cambridge: Polity Press.

Belmonte, R. and Cerny, P. G. (2021) 'Heterarchy: Toward Paradigm Shift in World Politics', *Journal of Political Power*, 14(1), pp. 235–257.

Besnard, P. (1987) *L'Anomie, ses usages et ses fonctions dans la discipline sociologique depuis Durkheim*. Paris: FeniXX.

Bohas, A. (2013) 'L'exceptionnalité des biens culturels. La destruction des mausolées de Tombouctou', in Laroche, J. (ed.) *Passage au crible de la scène mondiale. L'actualité internationale, 2012*. Paris: Editions L'Harmattan, pp. 35–39.

Bohas, A. (2016) 'La mondialisation d'un fanatisme. Les destructions culturelles de l'État Islamique', in Laroche, J. (ed.) *Passage au crible de la scène mondiale. L'actualité internationale, 2015*. Paris: L'Harmattan, pp. 23–27.

Bohas, A. (2019) 'Das Auto. A Case for Anomic Globalization Through Volkswagen's 'Made in Germany' Label', *Journal of Political Power*, 12(1), pp. 66–85.

Bohas, A., Morley, M. J. and Kinra, A. (2021) 'Perlmutter revisited: Revealing the anomic mindset', *Journal of International Business Studies*, 52, pp. 1695–1723.

Bourdieu, P. (1980) *Le Sens pratique*. Paris: Éditions de minuit.

Bourdieu, P. (1990) *The Logic of Practice*. Redwood City: Stanford University Press.

Cerny, P. G. and Prichard, A. (2017) "The New Anarchy: Globalisation and Fragmentation in 21st Century World Politics", *Journal of International Political Theory*, 13(3) (October), pp. 378–394.

Cox, R. W. (1981) 'Social Forces, States and World Orders: Beyond International Relations Theory', *Millennium*, 10(2), pp. 126–155.

Crumley, C. L. (1995) 'Heterarchy and the Analysis of Complex Societies', in Ehrenreich, R. M., Crumley, C. L. and Levy, J. E. (eds.) *Heterarchy and the Analysis of Complex Societies*. Arlington, VA: American Anthropological Association, pp. 1–5. https://doi.org/10.1525/ap3a.1995.6.1.1

Crumley, C. L. (2015) 'Heterarchy', in Scott, R. A., Kosslyn, S. M. and Buchmann, M. (eds.) *Emerging Trends in the Social and Behavioral Sciences: An Interdisciplinary, Searchable, and Linkable Resource*. Hoboken, NJ: John Wiley & Sons, Inc., pp. 1–14.

Durkheim, E. (1930/1897) *Le Suicide*. Paris: PUF.

Durkheim, E. (1967/1893) *De la division du travail social*. Paris: PUF.

Head, D. (1992) *Made in Germany: Corporate Identity of a Nation*. London: Hodder & Stoughton.

Jessop, B. (2013) 'Dynamics of Regionalism and Globalism: A Critical Political Economy Perspective', *Ritsumeikan Social Science Review*, (5), pp. 3–24.

Marcantonio, A., Abbott, D. and O'Driscoll, J. (2014) *Remember Those Great Volkswagen Ads?* London: Merrell Publishers.

McCulloch, W. S. (1945) 'A Heterarchy of Values Determined by the Topology of Nervous Nets', *Bulletin of Mathematical Biophysics*, 7, pp. 89–93.

Merton, R. K. (1964) 'Anomie, Anomia and Social Interaction: Contexts of Deviant Behavior', in Clinard, M. B. (ed.) *Anomie and Deviant Behavior. A Discussion and Critique*. New York: Free Press of Glencoe, pp. 213–242.

Neumann, I. B. and Pouliot, V. (2011) 'Untimely Russia: Hysteresis in Russian-Western Relations Over the Past Millennium', *Security Studies*, 20(1), pp. 105–137.

Orrù, M. (1998) *L'Anomie*. Paris: L'Harmattan.

Pieterse, J. N. (2009) *Globalization and Culture*. Lanham, ML: Rowman & Littlefield.

Robertson, R. (1992) *Globalization: Social Theory and Global Culture*. Thousand Oaks: Sage.

Robinson, W. I. and Sprague, J. (2018) 'The Transnational Capitalist Class', in Juergensmeyer, M., Steger, M. B., Sassen, S. and Faessel, V. (eds.) *The Oxford Handbook of Global Studies*. Oxford: Oxford University Press, pp. 309–327.

Rosenau, J. N. (1990) *Turbulence in World Politics: A Theory of Change and Continuity*. Princeton: Princeton University Press.

Rosenau, J. N. (2003) *Distant Proximities: Dynamics beyond Globalization*. Princeton: Princeton University Press.

Scholte, J. A. (2005) *Globalization: A Critical Introduction*. Basingstoke: Palgrave Macmillan.

Sklair, L. (2001) *The transnational Capitalist Class*. Oxford, UK: Blackwell.

Szerszynski, B. and Urry, J. (2002) 'Cultures of Cosmopolitanism', *The Sociological Review*, 50(4), pp. 455–481.

Talbot, M. (2022) 'Amy Coney Barrett's Long Game', *The New Yorker*, 14–21 February. www.newyorker.com/magazine/2022/02/14/amy-coney-barretts-long-game

Verdevoye, A.-G. (2015) 'Martin Winterkorn, impérial maître de Volkswagen', *Challenges*, 21 June.

Volkswagen. (2016) *Facts and Figures 2016, Moving Progress*. www.volkswagenag.com/presence/investorrelation/publications/annual-media-conference/2016/Navigator/englisch/NAVIGATOR_2016_WEB_englisch.pdf [Accessed 28 June 2017].

SECTION II

Issue Areas and Case Studies

9

NATIONALISM, CAPITALISM, AND HETERARCHY

Continuity and Change in the 21st Century World Order

Peter Rutland[1]

Introduction

Heterarchy is defined in opposition to two alternative structuring principles: hierarchy and anarchy, the state and the market (Belmonte & Cerny 2021). The state consists of rulers, bureaucrats, and citizens; and the market of corporations, consumers, and workers. The state is a vertical command structure, while the market involves horizontal exchange among equals. The statist paradigm has a distinguished lineage, from Machiavelli and Hobbes, through the Westphalian system, to contemporary Realists and Neorealists. Anarchy has two aspects: a utopian/communitarian side, from Jean-Jacques Rousseau to Jurgen Habermas; and a practical/commercial side, from Adam Smith and the Marquis de Condorcet to Friedrich Hayek and Milton Friedman.

The heterarchy approach warns against the intellectual laziness of taking the state as the default framework for political action, and the accompanying "methodological nationalism" (Beck 2007): taking the nation as the main framework for tracking political and economic activity, whether it be election results or economic performance. Heterarchy notes the increasing role played by non-state actors, including multinational corporations (MNCs), non-governmental organizations, private military companies, and a plethora of trans-national regulatory agencies. This fluid pluralism of actors on the global stage, across multiple dimensions, forces states into a reactive rather than proactive role. There is no teleological process of convergence on a single set of institutional arrangements at either the national or global level. Technological change—above all, the information revolution—is accelerating this process of pluralization. The spread of financialization and marketization complicates the role of the state, blurring public and private in the provision of public services. The decline of US hegemony since the 1990s has exposed

DOI: 10.4324/9781003352617-11

the instability of the global political and economic order: there is no longer a single dominant enforcer who can set and police the rules of the game.

These are all excellent insights to come out of the heterarchy approach, which takes us well beyond the paradigms that still dominate much of international relations scholarship. One important example: it is standard practice for elites in resource extractive regimes, from Angola to Russia, to park their assets and wealth in shell companies and property empires in other countries. They may even hire mercenaries or invite in troops from other countries to suppress popular unrest. This goes well beyond Putnam's two-level game (in which rulers interact with domestic constituencies at home and other states and foreign corporations abroad). The prototypical ruling elite is a hybrid actor bridging the national and global, akin to the mythic *centaur* (a creature with the upper body of a man and the lower body of a horse). They run their own country according to the brutal norms of the local political culture, while justifying their rule by appealing to national loyalty as the "father of the nation." At the same time, they use the stable institutions of the developed West to educate their children, hide their wealth, adjudicate their disputes, settle their divorces, and amuse themselves with football clubs. They hire PR firms to burnish their national brand (Rothkopf 2008; Bullough 2018).

That said, claims for heterarchy should not be pushed too far. The nation-state is still the dominant framework for political life in the 21st century. Critics of the state paradigm point to the increasing number of "failed states." But in fact, only a handful of countries fall into that category. The Fragile States Index lists 30 counties in their "alert" category (Fund for Peace 2021). North Korea is #30 and Pakistan #29: both are no doubt unpleasant places to live for much of the population, but hardly "failed states" (They both have nuclear weapons, for example). Those 30 countries have a total population of 1.2 billion. That means 85% of the world's population live in functioning states which have seen remarkable improvements in life expectancy, primary education, and poverty reduction in recent decades, much of that was due to improvements in state capacity to deliver public services (World Bank 2020). In Argentina, for example, corruption and populist politics have led it to default on its international debts nine times since independence in 1816, most recently in 2001 and 2020. Yet despite all the political and economic dysfunction, from 1990–2020 the average life expectancy rose from 71 to 76 years, just one year behind that of the US.[2] Finally, it is worth recalling that while economic inequality has been increasing *within* countries, it has been decreasing *across* countries, thanks to the rise of China and other late developers (Milanovic 2016).

Another claim of heterarchy that bears critical scrutiny is the argument that borders are increasingly porous, and national identity and citizenship matter less and less. Migrants trying to enter Europe or the USA would tell a different story. Moreover, although trans-national migration may be at an all-time high in absolute numbers, 96% of the world's population still live and work in the same country in which they were born (IOM 2020). National citizenship is the most important factor in determining one's chances in the lottery of life. Diaspora identities and cosmopolitan world views are much less important than national identities.

1. The Synergy of State and Market

There is both tension and synergy between the state and the market. States and markets sometimes work at cross purposes, but they can also work together. Similarly, political nationalism and economic globalization can sometimes be mutually destructive, but also sometimes mutually reinforcing.

A successful state needs a competitive market economy to generate the wealth which funds its capacity to establish a monopoly of violence and to protect the country from foreign rivals (Tilly 1992). At the same time, in the age of imperialism capitalist entrepreneurs needed a strong state to help them gain control over resources and markets abroad, while securing their property rights from challengers and social unrest at home. There was always the danger that the state would use its power to expropriate the capitalists.

Marxism represented the most serious challenge to the world order of sovereign states and capitalist economies. But once Communists seized power in Russia and China, their revolutionary ardor was channeled into building powerful states that became pillars of the global system, competing with the United States for a position at the top of the power hierarchy.

The two world wars raised doubts about the capacity of the European state system to provide a stable environment for the functioning of capitalism. Hence neoliberal critics of the state such as Friedrich Hayek explored the possibility of creating trans-national institutions to provide the framework for the functioning of a capitalist market (Slobodian 2018). That culminated in the creation of the European Economic Community. However, as Alan Milward (1992) noted, the EEC was designed to "rescue" the nation-state in the aftermath of World War II, which had shattered their economies and discredited or eliminated their pre-war national political elites. It was not until the 1980s that Europe and the world had regained the level of cross-border trade that had been achieved in 1914.

The post-war European recovery showed that capitalism, nationalism and democracy were mutually compatible. The Scandinavian countries are widely seen as the best-governed countries in the world. As small economies, the Scandinavians had no choice but to open up to foreign trade, and they concentrated on developing a narrow range of firms able to compete in international markets. At the same time, under pressure of electoral competition and organized labor they increased taxation, to invest in infrastructure and human capital and also redistribute income and wealth, to keep inequality in check and create a more solidaristic identity. Hence the economies most open to foreign trade were also those with the highest proportion of state taxation and spending (Rodrik 2012). This is a paradox, because free-market theorists would have predicted that capitalists would choose to invest in other countries with a lower tax burden. But the post-war European state turned out to be more a "helping hand" than a "grabbing hand"—helping capitalists to become more competitive, helping workers and citizens to share in the fruits of that success, and establishing a virtuous cycle of high productivity and high incomes (Cerny 2010). The European Union ensured the free flow of goods, capital and finally labor across all member-states—while leaving all other questions of taxation, citizenship, defense, etc., in the hands of the sovereign national governments. Except for a small cosmopolitan elite, the primary political identity remained national, with European identity as a secondary attribute (Risse 2011).

Over time, the European model came under strain. Automation and competition from low-wage rivals in the developing world led to the loss of high-paid manufacturing jobs, while an influx of migrant labor led to the rise of more ethnically diverse societies, which challenged the social solidarity welfare-state model. Globalization accelerated in the 1990s, with the international trade in goods going from 20% of global GDP in 1960 to 33% in 1990 and 61% in 2008.[3] This was accompanied by accelerating social change, intensified competition and greater social inequality. The problems were more acute in the United States, with weaker social safety nets and redistributive mechanisms than the Europeans. The traditional political party systems, which were based on the post-war welfare state economic agenda and social structure, also started to break down.

The deepening globalization over the past 30 years led to some policy convergence across states, but there is still a broad variation in local conditions and in the strategies adopted by corporate and national actors—contrary to Thomas Friedman, the world is still not "flat." The variety of regulatory regimes has led to venue-shopping, with MNCs taking advantage of looser tax and regulatory regimes to offshore many of their revenues (Clausing 2018; Doremus et al. 1998). US corporations such as Apple or Amazon are just as likely to indulge in these practices as the oligarchs running Third World kleptocracies. A change in US law in the 1990s, for example, enabled US corporations to shift profits offshore by licensing intellectual property to subsidiaries overseas. That said, few corporations are completely de-territorialized: they each remain attached to a home base to some degree. They need states to protect their property rights, to provide a disciplined and educated labor force, and a location for the headquarters where the core management team are housed. In times of crisis, such as the 2008 financial collapse or COVID-19 epidemic, they turn to their national governments for bailouts.

There are signs that globalization may have peaked in the 2010s. Trade peaked at 61% of global GDP in 2008, falling to 52% in 2020.[4] This is mainly because automation cut the cost of manufacturing in high-wage economies: some robots that can replace an individual worker only cost $4 an hour to run (Hammes 2019). Reshoring of manufacturing closer to final consumer markets has other advantages—it cuts inventory and transport costs; lowers political risk; and minimizes the opportunities for intellectual property theft.

2. The Trilemma of Nationalism, Democracy and Globalization

Dani Rodrik (2012) and Arthur Stein (2016) argue in different ways that advanced industrial democracies face a trilemma between national sovereignty, democracy and globalization. You can have two of the three at any one time, but not all three. Globalization means accepting some rules that are established at trans-national level and policed by organizations such as the EU or World Trade Organization. So you have to sacrifice sovereignty. However, if a country has given up some sovereignty, in what sense can there be democratic control—if the decisions are being made not in the national parliament, but in arbitration courts in Sweden, or the bureaucratic chambers of Brussels. One argument is that democracies all share core values, so can happily pool their sovereignty over those issues. Another argument is that a nation can democratically decide to delegate part of its sovereignty to international institutions. But contra Rodrik, it can be argued that the democracy-globalization pairing is hard to realize in practice.

Stein (2016) has a different argument for the incompatibility of democracy and globalization. Globalization results in widening inequality within countries, with the losers outnumbering the winners. In a democracy sooner or later power shifts to parties representing the median voter—who will want to limit free trade ("protectionism from below"). The gains from trade are often dispersed (amongst consumers for example) while the gains from protectionism are concentrated in certain industries, threatened by competition. The dynamics of lobbying, especially in a political system such as the US with multiple veto points and a large role for money, favor the protectionists over the free traders.

3. Beyond the Trilemma

Arguably, there is really no trilemma at all, just a dilemma—the tension between the global and the national (Palley 2021). Moreover, it can be argued that there is not even really a dilemma between globalism and nationalism, since the two often operate in synergy with each other, and only sometimes work at cross-purposes. A successful nationalist leader is one who improves their nation's competitive position in the global market, and/or moves up the ladder in the hierarchy of power, thus improving their bargaining position. Nationalist narratives portray their own nation as the product of a unique history, in reality modern nation-states emerged from an international system of states in competition with each other—initially in Europe, and then world-wide. Successful nation-builders learned from the experience of other states. The very building blocks of the modern nation-state, from anthems to the notion of citizenship, came out of ideas and techniques that were internationally circulating.

The reverse is also true. A capitalist will tend to invest in stable and predictable states in which the rules of the game are clearly established, and where the local political leaders (be they democratic or authoritarian) can guarantee property rights and a stable business environment.

If the Scandinavian model represents one equilibrium solution to the globalism/nationalism dilemma, the developmental state of an authoritarian regime like China, or a petrostate flush with oil revenue such as Saudi Arabia, represents another. Both these authoritarian variants typically rely on integration with the global economy. We often hear that oil is a "curse" that hinders long-term development, but despite that the petrostates seem politically stable—riding out the Arab Spring for example. Despite economic stagnation and massive levels of corruption and incompetence in Venezuela or Russia, authoritarian rules have managed to stay in power through media control and repression of the political opposition. The past 200 years of Enlightenment thinking in the West has assumed that political and economic freedom go together, are two sides of the same coin. Political authoritarianism does not allow entrepreneurs the space they need to innovate; and the lack of rule of law means that capitalists can be expropriated at any moment. Despite that, over the past 30 years China has seen rapid growth thanks to capitalist institutions and global integration, while maintaining largely unchanged the political monopoly of the Communist Party.

The collapse of communism in Europe gave rise to widespread optimism in the West that the arc of history was curving towards democracy. The number of democracies in the world steadily increased, passing the 50% mark around 2000, but since 2010 there has been democratic backsliding. Consequently, with the failure of the Arab Spring; the Brexit referendum and Trump election in 2016; and democratic retreat in Poland, Hungary and elsewhere; there is no longer much confidence that the future belongs to democracy.

4. Responding to Systemic Threats

Global capitalism is typically treated as if it is a hermetically-sealed, logically-grounded system in which actors respond in a rationally and predictable way to Newtonian forces of supply and demand, electoral competition, the balance of power, or whatever.

However, the twin crises of the COVID-19 pandemic and climate change remind us that human activity is also shaped by forces beyond our control. They oblige us to act in ways that go well beyond the equilibrating models upon which social scientists depend.

Climate change and COVID-19 are directly connected. The mass destruction of habitats during the Anthropocene has led to more interactions between humans and animal species, and hence pathogens jumping the species barrier (Duara 2021).

In many respects the response to COVID-19 has strengthened the role of the state. States have thus far been ineffective in rising to the challenge of climate change, leaving space for non-state actors to play a prominent role, from Greenpeace to Greta Thunberg, strengthening the heterarchy argument. But progress against climate change long-term will crucially depend on the coordinated action of states.

5. Nationalism and the COVID-19 Pandemic

The COVID-19 pandemic has vividly brought out the persistence of nationalism in the 21st century (Elias et al. 2021). In just about every country on the planet, the response to COVID-19 was profoundly nationalist, both in the policies adopted and the rhetoric used by state leaders to justify those policies. The typical policy responses included bans on international travel; lockdowns; mask and vaccine mandates; bans on the export of medical equipment and vaccines; and feverish efforts to promote the manufacture of equipment and vaccines within national borders. The phrase "vaccine nationalism" entered the vocabulary, as countries scrambled to secure supplies for their own population. Countries that manufactured vaccines and provided them to others made sure to exploit the opportunity as a display of their beneficence and to project their "soft power."

Disruptions in supply chains led to stoppages in the manufacturing industry and shortages of everything from toilet paper to microchips. This led to growing support for deglobalization and onshoring of production capacity in the future, both to protect corporate profits and as a national security priority (Tooze 2021). It would be premature, however, to judge whether such policies will actually be followed through. The international division of labor brought about profound cost-savings, and reshoring manufacturing to Europe and the U.S. would be expensive. It may be more cost-effective just to increase stocks.

In almost all cases the pandemic led to a dramatic expansion in the role of the state in regulating people's lives and deficit spending on an unprecedented scale in a bid to keep businesses afloat (Bieber 2020). In many countries, nationalism helped to rally public support for radical responses to the pandemic, providing a focal point for collective action (Mylonas & Whalley 2022).

The rhetoric justifying these radical and often unpopular policies was often couched directly in patriotic language—appealing to people to put the collective interest over the individual, and to take pride in the fact that their nation was handling the crisis more responsibly than others. We also unfortunately saw heightened exclusionary nationalism (hostility towards certain ethnic groups) and increased social polarization. Some right-wing leaders were dismissive of COVID-19 (Trump in the US, Bolsonaro in Brazil) while others were quite proactive in reacting to the pandemic (e.g., Modi in India). The most effective state policies are generally to be found in countries with a strong sense of national identity—from China, South Korea and Singapore to Australia and New Zealand. It can even be argued that the ineffective response in places like Brazil and the US—often portrayed as hotbeds of far-right nationalism because of the antics of Bolsonaro and Trump—was a sign of the relative weakness of national solidarity and willingness to sacrifice for the sake of the common good in those countries. The pandemic has generally strengthened authoritarian leaders (who are not accountable for bad policies, and who used it as an excuse to ban protests) and weakened democratic leaders, who are held accountable by the public for their policy failings (V-Dem 2021).

At the same time, however, this resurgence of nationalism is an obstacle to effective collective responses to the pandemic at the global level. Countries secured vaccines for their own citizens first, and vaccination rates varied greatly between the Global North and the Global South. Countries and private companies that developed vaccines generally asserted ownership rights and did not grant permission for production at low cost in poor countries.

One modest silver lining to the COVID-19 cloud was the fact that it showed that the majority of people can change their behavior radically, and quickly. Also, it gave a new prominence and respect for scientific expertise. The information technology revolution meant that both state and non-state actors were able to speedily gather data to track the spread of the pandemic and the effectiveness of state responses to it, exponentially more effectively than in previous years. All of those factors bode well for the major long-term challenge facing humanity: climate change.

6. Nationalism and Climate Change

The catastrophic effects of human-induced climate change are now all too clear. Climate change has arguably displaced nuclear war as the main threat to the future of humanity. Over the past two centuries, extractivism in the name of national progress—and personal enrichment—has locked the world into the reckless exploitation of fossil fuels, causing catastrophic global heating. Capitalism has been the engine of climate change—as was Soviet and Chinese communism, which also wholeheartedly embraced industrialization as the measure of human progress (Wainwright & Mann 2018; Monbiot 2021).

Capitalism arose within an international system of sovereign states. Initially in the 19th century the dominant form of political organization was that of multinational empires, but in the course of the 20th century empire was replaced by the nation-state, and nationalism became the most pervasive political ideology (Duara 2021). Capitalism and nationalism also worked together to birth the rise of democracy. Timothy Mitchell (2011) argued that the rise of the coal industry in Britain was key to the working class's ability to win the right to vote in the 19th century, given the large number and strategic location of the coal miners. But in the 20th century of oil and gas, the connection between energy and democracy has been sundered. Instead we may be facing what Andreas Malm (2021) calls "fossil fascism," with authoritarian rulers using repression of their own population and bribery of global elites to maintain the status quo. Since 1990 the acceleration of globalization led to an intensification of economic growth and of fossil fuel use.

The accompanying political philosophy of nationalism was very bad for climate change, since it turned GDP growth into a symbol of national success, while treating other nations as rivals (Conversi 2020). Likewise, the doctrine of neoliberalism heavily discounts the future in favor of net present value, and prioritizes individual rights and choices over collective responsibility to one's fellow humans, present and future. Liberal democracy also has some negative aspects from the climate change point of view—it institutionalizes individual property rights; favors satisfying current desires over long-term needs; and it generally makes radical change difficult, favoring compromise and consensus over painful, costly decisions. Monbiot (2021) points out for example that "cake" was mentioned 10 times as often as "climate change" on UK television programs in 2020. Of course, that is not to say that the record of authoritarian regimes dealing with the environmental and ecological impact of climate change has been any better.

The rise of China and India as manufacturing platforms for the global economy meant that many dirty and energy-intensive industries were relocated to those countries from the advanced economies. In effect, the West was outsourcing its pollution. That process included exporting waste from Europe and the US to poor countries for recycling or dumping. This leads to an unfortunate asymmetry which makes international cooperation very difficult. China and India point out that while the current *flow* of greenhouse gases (GHG) is coming from their countries, the *stock* of GHG in the atmosphere was put there by the early industrializers of North America and Europe. On top of which, the Global North enjoys a higher standard of living thanks to their early mover advantage. So China and India demand financial compensation from the developed world in order to help fund their transition away from fossil fuels.

In addition to questions of international equity, there are also severe political obstacles to dealing with climate change *within* each country. The vested interests of the fossil fuel lobby and the political constituencies which depend on them put up a fierce resistance to efforts to transition away from fossil fuels. Even in Germany, which has been at the forefront of efforts to decarbonize their economy, the interest of the Social Democratic Party in protecting their political base in the Saar region has delayed their willingness to phase out coal. Although Germany aims to cut GHG emissions by 65% by 2030, it will not eliminate coal production until 2038 (Morris 2021).

As a result of these political obstacles at national and international level, global society has been painfully slow to meet the challenge. From the 1992 United Nations Framework Convention on Climate Change, through the Kyoto Protocol (1997), COPS 19 in Copenhagen (2009), COPS 21 in Paris (2015), and COPS 26 in Glasgow (2021), the international community has been unable to come up with binding commitments to curtail greenhouse gas emissions. The move away from fossil fuels is proving too little, too late, to prevent irreversible climate change.

China's authoritarian regime enables the state to focus resources on tackling specific problems. The concentration of coal power stations and other high emission industries means that pollution is a serious problem for China's cities (as it is in India). This stimulated the government to make a serious effort to curb emissions, pouring massive investment into renewable technologies. They have been able to corner the global market in solar cells, batteries and to a lesser extent wind turbines, leading amongst other things to a 70% drop in the cost of solar cells (Liu 2015; Stalley 2021). This process has also created new business constituencies favoring the green economy, though they still face strong resistance from vested interests in the fossil economy that may fatally slow the transition (e.g. the continued reliance on coal for power generation). It is to be hoped that President Xi's commitment to "ecological civilization" will continue, and widen. However, there is a risk that the slowdown in economic growth which China is experiencing will lead to intensifying authoritarianism to control social unrest. That would have the collateral effect of shutting down the critical thinking and international collaboration which tackling climate change requires.

Benjamin Cashore and colleagues have a promising approach which could be a way out of the policy dead-end in which we find ourselves (Cashore & Bernstein 2020; Rosenbloom et al. 2018). They lay out four policy analysis frames:

- Type 1 tragedy of the commons (a specific type of economic problem);
- Type 2 optimization (the economists' general equilibrium approach);
- Type 3 compromise (the general approach favored by politics); and
- Type 4 prioritization (which is political and specific, goal oriented).

The mainstream approach to tackling climate change is that reflected in the Paris Accord: a classic Type 3 approach, based on compromise and trading over costs and benefits. It assumes that existing social, political and economic institutions have to be taken as given, and new policies must be introduced as add-ons to the status quo institutional landscape. Neoliberals advocate the introduction of new markets to monetize the externalities: carbon pricing, emission trading, etc. In contrast, the Type 4 approach requires bold critical action that sets up a new dynamic. Some old institutions and interests will have to be retired, and some new ones created. This approach starts with the recognition of the trajectory of past history that has led to the present state of affairs—that is, the path dependency that has created the problematic and unsatisfactory institutional structure that we have today. It then posits that we are at a critical juncture, that we must take radical steps to get off the current path and on to a new path, defined by our future goals. This Type 4 approach goes well beyond the Type 1 collective action metaphor. It recognizes that political decisions need to be taken which confront head-on the redistributional conflicts involved in implementing effective politics to stop climate change. These new policies will in turn create new constituencies who defend them.

7. Conclusion

Idealists on both the political Left and the pro-business Right may look forward to a future global order that transcends nationalism, in which governments and companies conform to universal rules administered through trans-national regulatory structures. But this seems hopelessly utopian. A more realistic approach may be to try to re-frame climate change as part of a nationalist narrative; not to disconnect climate change from the nation-state, but reconnect it to a politically appealing narrative of national renewal. In Europe, some far right parties are indeed embracing climate change as a policy issue (Ruser & Machin 2019). Unfortunately it is the Left that is most willing to embrace climate change as a priority—but the Left is generally hostile to the rhetoric of nationalism.

The heterarchy approach helps us understand that we cannot expect to see solutions to global problems coming from sovereign states acting individually in the territories they control or through cooperation with other sovereign states. We need fresh approaches that bring in a role for non-state actors at both the sub-state and trans-state levels. That will necessarily involve further changes in the way that states themselves operate, including tackling the common pattern of "state capture" by business elites that we see across a broad range of states, both rich and poor.

Notes

1 Thanks to Phil Cerny, Giulio Gallarotti and Andrei Kazantsev for comments on an earlier draft.
2 https://data.worldbank.org/indicator/SP.DYN.LE00.IN?locations=AR
3 https://data.worldbank.org/indicator/NE.TRD.GNFS.ZS
4 https://data.worldbank.org/indicator/NE.TRD.GNFS.ZS

References

Beck, Ulrich. 2007. "The cosmopolitan condition: Why methodological nationalism fails." *Theory, Culture & Society* 24 (7–8): 286–290.
Belmonte, Rosalba & Philip G. Cerny. 2021. "Heterarchy. Towards a paradigm shift in world politics." *Journal of Political Power* 14 (1).
Bieber, Florian. 2020. "Global nationalism in times of the COVID-19 pandemic." *Nationalities Papers* 1–13.
Bullough, Oliver. 2018. *Moneyland. Why Thieves and Crooks Now Rule the World, and How to Take It Back.* London: Profile Books.
Cashore, Benjamin & Steven Bernstein. 2020. "Why experts disagree on how to manage COVID-19." *Global Policy*, April 7. www.globalpolicyjournal.com/blog/07/04/2020/why-experts-disagree-how-manage-covid-19-four-problem-conceptions-not-one
Cerny, Philip G. 2010. "The competition state today: from raison d'État to raison du Monde." *Policy Studies* 31 (1): 5–21.
Clausing, Kimberly. 2019. *Open. The Progressive Case for Free Trade, Immigration and Global Capital.* Cambridge, MA: Harvard University Press.
Conversi, Daniele. 2020. "The ultimate challenge: Nationalism and climate change." *Nationalities Papers* 48 (4): 625–636.
Doremus, Paul N., William W. Keller, Louis W. Pauly & Simon Reich. 1998. *The Myth of the Global Corporation.* Princeton, NJ: Princeton University Press.
Duara, Prasenjit. 2021. "Nationalism and the crises of global modernity." *Nations and Nationalism* 1–13.
Elias, Amanuel, Jehonathan Ben, Fethi Mansouri & Yin Paradies. 2021. "Racism and nationalism during and beyond the COVID-19 pandemic." *Ethnic and Racial Studies* 44 (5): 783–793.
Fund for Peace. 2021. *Fragile States Index 2021.* https://fragilestatesindex.org/2021/05/20/fragile-states-index-2021-annual-report/

Hammes, T.X. 2019. *Deglobalization and the Fourth Industrial Revolution*. Amherst, NY: Cambria Press.

International Organization for Migration. 2020. *World Migration Report*. Geneva. https://worldmigrationreport.iom.int/wmr-2020-interactive/

Liu, Zhu, et al. 2015. "Climate policy: Steps to China's carbon peak." *Nature* 522: 279–281.

Malm, Andreas. 2021. *White Skin, Black Fuel. On the Danger of Fossil Fascism*. London: Verso.

Milanovic, Branko. 2016. *Global Inequality: A New Approach for the Age of Globalization*. Cambridge, MA: Harvard University Press.

Milward, Alan S. 1992. *The European Rescue of the Nation-State*. London: Routledge.

Mitchell, Timothy. 2011. *Carbon Democracy. Political Power in the Age of Oil*. London: Verso.

Monbiot, George. 2021. "Capitalism is killing the planet." *Guardian*, October 30.

Morris, Loveday. 2021. "Germany portrays itself as a climate leader." *Washington Post*, October 23.

Mylonas, Harris & Ned Whalley. 2022. "Pandemic Nationalism." *Nationalities Papers* 1–10.

Nordhaus, William. 2020. "The climate club." *Foreign Affairs* 99 (3).

Nordhaus, William. 2021. "Why climate policy has failed." *Foreign Affairs*, October 12.

Palley, Thomas I. 2021. "National policy space: Reframing the political economy of globalization and its implications for national sovereignty and democracy." *Brazilian Journal of Political Economy* 41 (3).

Risse, Thomas. 2011. *A Community of Europeans? Transnational Identities and Public Spheres*. Ithaca, NY: Cornell University Press.

Rodrik, Dani. 2012. *The Globalization Paradox: Democracy and the Future of the World Economy*. New York: W.W. Norton.

Rosenbloom, Daniel, James Meadowcroft & Benjamin Cashore. 2018. "Stability and climate policy." *Energy Research & Social Science* 50: 168–178.

Rothkopf, David. 2008. *Superclass: The Global Power Elite and the World They are Making*. New York: Farrar, Straus and Giroux.

Ruser, Alexander & Amanda Machin. 2019. "Nationalizing the climate. Is the European far right turning green?" *Green European Journal* September 27. www.greeneuropeanjournal.eu/nationalising-the-climate-is-the-european-far-right-turning-green/

Slobodian, Quinn, 2018. *Globalists: The End of Empire and the Birth of Neoliberalism*. Cambridge, MA: Harvard University Press.

Stalley, Philip.2021. "In the fight against climate change China is doing more than you think." *The Conversation*, December 6.

Stein, Arthur. 2016. "The great trilemma: Are globalization, democracy, and sovereignty compatible?" *International Theory* 8 (2): 297–340.

Tilly, Charles. 1992. *Coercion, Capital, and European States, A.D. 990–1990*. Oxford, UK: Wiley Blackwell.

Tooze, Adam. 2021. "Has Covid ended the neoliberal era?" *The Guardian*, September 2.

V-Dem. 2021. *Pandemic backsliding*. Varieties of Democracy Project, June. www.v-dem.net/pandem.html

Wainwright, Joel & Geoff Mann. 2018. *Climate Leviathan: A Political Theory of Our Planetary Future*. London: Verso.

World Bank. 2020. *World Development Report 2020*. www.worldbank.org/en/publication/wdr2020

10

HETERARCHY AND THE LIMITS OF GLOBAL GOVERNANCE

Philip G. Cerny

Introduction

The concept of "governance" denotes not formal institutions but informal forms of social control and loose and fungible structures of power. Interest group theory, public policy analysis, bargaining approaches, pluralism and neopluralism, elite theory, capture theory, and the like suggest that such processes are at the heart of policymaking and implementation. Global governance institutions are not the structurally differentiated, relatively autonomous, multifunctional institutions represented in modern state theory; indeed, they are moving in the opposite direction through the "fragmentation of global governance architectures," "forum shopping," and the hybridization of public and private characteristics of heterarchical world politics. Global economic growth, environmental policymaking, new wars, uneven development, etc., involve complex dialectics of bottom up/ top down, inside/out, endogenous and exogenous variables, not a coherent institutional shift to global governance—i.e., heterarchy

1. Governance as a Contested Concept

Coen and Pegram argued in an issue of *Governance* in 2015 that "Global governance is not working." They identified a "first generation" of global governance research that "focused almost exclusively on formal mechanisms of interstate relations within public multilateral institutions. . ... With these structures apparently in gridlock, observers now regard global governance to be in crisis" (Coen and Pegram 2015). Similar arguments were also made in a symposium in *Public Administration* entitled Global Public Policy and Transnational Administration, edited by Stone and Ladi (2015). At the same time, the word itself is characterized

DOI: 10.4324/9781003352617-12

by a particular ambiguity that has run through the political and social sciences generally since their early development.

For example, Randall Stone's book *Controlling Institutions* frames global governance as a set of complex, problematic institutions represented by international—or, more properly, intergovernmental or interstate—organizations (Stone 2011). He argues that they are characterized by a trade-off between more formalized and legalized decision-making processes, on the one hand, and an accepted safety valve for the most structurally powerful states to manipulate outcomes in favor of their own perceived—especially their most "intense"—interests, policies, alliances, and other special relationships, on the other. In this context, more powerful states, reluctant to give up their positions when they see their own interests at stake, are happy to allow these formal/legal processes to develop as long as they have a kind of safety valve or virtual opt-out when they decide they want or need it. But if other countries raise the barriers to the influence of the United States—especially if U.S. structural power declines in a globalizing world—then the U.S. will pull back its commitment, leading to "institutional decline." This reflects a fundamental problem with some main assumptions of international relations theory—that is, that there is an underlying "levels of analysis distinction" that makes world politics different from domestic politics (Hollis and Smith 1990).

But a familiarity with longstanding—mainly domestic—pressure and interest group theory, public policy analysis, bargaining approaches, pluralism and neopluralism, corporatism and neocorporatism, elite theory, capture theory, and the like might suggest that such a trade-off is not only a normal state of affairs but, even more so, a condition for political processes to work in the first place. However, this has led to the central conundrum of global governance today. To what extent are states themselves the Waltzian "unit actors," the interaction of which determines outcomes (Waltz 1979)? Global governance institutions are not the kind of structurally differentiated, relatively autonomous, multifunctional institutions represented in political theory, at least, by modern states (Cerny 1990). Authors such as Stone underestimate the roles of private actors in shaping state actors' conceptions of what is in the "national interest" of states and what states' policy priorities might be. Moreover, non-state actors—often in regular interaction with actors in a Slaughterian "disaggregated state" (Slaughter 2004)—may be the true "independent variables" in any analysis of how states and I.O.s really operate.

It is necessary to move beyond realism and consider global governance as a political process more like that of a *pre-state* world, as Subrahmanyam and Spalińska argue in this book. Indeed, recent history suggests that the further development of an effective global governance structure is unlikely, even moving in the opposite direction. Biermann et al. (2009), for example, refer to the "fragmentation of global governance architectures" as the dominant trend in the 21st century. The International Monetary Fund, as a result of its imposition of conditionality (often at the behest of the United States), especially in the wake of the Asian financial crisis of the late 1990s, is today treated with caution in the developing world. As a result, the organization has turned back to Europe—its original remit in the 1940s—but has limited clout there. The World Trade Organization found the Doha Round to be a non-starter, and the proliferation of preferential trade agreements, from the Trans-Pacific Partnership and the Transatlantic Trade and Investment Partnership to myriad bilateral and minilateral pacts, to be the wave of the present, perhaps of the future. And the European Union is caught up in the Eurozone and migrant crises, along with Brexit, challenging the very cooperative core of the union itself, although the current crisis in Ukraine seems to be bringing the EU further together. International organizations may be increasingly vulnerable to capture—and to trying to impose reverse capture on the private sector actors and national regulators with whom they will increasingly be interacting.

2. Toward a Heterarchical Approach

Policymaking and implementation in the world today can no longer be analyzed through the lenses of either "methodological nationalism"—which has dominated the study of public administration and public policy, prioritizing the domestic arena—or "methodological internationalism" (or, more properly, what might be called "methodological inter-statism")—which has dominated international relations theory (Stone and Ladi 2015). Stone and Ladi identify several key issues, including questions of scale and multiscalarity, geographical limitations, diverse socio-political and historical contexts, the "negative externalities of complexity . . . [e.g.] inconsistency, duplication and regulatory arbitrage," and that "global" "public" policy is not necessarily "public," as well as problems of coordination and the rise of "closed, technocratic transnational administrations." They also identify key sets of actors: business, international civil servants, scientific and expert groups, philanthropic actors and management consultants—as well as policy entrepreneurs and policy brokers. The policy "toolbox" they identify includes legal and regulatory, financial, information, and organizational tools: "In short, transnational administration operates with different patterns of instrumentation." Policy diffusion and policy transfer are also crucial processes.

However, they do not go far enough. What globalization, seen as a process and not as an end point, does in the policy field is to open up the process to precisely the kinds of special interests that have been identified in the longstanding critical domestic interest group, elitist, corporatist, and neopluralist literature mentioned earlier. In other words, the processes of *capture* and *reverse capture* that have most recently been explored by Dauvergne and Lebaron in the case of nongovernmental organizations (NGOs) have, if anything, proliferated more widely in the transnational sphere precisely because of the fragmented institutionalization and crosscutting linkages and networks characteristic of that sphere (Dauvergne and Lebaron 2014).

Davies, in what is seen as the definitive history of international NGOs (INGOs), argues that the burgeoning constellation of such organizations in the 1980s and 1990s has been declining and fragmenting in the 21st century, with some limited exceptions (Davies 2013). And the proliferating literature on multinational corporations and transnational production chains, the advances of information and communications technologies, and, in particular, the power of quasi-globalized financial markets and institutions (Cerny 2014), demonstrates that global governance can be even more vulnerable to whipsawing, bypassing, capture, manipulation, and even corruption (as with the Federation of International Football Associations), than the traditional domestic public policy sphere. At the core of these processes is the interaction of two equally inextricably intertwined categories that are also at the core of the political and social sciences—the public and the private. Governance in a globalizing world is like domestic politics, or, as Robert Dahl so famously put it, "who governs?" (Dahl 1961).

3. From Pluralism to Heterarchy

Since the early 20th century, another key paradigm has been at work in the study of politics, although mainly limited to the domestic field—pluralism. Pluralism as a paradigm itself has a checkered history, challenged by other paradigms, including Marxist class analysis, theories of elitism and corporatism, and the revival of sociological theories of the state in the tradition of Max Weber. For my purposes, however, the key development is heterarchy. The outcomes of various political processes stem from the interaction of a range of specific, powerful individual and collective (group) actors below, outside, surrounding, cutting across, and populating states and societies. These actors—the more powerful economic interest groups, state actors in particular issue areas, certain NGOs (but see below), etc.—have very different kinds of social bonds, levels of social, economic, and political power resources, understandings of how to use that power, material interests, normative values, political projects, and, of course, the determination to pursue those interests, values, and projects in a range of public and private arenas. They have differing and sometimes incompatible interests as well as common interests, and they engage in processes of conflict, competition, and coalition-building in order to pursue those interests.

In this process, actors depend upon the capacities of real-world, crosscutting "interest" groups—including both "sectional" (or "material interest") and "value" groups (Key 1953), including civil society groups, non-governmental organizations (NGOs), and social movements—to manipulate constraints, to identify and take advantage of opportunities, and to shape new directions through processes of competition and coalition-building. What is new, however, are the rapidly growing linkages among groups in a growing range of crosscutting, uneven yet crucial, political processes above, below, and cutting across states and transnational institutions—what I call the "dialectic of globalization and fragmentation" (Cerny and Prichard 2017). This is not a "borderless world" (Ohmae 1990). Instead, these linkages are crystallizing into complex and uneven webs of power. In particular, Lindblom's (1977) concept of the "privileged position of business" reflects the skewed distribution of resources, network connections, and positional power of such groups.

The most important movers and shakers are no longer simply domestic political forces, institutions, and processes, but multi-level and multi-nodal ones—whether in terms of economic interdependence, including multinational firms and global financial markets, as well as production, distribution, and consumption chains; social interconnections, migration, and the movement of people; relationships of violence and force (including terrorism); "transgovernmental networks" cutting across governments; problem-solving "epistemic communities"; technological change from the internet to a growing variety of human activities; ideological conflict and competition; and a whole range of other deep trends. The most influential actors are those who can coordinate their activities, convince and/or bully governments, other competing actors, both public and private, and mass publics alike, thereby shaping in this process not merely transnational—even global— outcomes but also local and regional micro- and meso-politics.

4. Complex Globalization and the Diffusion of Power

Governance is therefore being transformed into a "polycentric" or "multinucle-ated" global political system operating within the same geographical space—and/ or overlapping spaces—in a way analogous to the emergence of coexisting and overlapping functional authorities in metropolitan areas and subnational regions (Ostrom et al. 1961; see Antonescu, this book). On the one hand, it becomes harder to maintain the boundaries that are necessary for the efficient "packaging" of public or collective goods; and second, it becomes harder to determine what collective goods are demanded or required in the first place—i.e., even to measure what is the "preferred state of affairs" (Ostrom et al. 1961: 832–835; cf. Cerny 1999 and Lowi 1964). On the other hand, state actors themselves paradoxically act in routine fashion to undermine the holistic and hierarchical character of traditional state sovereignty, authority, or *potestas*—leading to a "hollowing out of the state" (Jessop 1997). Different 'groups' are often interconnected with each other in complex ways that reflect diverse, even contrasting, identities, and belongings, cutting across territory, class, gender, ethnicity, family ties, and the like.

This changing environment is leading to a dialectic of stabilization and desta-bilization, especially among so-called "overlapping" and collusive groups (Coser 1956; Simmel 1922/1955) as well as competing and conflicting ones. At one level, the physical or material environmental bases of certain types of interest group associations have been transformed by both technological change and greater awareness of the interconnectedness of environmental and other issues. In particular, the multinationalization of industry, the expansion of trade, and the globalization of financial markets, along with the development of a transnational consumer society, have transformed many of what V.O. Key (1953) called "sectional groups" into transnational interest groups, operating across borders and involved in complex competition and coalition-building with each other, with state actors, with so-called "global governance" regimes, and increasingly with mass publics.

Within and across states, too, bureaucrats, politicians, and other officials or "state actors" have become more and more imbricated with groups of their counterparts in other countries through transgovernmental networks, policy communities, and the like. In the economic sphere, post-Fordist forms of production based on flexibiliza-tion have transformed "techniques of industry," labor markets, and finance. And the rediscovery of ideas has transformed the everyday content of both formally organized and informal groups, as well as that of political actors and intellectuals, into forums for developing increasingly global or transnational understandings of the major challenges of the day, year, or millennium—what I have elsewhere described as a post-Foucauldian *raison du monde* (Cerny 2010b, chapter 8).

5. Strategically Situated Actors

At the same time, however, such changes also give rise to adaptive as well as transformational modes of behavior. Therefore the particular shape a transformed international system is likely to take will be determined primarily by whether particular sets of groups—in particular, those competing groups led by "institutional entrepreneurs" or "change masters" (Kanter 1985)—are best able, either strategically or accidentally, to exploit the manifest and latent structural resources or political opportunity structures available to them most effectively in a period of flux. A key variable in explaining group-led change is thus the presence of strategically situated groups in a flawed and/or fluid structural context. Their presence constitutes a necessary—but not sufficient—condition of structural change.

Key sets of groups that have in the past been closely bound up with the territorial nation-state are increasingly experimenting with new forms of quasi-private regulation of their activities, especially in the context of neoliberal ideology and approaches to governance. And state actors themselves, once said to be "captured" by large, well-organized domestic constituencies, are increasingly captured instead by transnationally-linked sectors. These actors not only set state agencies and international regimes against each other—a process sometimes called "venue shopping" (or "forum shopping") or "regulatory arbitrage"—in the desire to "level the playing field" for their domestic clients in the wider world, on the one hand, but they also cause them simultaneously to try to network in an increasingly dense fashion with their peers in other states, on the other. Among the major losers are trade unions and other groups with few transnational linkages, although they are sometimes still in a position to demand and obtain compensatory side payments from national governments.

Alongside these economic developments has come a range of meso- and micro-social and political developments. Major social movements and cause groups are increasingly focused on transnational issues, whether seeking to address and resolve problems such as the environment, human rights, women's issues, the international banning of landmines, opposition to the holding of political prisoners, promoting "sustainable development," eliminating poor countries' international debts and the like, but also populist reactions seeking to restore the nation-state to its previous (supposed) structural hegemony. Growing pressures for migration, along with new possibilities for international communication, have not only led to the growth of active diasporas as well as of "global tribes" (Kotkin 1992) but also to major movements of refugees and asylum seekers attempting to escape the civil wars and unrest of the current decade. The key driving force in this transformation and reconstruction will consist of actors engaging in crosscutting competition and coalition-building behavior, exploiting the growing institutional loopholes of global politics, constructing new power games, creating new networks and changing people's perceptions of how world politics works.

6. Transnational Policy Issues

The main variable propelling this process of change is usually seen to be the nature of the policy issues and challenges that face both states and international organizations today. These challenges include global economic growth, climate change and pollution, cross-border civil and insurgent wars, increasing relative inequality and the growing public salience of poverty and uneven development—not to mention a range of significant issues concerning particular transnationally-networked economic and financial sectors, crosscutting transportation and infrastructure issues, technological changes with global implications, such as governing the internet, and the like. Operating in such a changing world is leading to new problems of management and control, what Lake has called "the privatization of governance" (Lake 1999; Kahler and Lake 2003) and others have identified as the emergence of "private authority" in international affairs (Cutler et al. 1999; Ronit and Schneider 2000; Hall and Biersteker 2003). Institutions and formal processes of "global governance" simply do not have the direct sanctioning power that has been at the core of state development and power in the modern era—especially in the form of Weber's "monopoly of legitimate violence."

In this world, even small firms that seem ostensibly "local" are not immune, being dependent upon "foreign" raw materials, export markets, investment finance, migrant labor and the like, and both increasingly form nodes of wider networks and coordinate their actions. Less formal networks and more formal interaction among firms, "private regimes," "alliance capitalism" and the ability of non-state actors in general to develop a range of formal and informal interconnections, both economic and political, have led to significant degrees of policy transfer both across states and in terms of shaping the evolution of global governance more broadly (Higgott et al. 1999; Evans 2005). Significant issue-areas, such as accountancy, auditing and corporate governance, have witnessed ongoing negotiation processes among firms, private sector organizations representing particular industrial, financial and commercial sectors, as well as governments and international regimes, in order to reconcile conflicting standards and move toward a more level playing field (Mügge 2006).

Ordinary people in everyday life are growing more and more aware that their fates depend not so much on decisions taken at national level, but on wider developments and transformations at international, transnational and translocal levels (Hobson and Seabrooke 2007). Perhaps most salient of all, given the recent growth of concern with issues like climate change and the Coronavirus pandemic have been environmental groups, which have come to occupy a central place in the claim to represent people in general across borders, calling for global solutions to deal with a growing, imperative crisis (Kütting and Cerny 2015). In sum, world politics is coming to be increasingly characterized by what sociologists call "functional differentiation," governance organized around different social, economic and political "functions" or crosscutting issue-areas (Albert et al. 2013; Cerny 2013b).

7. Dimensions of Transformation

This overall process of transformation has three main interlocking dimensions. The first involves a change in the character of the state's domestic functions, especially how so-called "public goods" and "social justice" are perceived, pursued and provided, challenged by the marketization and transnationalization of economic activities (and of the state itself). Second, state actors are increasingly concerned with promoting the competitive advantages of particular production and service sectors in a more open and integrated world economy—the "Competition State" (Cerny 1990, 2000, 2010a; Horsfall 2011). Third, rather than continuing path dependency, these effects generate multiple equilibria, creating the possibility of new "branching points," thus opening the way to potential path modification and reconstruction of the system itself. The economic mission of the state has shifted considerably from its traditional role as a "decommodifying agent" to that of a "commodifying agent" (Cerny 1990).

Globalization is itself increasingly constituted by the very political processes identified here. At the base, we find such factors as: the distribution of resources in society; the kind of processes of production, distribution and exchange prevalent therein; the state of consciousness or the perception of interests, values and possibilities of the various individual and group actors; and the sorts of basic solidarities and alliances of a more political nature that emerge from all of these taken together. The second level concerns the character of "intermediaries," sometimes called the power structure. Is public policy made by "iron triangles," closed policy communities, wider policy networks, or transparent, competitive, pluralistic processes? The third level concerns the structure of the institutional playing fields themselves, whether concentrated or diffused, unitary or fragmented, and the sorts of rules and practices that have evolved to coordinate different levels and/or pillars of the political system.

The power of latent or potential groups or categories has been growing. New categories of losers have been created as well, although in some cases these are groups that have already long been disenfranchised, suppressed or subsumed in authoritarian social hierarchies, such as tribes or clans—they now confront "centralizing elites" through more localized, quasi-tribal resistance (Ahmed 2013). Meanwhile, recent attempts to reform financial regulation are increasingly facing obstacles stemming from the lack of a coherent transnational response (Goldbach 2015). The blurring of these traditional lines between what once formed the basis for the left-right divide at national level has switched the focus of group politics toward other kinds of linkages, whether the translocal restructuring of influence around multiculturalism and/or mutually exclusive but cross-border religious and ethnic identities, diaspora communities, world cities and the like, on the one hand, or the transnational/global reorganizing of businesses and market structures around more extended networks, the development of epistemic communities of scientists and experts, the rapid growth of transnational advocacy coalitions and networks (NGOs, civil society, environmentalism, etc.), on the other.

Long-term left/right blocs are giving way to mixed coalitions, leading to political cognitive dissonance and, at times, to strange alliances that can distort preferences rather than effectively pursue them. This is reflected in the support for less well-off "social conservatives" (Frank 2004), as currently evidenced by support for the Tea Party and for Donald J. Trump. When governmental leaders go home from major international meetings like the G20 or the COP26 climate change conferences, they are immediately faced with such domestic pressures, making the transnationalization of policy something that often has to be pursued surreptitiously and legitimated indirectly—or "depoliticized"—especially when the light of crisis or disruptive change is shone on particular domestic sectors and interests.

8. Conclusion

Therefore, there is unlikely to emerge a broad-based, public interest oriented "global civil society" that would permit social actors to develop an overall structural impact of a kind that could transform the international system itself. Each set of actors faces not only promising opportunities, but also significant constraints in pursuing their group goals, veering between convergence and divergence, between a widening process of relatively stable horse-trading and bargaining, on the one hand, and a neomedieval "durable disorder" (Minc 1993; Cerny 1998; Spalińska, this book), on the other. Globalization is not an exogenous variable, imposed on states from outside (*pace* Pierre 2013). It is a complex dialectic of bottom up/top down, inside/out, endogenous and exogenous variables that come as much—or even more—from within states and societies as from the "international" level of analysis. Reframing political action and process through heterarchy and bringing that to center stage will provide the best way to conceptualize the restructuring of governance during the rest of this century.

References

Ahmed, Akbar (2013). *The Thistle and the Drone: How America's War on Terror Became a Global War on Tribal Islam* (Washington, DC: Brookings Institution Press).
Albert, Mathias, Barry Buzan and Michael Zürn, eds. (2013). *Bringing Sociology to IR: World Politics as Differentiation Theory* (Cambridge: Cambridge University Press).

Biermann, F., P. Pattberg, H. van Asselt and F. Zelli (2009). 'The Fragmentation of Global Governance Architectures: A Framework for Analysis," *Global Environmental Politics*, vol. 9, no. 4, pp. 14–40.

Cerny, Philip G. (1990). *The Changing Architecture of Politics: Structure, Agency and the Future of the State* (London: Sage).

Cerny, Philip G. (1998). "Neomedievalism, Civil Wars and the New Security Dilemma: Globalization as Durable Disorder," *Civil Wars*, vol. 1, no. 1 (Spring), pp. 36–64.

Cerny, Philip G. (1999). "Globalization, Governance and Complexity," in Aseem Prakash and Jeffrey A. Hart, eds., *Globalization and Governance* (London: Routledge), pp. 188–212.

Cerny, Philip G. (2000). "Restructuring the Political Arena: Globalization and the Para-doxes of the Competition State," in Randall D. Germain, ed., *Globalization and Its Critics: Perspectives from Political Economy* (London: Macmillan), pp. 117–138.

Cerny, Philip G. (2010a). "The Competition State Today: From *raison d'État* to *raison du monde*," *Policy Studies*, vol. 4, no. 1 (January), pp. 5–21.

Cerny, Philip G. (2010b). *Rethinking World Politics: A Theory of Transnational Neoplural-ism* (New York and Oxford: Oxford University Press).

Cerny, Philip G. (2012). 'Globalization and the Transformation of Power,' in Mark Hau-gaard and Kevin Ryan, eds., *Political Power: The Development of the Field* (Lev-erkusen/Opladen: Barbara Budrich for the International Political Science Association, Research Committee No. 36, Political Power), pp. 185–214.

Cerny, Philip G. (2013a). "The Paradox of Liberalism in a Globalizing World," in Rebekka Friedman, Kevork Oskanian and Ramon Pacheco Pardo, eds., *After Liberalism? The Future of Liberalism in International Relations* (Basingstoke and New York: Palgrave Macmillan), pp. 189–214.

Cerny, Philip G. (2013b). "Functional Differentiation, Globalization and the New Transna-tional Neopluralism," in Mathias Albert, Barry Buzan and Michael Zürn, eds., *Bringing Sociology to International Relations: World Politics as Differentiation Theory* (Cam-bridge: Cambridge University Press), pp. 205–227.

Cerny, Philip G. (2014). "Rethinking Financial Regulation: Risk, Club Goods and Regu-latory Fatigue," in Thomas Oatley and W. Kindred Winecoff, eds., *Handbook of the International Political Economy of Monetary Relations* (Cheltenham and Northampton, MA: Edward Elgar, May), pp. 343–363.

Cerny, Philip G. and Prichard, Alex (2017). "The New Anarchy: Globalisation and Frag-mentation in 21st Century World Politics", *Journal of International Political Theory*, vol. 13, no. 3 (October), pp. 378–394.

Coen, David and Tom Pegram (2015). "Wanted: A Third Generation of Global Governance Research," *Commentary, Governance: An International Journal of Policy, Administra-tion and Institutions*, vol. 28, no. 4 (October), pp. 417–420, 417.

Coser, Lewis A. (1956). *The Functions of Social Conflict* (London: Routledge and Kegan Paul).

Crozier, Michel and Erhard Friedberg (1977). *L'Acteur et le système: les contraintes de l'action collective* (Paris: Éditions du Seuil).

Cutler, A. Claire, Virginia Haufler and Tony Porter, eds. (1999). *Private Authority and International Affairs* (Albany, NY: State University of New York Press).

Dahl, Robert A. (1961). *Who Governs? Democracy and Power in the American City* (New Haven: Yale University Press).

Dauvergne, Peter and Genevieve Lebaron (2014). *Protest, Inc.: The Corporatization of Activism* (Cambridge: Polity Press).

Davies, Thomas (2013). *NGOs: A New History of Transnational Civil Society* (London: C. Hurst).

Durkheim, Emile (1893/1933). *The Division of Labor in Society*, trs. George Simpson (New York: Free Press, Original French Edition 1893).

Evans, Mark G. (2005). *Policy Transfer in Global Perspective* (London: Ashgate).

Frank, Thomas (2004). *What's the Matter with Kansas? How Conservatives Won the Heart of America* (New York: Henry Holt).

Goldbach, Roman (2015). *Global Governance and Regulatory Failure: The Political Economy of Banking* (Basingstoke, Hants: Palgrave Macmillan).

Hall, Rodney Bruce and Thomas J. Biersteker, eds. (2003). *The Emergence of Private Authority in Global Governance* (Cambridge: Cambridge University Press).

Higgott, Richard, Geoffrey R.D. Underhill and Andreas Bieler, eds. (1999). *Non-State Actors and Authority in the Global System* (London: Routledge).

Hobson, John M. and Leonard Seabrooke, eds. (2007). *Everyday Politics of the World Economy* (Cambridge: Cambridge University Press).

Hollis, Martin and Steve Smith (1990). *Explaining and Understanding International Relations* (Oxford: Clarendon Press).

Horsfall, Daniel (2011). *From Competition State to Competition States? An Empirical Exploration*, unpublished Ph.D. thesis, Department of Social Policy, University of York.

Jessop, Bob (1997). "The Future of the National State: Erosion or Reorganization? Reflections on the West European Case," Paper Presented at a Conference on Globalization: Critical Perspectives, University of Birmingham (14–16 March).

Kahler, Miles and David A. Lake, eds. (2003). *Governance in a Global Economy: Political Authority in Transition* (Princeton: Princeton University Press).

Kanter, Rosabeth Moss (1985). *The Change Masters: Innovation and Entrepreneurship in the American Corporation* (Glencoe, IL: Free Press).

Key, V.O. Jr. (1953). *Politics, Parties, and Pressure Groups* (New York: Thomas Y. Crowell).

Kotkin, Joel (1992). *Tribes: How Race, Religion and Identity Determine Success in the New Global Economy* (New York: Random House).

Kütting, Gabriela and Philip G. Cerny (2015). "Rethinking Global Environmental Policy: From Global Governance to Transnational Neopluralism," *Public Administration*, vol. 93, no. 4 (December), pp. 907–921.

Lake, David A. (1999). "Global Governance: A Relational Contracting Approach," in Aseem Prakash and Jeffrey A. Hart, eds., *Globalization and Governance* (London: Routledge), pp. 31–53.

Lindblom, Charles E. (1977). *Politics and Markets: The World's Political Economic Systems* (New York: Basic Books).

Lowi, Theodore J. (1964). "American Business, Public Policy, Case Studies, and Political Theory," *World Politics*, vol. 16, no. 4 (July), pp. 677–715.

McFarland, Andrew S. (2004). *Neopluralism: The Evolution of Political Process Theory* (Lawrence, Kansas: University of Kansas Press).

Minc, Alain (1993). *Le nouveau Moyen Âge* (Paris: Gallimard).

Mügge, Daniel (2006). "Private-Public Puzzles: Inter-Firm Competition and Transnational Private Regulation," *New Political Economy*, vol. 11, no. 2 (June), pp. 177–200.

Ohmae, Kenichi (1990). *The Borderless World: Power and Strategy in the Interlinked Economy* (Pensacola, FL: Ballinger Publishing).

Ostrom, Vincent, Charles M. Tiebout and Robert Warren (1961). "The Organization of Government in Metropolitan Areas: A Theoretical Inquiry," *American Political Science Review*, vol 55, no. 3 (September), pp. 831–842.

Pierre, Jon (2013). *Globalization and Governance* (Cheltenham and Northampton, MA: Edward Elgar).

Ronit, Karsten and Volker Schneider, eds. (2000). *Private Organizations in Global Politics* (London: Routledge).

Rosenau, James N. (1997). *Along the Domestic-Foreign Frontier: Exploring Governance in a Turbulent World* (Cambridge: Cambridge University Press).

Simmel, Georg (1922/1955). *Conflict and the Web of Group Affiliations* (New York: Free Press).

Slaughter, Anne-Marie (2004). *A New World Order* (Princeton, NJ: Princeton University Press).

Stone, Diane and Stella Ladi (2015). "Global Public Policy and Transnational Administration," *Public Administration* (Wiley Early View, 7 September), p. 1. doi: 10.1111/padm.12207

Stone, Randall W. (2011). *Controlling Institutions: International Organizations and the Global Economy* (Cambridge: Cambridge University Press).

Waltz, Kenneth (1979). *Theory of International Politics* (Reading, MA: Addison-Wesley).

11

METROPOLITAN DIPLOMACY

Global Metropolitan Law and Global Cities Seen from the Heterarchy Perspective

Mădălina Virginia Antonescu

Introduction

This chapter seeks to develop a perspective about the deep, complex, and multi-dimensional order of the 21st century as an order dominated by the rise of new non-state actors: the metropolises. The megacities/megalopolises of this "urban century," as defined by the United Nations, will behave as key actors by shaping the overall profile of the international order. Metropolises will develop a special form of diplomacy and particular regulations, thus progressively creating a holistic body of normative rules—a genuine metropolitan law. This chapter explores the new global world of rising non-state actors as an alternative to the hierarchic dominant pattern, without admitting a total exclusion of the latter from the new global world. Heterarchy is approached as a specific reality of two or many imbricate orders, co-existent with the Westphalian official order. Heterarchy will progressively shape the new mega-reality as a result of the interconnections between such orders with the emancipation of actors from the state umbrella and with the creation of mega or infra-entities linked in distinct types of legal, political, or alter-political networks that need new concepts to be defined. In particular, private sector actors benefiting from the dialectic of globalization and fragmentation will dominate megalopolistic policy processes.

1. Megacities in the 21st Century—The Urban Century in Historical Perspective

Heterarchic structural patterns can be revolutionary, alternative, post-state patterns used in the present wave of globalization in order to describe a new political reality, a post-political or a super-political reality. Heterarchy into the 21st century needs to take into account the rise of new non-state actors, such as civilizations,

DOI: 10.4324/9781003352617-13

metropolises, and megalopolises, and their capacity and will to conquer much autonomy from the state, to surpass the state world and to create new types of systems and networks—a post-United Nations world. Heterarchy in the 21st century states that two or many kinds of orders will co-exist and interfere with each other, putting an end to the Westphalian world monopoly of one world, one system, and one law (i.e., international law). Heterarchy comes to put order where at present is a chaotic field.

Especially during the second part of the 21st century, the inter-metropolitan order will become a specific order, characterized by exclusive relations among the metropolises, with geopolitical and geo-economic effects, considering the struggles for power and supremacy among the megacities—which will become stakeholders. We refer to the neo-medieval hypothesis (see Spalińska, this volume) as the creation of *city leagues*, the creation of federations of free cities, which can also lead to forms of empires dominated by a single city—that is, a decision-making center (Griffiths, 2005: 591–592). In ancient times, cities such as the Mesopotamian cities, also known as *state-cities*, created *hydraulic/agrarian empires*—for example, the Sumerian thalassocratic empire, the Babylonian empire (Antonescu, 2008: 105–106) or the imperial Rome—in which case a state-city produced an imperial form expanded at the global level of the age (Held et al., 2004: 373–376). Other cities such as Athens or Sparta created thalassocratic *military-commercial empires* (Lévêque, 1987: 5–29). Later on, during medieval times, republic-cities such as Venice, Florence, and Genoa formed *military-commercial empires* (Rendina, 2003: 8–11; Morris, 2016: 24–27; Toynbee, 1979: 81–84).

Cities have also taken the form of *fortified states*, organized into alliances, federations, or different association forms, based on the criterion of their autonomy (Giurescu and Giurescu, 1974: 76–125, quoted in Malita, 1975: 82). For example, in imperial Rome, in its last stage of evolution, when the empire was transformed into a federation, unity was ensured by the form of administration, which ensured a high level of local autonomy despite being part of the same civilizational area. The cities of the Roman Empire were quasi-autonomous from the imperial center, as they had the right of "legation" (*ius legationis*), being able to accredit envoys to obtain tax deductions, aid, and administrative benefits. They observed a municipal law, they had administrative privileges, although they were parts of a single system, i.e. the imperial system controlled by Rome, the imperial city (Giurescu and Giurescu, 1974, vol. I: 76–125, quoted in Malita, 1975: 82). Cities created a permanent map of civilizations and of the interactions among empires. They were centers of culture, storing unique cultural and traditional identities. The great routes of world commerce existed due to cities, and so did the great military centers of expansionist decision-making, leading to the creation of empires that covered territories beyond the civilizational area of the imperial city. Throughout history, cities have been associated with the state concept, the imperial concept, and the confederative concept (confederations, leagues, federations of cities), with coalitions of cities involved in various projects, such as expansion military projects, defensive military projects, commercial projects, etc. (McNeill, 2000: 112–113).

Particularly in the 20th century, the direct impact of the waves of globalization was an increase in the urbanization pace (Lee, 2008: 3–9), at a level that also includes geographic spaces outside the global economic-financial flows. According to the UN estimates and determinations, the 21st century is already "an urban century," when over 50% of the world's population lives in the urban environment.[1] Under the impact of these phenomena specific to the 21st century, the doctrine even proposed new terms, such as "metropolization"[2] and "durable urbanization."[3] As of the second part of the 21st century, following this trend, i.e. consolidation of the global urban world, we will be able to talk about the creation of a specific type of political-legal-economic order, considering the proliferation of megacities, of the new non-state actors, i.e. *the inter-metropolitan order*— which will be complementary at first and will subsequently substitute the traditional international order dominated by nation-states. Far from slowing down, the global urbanization trend is rapidly growing, hence the proliferation of megacities, which often put the political stakeholders and decision-makers—accustomed to a traditional framework in which the rural environment dominates the urban environment—in situations that make it difficult for them to understand the need to quickly adjust certain policies for the sustainable and controlled urban development of the 21st century.

Megacities continue to be considered simple units without administrative identity, without their own policy, unable to compete against the state and to influence world geopolitics (determined by the states, not by other actors). In addition, there is an obsolete view that the world of states continues to express a type of mainly rural order or an order in which the *rural regions* or the industrial regions (named differently) have a specific cultural identity, as they represent the infra-national level, instead of the metropolises they include (if the latter exist). The *inter-metropolitan order* can be defined as an order in which the metropolises become globally dominating actors, original, main subjects of inter-metropolitan law, the entities generating the legal regulations governing the actual metropolitan order.

2. Development of Megalopolises in the Second Half of the 21st Century: Region-Megalopolises

Starting with the 21st century, the urbanization trend of human societies all over the globe will be further on the rise, with a demographic and urban explosion in Asia forecast. Continent-countries such as Asia will be confronted with two main challenges: the rapid demographic increase and the urbanization of poverty, entailing the uncontrollable expansion of the information urban settlements, which are not included in architectonic urbanization plans and which highlight a world of social and cultural differences between the outskirts and the residential areas (Bonnet, 2000: 24–25).

A distinction needs to be made between "*metropolization*"—a term which refers to the urbanization of territories that participate in the global economic flows, therefore they are integrated in the global economy—and "*megalopolization*"—a term which refers to the urbanization phenomenon on territories *less integrated* in the global economy, with increased risks of higher levels of poverty and lack of sustainable policies regarding the urban environment), (Bonnet, 2000: 8–9; Gorra-Gobin, 2006: 242–243). At the same time, there is the possibility that certain non-state actors (at the same time infra-state, as well as trans-national) emerge, go beyond and challenge the traditional concept of nation-state: the *region-megalopolises*. We are discussing an advanced type of metropolises and megalopolises, which add sufficient surrounding areas, until they create their own outskirts belts, being capable of supporting their economic development, to ensure their green areas, amusement parks, malls, and factories, which can no longer be included in the "old town center." The old town center areas are now saved for the preservation of urban cultural traditions, of the city's cultural identity, historical areas that are part of the city's cultural heritage. However, these metropolises and megalopolises are advanced in the sense that they have managed to absorb a significant number of surrounding areas and transform them into urban outskirts, thus changing the administrative configuration of a territorial unit (county, region).

The region itself will borrow the name and identity of the center-megalopolis that generated it, which demonstrates its affiliation to the metropolitan decision-making nucleus. Paris—the Parisian region; Buenos Aires—the Buenos Aires region; Beijing—the Beijing region, Calcutta—the Calcutta region, Rio de Janeiro—the Rio de Janeiro region, Jakarta—the Jakartan region, Mexico City—the Mexico City region, New York City—the New York City region, Los Angeles—the Los Angeles region, London—the London region, Manila—the Manila region, Osaka—the Osakan region—are all examples of region names with which we are not accustomed and which will define the new geopolitical realities of a future order of metropolises, transforming the current territorial units, at infra-state level, into a world urbanized and regional-urbanized map. Infra-national actors such as megacities will be decisive in the fight for supremacy among the states, while the Westphalian order will be duplicated (if not fully replaced) by the new order, that is, the order of metropolises. Non-state actors seem to compete against the nation-state, in the early 21st century, until they weaken it and replace it with new forms of organization (transnational corporations, transnational terrorist groups, global NGOs, etc.) and are replaced with a type of actors to which the doctrine of "international relations" has not paid sufficient attention and which it has not taken into consideration as distinct actors. These changes, which currently seem inconceivable given the current dominant paradigms of the academic study of international relations and the state-centered practices of diplomacy, will in turn influence the traditional organization of nation-states and implicitly the neo-Westphalian order, as the proliferation of metropolises becomes consolidated at the global level, creating an *inter-metropolitan order*.

Crucially, the most important states will include a large number of metropolises able to act in the 21st-century global economy—an economy based on knowledge, an informational economy, a durable urbanization-oriented economy, focused on attracting global urban economic and commercial flows. These megacities will have the capacity to become distinct actors in an international order progressively influenced, if not determined by metropolitan decisions and policies, by the capacity of the metropolises to attract, manage, use, and invest funds, human resources, creativity, and innovation. In the 21st-century world, the more powerful states or the states dominating the world at the continental or global level will those with the most powerful/largest number of metropolises capable of influencing the global economy (from the viewpoint of state-of-the-art technologies, inventions, and sciences, from the perspective of know-how transfer, informational economy, and durable urbanization). Based on the number and power of its metropolises (economic, scientific power), we will be able to estimate whether a state is a "powerful state," in terms of 21st-century economy and geopolitics. Countries that are rural by nature, as well as those countries confronted by significant migration levels toward the cities, with a predominantly rural economy, with metropolises outside/little integrated with the economic, investment flows or the world technologies, cannot become significant actors of the 21st century world; neither them, *nor* their metropolises.

If we encounter suprastate entities in today's world, such as the European Union, with clear suprastate characteristics, considering the process of transferring competences to the European decision-making level (Antonescu, 2005: 24–26), the second half of the 21st century will witness the proliferation of *supra- or pluri-metropolitan entities*, of metropolis agglomerations forming a regional/megalopolis entity or metropolis networks organized in a trans-regional metropolitan arc. In other words, as the second part of the 21st century evolves, the world becomes a world of *Regional City Archipelagos (RCA)*, which form a World City Archipelago (WCA) in the second stage. This term is used to define the connections among the cities that belong to the same region and the connections among the great world urban poles (visible on the air traffic maps and the telecommunication flow maps). According to this theory, the WCA currently includes six poles, which shape a metropolitan geopolitical map of the distribution of metropolitan power in the 21st-century world: (1) the urban entity from Boston to Washington; plus (2) the metropolises from the Great Lakes region, from Chicago to Toronto; (3) the metropolises facing the Pacific, from San Diego to Seattle, including Los Angeles and San Francisco; (4) the fourth urban pole comprising the Western Europe metropolises—from London and Paris to Catalonia and Munich. The fifth urban pole includes the Japanese megalopolises of Tokyo and Osaka, while the sixth pole, currently in the process of forming, covers a territory from Seoul to Singapore, from the seas of China and the Yellow Sea, closing continental China in the East, and the four urban entities: Beijing, Tianjin, Shanghai, Canton (or *the Great Asia-Pacific Arc*: Gorra-Gobin, 2006: 243).

In the legal order of the early 22nd century, and following the global proliferation of the urbanization phenomenon and the increase in the number of metropolises, as well as the developing megalopolises and their tendency to connect, we
will have to add a tendency to create new actors—*region-metropolises*—in the
21st century. Thus, we will see the creation of a new statalized order, because
metropolises and megalopolises can be statalized based on the model of the
ancient citadel-cities. *Transregional Metropolitan Arcs* will be defined as new
trans-state actors. They will have their own legal personality, special diplomatic
representatives, specific institutions, and their own budgets, based on the contributions of the region-metropolises participating in such an Arc.

3. From the 21st to the 22nd Century: Metropolitan Diplomacy

We can define metropolitan diplomats as special envoys with special competences, assigned directly by the region-metropolises, by the Great TransOceanic
City Arcs (TOCA) and the TransContinental City Arcs (TCCA), entities with
distinct legal personalities, based on an inter-metropolitan body of laws, called
inter-metropolitan law. We are using this term because we take into consideration the development of a set of legal regulations in a post-state world in which
the current international law is obsolete. Due to the ascension of the metropolises
and megalopolises, the legal and political order of the world will be decided by
the new power center of these actors, as the ancient state-cities or imperial-cities
did, building terrestrial imperial or thalassocratic superstructures, starting from
the decision-making nucleus, the initiating state-city. Therefore, the metropolitan
diplomats are the special public servants appointed by the Councils of the Region-
Metropolises and by the Foreign Policy Councils of the TransOceanic and Trans-
Continental City Arcs (TOCA and TCCA) and validated by the General Mayors
of the Region-Metropolises and by the TOCA and TCCA Doges/Dogessas (Governors, Governors-women). They have special legal and political status, based
on inter-metropolitan law treaties and the Charter of Fundamental Principles of
Metropolitan Diplomacy, signed and assumed by all the region-metropolises and
by all the TOCAs and TCCAs.

Thus, several categories of metropolitan diplomats can be determined, depending on the level and the legal-political entity represented, in a world of statalized
or quasi-statalized metropolises:

- *Diplomats of the state-metropolises* (lower level of direct, diplomatic representation in the region-metropolises);
- *Diplomats of the region-metropolises* (second level of diplomatic representation, i.e., region-metropolises in TCCAs and TOCAs);
- *Diplomats of the TCCAs and the TOCAs* (third level of diplomatic representation, i.e., TCCA and TOCA, in the relationship with the Great Transre-
gional/Global City Arc or GGCA);

- *GGCA diplomats* (representing GGCA in relation with any other low-level legal entity, as well as in relation with non-metropolitan political entities, such as the Rural Networks (RNs), the Chaotic Elements (such as the CEs, in relation to the chiefs of migrating hoards that control the migratory movements and determine the massive migration routes clandestine or forced by various situations). The level of GGCA diplomatic representation is the ultimate level and the authority represented by these diplomats is the ultimate level of diplomacy.

4. A Hybrid World Structure, Balancing Between International and Global Orders

The early 21st century globalization processes have added unprecedented pressure on nation-states and the Westphalian order. One could say that the nation-states face situations, relations, contexts, practices of the non-state actors, at infra-local, regional, international, and global level, relations in which there is the risk of assuming a subordinated position (economic, financial, commercial, or even political). Thus, in many ways, nation-states become "captive/reactive states," i.e., they are held captive under the practices, situations and relations controlled by the non-state actors, academics using various terms as "amorphous neo-medievalism" or "durable disorder" (Cerny, 1998; Spalińska, this volume). For the states, the global world is a world prone to uncertainty and hazard, which dampens the worldwide business management processes (Vlad, 2001: 90).

The impulse towards globalization comes from the economic-financial sector, under the pressure of the interests and strategies specific to the non-state actors. One can even consider *an alliance sui generis* of the transnational companies, the banks, and the stock exchanges, which would act to control the state policies in the area of foreign economic relations and more (Vlad, 2001: 91). Another notable aspect is the proliferation and expansion/conquering of the national markets (which would lead to a phenomenon of economic-financial captivity of the states) by the banks, transnational corporations, during the past couple of decades, which has changed the mainly inter-national nature of the economic and political order into a predominantly a *post-international* one (see Ramjit, this volume), impacted by the action, the strategies and the group interests—forming authentic cartels on specialized markets, at the level of regional or even global markets—of such non-state actors. The 21st century global order is more likely to witness a conflict between the state (traditional) actors and their Westphalian order (based on a specific set of principles included in the UN Charter, which only acknowledges nations and states) on one hand, and non-state actors on the other. Non-state actors are evolving progressively into an economic-financial order which will be granted the legal-political recognition suitable for this new profile (the post-state or global law), in a final stage—a form of quasi-private "global governance."

In our opinion, the great conflict of the first half of the 21st century, which will decide the nature of the political order of this century, will be the conflict between the *nation-states* (the coordinating, Westphalian model) and the non-state actors (shaping a model which is still studied, either leaning towards *a new hierarchical pattern*, with institutions specific to non-state actors at the top—e.g., a global council of corporations or banks, a global, unique, multi-sector stock exchange, a board of presidents of the private banks, with the global or continental capacity to influence the captive financial markets—or leaning towards *a heterarchical pattern*, which entails the forced, often tense coexistence with the states and the states authorities. In the latter case, we may witness the creation of mixed, hybrid institutions, at global level, institutions such as the global council of national bank governors and of the chairmen of boards of directors for the private banks, expanding regionally/continentally and having the capacity to maintain control over these captive markets for over two decades; stock exchanges with markets controlled at regional or continental level by "inter-allied" boards of directors of the states, in order to counter the non-state actors' attempts to centralize and weaken the states.

Lack of legal regulation will contribute to an increase in the degree of economic instability and insecurity among the nations, generating the risks of hyper-conflict. Converting the Westphalian order into a post-state economic order, focused exclusively or predominantly on the meta-symbolic economy (electronic capital, electronic money, virtual speculative flows) entails the risk of a global hyper-conflict. Thus the 21st century Westphalian order is fundamentally different from the late 20th century inter-state order. In this context, the Westphalian order is entangled and interconnected at various levels (infra-local, national, regional, multilateral, international) through a series of webs designed and controlled by the non-state actors. The states (irrespective of their power) are captive in structural dependence on the non-state actors they once used to control or ignore; the new webs form the underlying structure of the 21st—22nd century global order. The traditional power of the states has been undermined and both hard and soft power are defined and implemented by non-state actors. This unique pattern of heterarchy is currently controlled mainly by the non-state actors and very little by the states according to the rules and regulations of the contemporary international law.

Currently, international law does not have the tools to handle the new profile of economic-political order controlled by the non-state actors. Non-state actors cannot be held accountable internationally, before international courts (the International Court of Justice does not have responsibilities concerning the non-state actors), neither globally (there is no body of global regulations assumed by the non-state actors and by the states, a global convention of non-state and state actors, which stipulates the underlying principles, institutions, legal rights and obligations specific to the non-state actors, either in the current international order or in the global order). There is no Council of the States for the relations with the non-state actors, within or outside the UN framework. There is no Mixed Court of Justice (to cover litigations between the states and the non-state actors, based on clear legal regulations). There is no precise mechanism to hold accountable or to control the community of states in relation to the non-state actors, in relation to their autonomous, transnational interests and actions. The large international financial cartels and transnational companies are a potential risk to the stability of the states from which they separated by becoming autonomous and which they can control both directly and indirectly (governments, parliaments, presidents, local decision-making institutions etc.). We are looking at *underground empires*, at *private empires*, at *pseudo-political empires* or at *post-historical empires*, based on the webs controlled by the non-state actors, webs in which the states are caught irrespective of their power (Antonescu, 2004: 228–236. Antonescu, 2005: 16–18, 26–28. Antonescu, 2008: 18, 30, 31).

Tech monopolies, social media, or information monopolies (databases built on information received from the social media platforms) are currently removed from the state control, based on the premise that the market is absolutely free; they are under the control of the private actors. A state's attempt to manage or control the activity, the profile of companies which own tech or information monopolies, which have recorded speculative activities, or which transfer the databases acquired and considered their property, and to limit them is considered a "totalitarian act." The models in which the state authorities are penetrated by multiple (sometimes competing) non-state/under-state authorities (Cerny, 2021), configured in webs and counter-webs, as result of struggles for supremacy amongst them or with the states, may vary, from decentralized models to models in which the non-state command structures form a decision-making peak looking over a global/regional command mini-structure, which represents the large financial, commercial cartels or cartels from other areas—"the large transnational command network," to name it by convention). Organizations specific to the Westphalian order, such as the UN, become parallel, interpenetrated or connected to these webs. The absence of new international or global institutions, adjusted by the states to the new situation—for example, some sort of global council—is currently impossible, given the residual power of nation-states to block such initiatives. The international order, interpenetrated by webs controlled by the private actors, creates the risk of dissipation and fragmentation of the Westphalian order (Cerny, 2021), and the risk of hyper-conflict (as a last resort type of extreme reaction of the states to the total loss of their independence and to the rise of the new order).

Notes

1 *Istanbul+5,* The UN Special Session of Great Assembly, Urban Habitat. *State of the World's cities, 2012–2013. Prosperity of cities*, UN-HABITAT, *For a better urban future*, Routledge, 2013, US, Canada, www.unhabitat.org.
2 Idem, p. 242.
3 Many key-documents adopted at international level on this issue, as: Istanbul+5, Urban Millennium, New York, 6–8 June 2001, United Nations, UNCHS. Johannesburg Declaration on Sustainable Development, 4 September 2002. United Nations Millennium Declaration 55/2, Resolution adopted by the General Assembly, 6 September 2000. Incheon Communiqué, November 16, 2012, Strengthening planning and implementation capacities for sustainable development in the post-Rio context, UNCSD. Agenda 2030, https://sustainabledevelopment.un.org. The Millennium Development Goals Report, 2014, We can end poverty 2015, www.undp.org/content/undp/en

References

Agenda 2030. UN. https://sustainabledevelopment.un.org.

Antonescu, Madalina Virginia (2004). *Uniunea Europeană, un imperiu al sec. XXI? Spre o civilizatie a Uniunii Europene.* Bucharest: Ed. Cartea Universitara.

Antonescu, Mădălina Virginia (2005). *Uniunea Europeană, un imperiu modern?* Bucharest: Ed. Cartea Universitară.

Antonescu, Mădălina Virginia (2008). *Uniunea Europeană, imperiile antice si imperiile medievale. Studiu comparativ.* Iasi: Ed. Lumen.

Antonescu, Madalina Virginia (2015). "New Legal Concepts in the XXIst Century Global Society: From "Global Good Governance" to "Global Eco-diplomacy", *Polis Journal*, vol. 3, no. 9, pp. 239–256. Petre Andrei University, Iasi, year III, ISSN 12219762.

Antonescu, Madalina Virginia (2017a). "Global Diplomacy, in the Context of Global Governance", *Logos Universality Mentality Education Novelty, Section: Law*, vol. V, no. 1, pp. 29–42. http://dx.doi.org/10.18662/lumenlaw.2017.0501.03

Antonescu, Madalina Virginia (2017b). "Global Eco-Diplomacy and New Evolutions in the International Law", *Univers Strategic Journal*, vol. 2, no. 30, pp. 185–197. Ed. Universitatea Crestina "Dimitrie Cantemir", Bucharest, year VIII.

Antonescu, Madalina Virginia (2017c). "The Century of Mega-Daguos. The Charter of Peaceful Coexistence among the Mega-Daguos", *Annals of the Academy of Romanian Scientists, Series on History and Archaeology Sciences*, vol. 9, no. 2, pp. 121–138. ISSN 2067–5682.

Antonescu, Madalina Virginia (2018a). Communicating the Scientific Paper *Metropolitan Diplomacy. The Global Metropolitan Law and Principles of Metropolitan Diplomacy*, International Conference RSACVP Lumen, Suceava, 26–29 aprilie 2018. http://conferinta.info/wp-content/uploads/2018/04/BT1_Working-papers_LUMEN-RSACVP2018ESDPAL2018_Conferences.pdf

Antonescu, Madalina Virginia (2018b). Communicating the Scientific Paper, *Regional and Global Institutions in a Global Order of Megacities*, International Conference RSACVP Lumen, Suceava, 26–29 aprilie 2018. http://conferinta.info/wp-content/uploads/2018/04/BT1_Working-papers_LUMEN-RSACVP2018ESDPAL2018_Conferences.pdf

Antonescu, Madalina Virginia (2018c). Communicating the Scientific Paper, *The Global Order of Civilizations. Institutions of the Global Order of Civilizations: The GMC/ Global Mediator of Civilizations)*, Participation at the 5th Central and Eastern European Lumen Scientific Conference, Hradec Kralove, Czech Republic, 20–21 September 2018, The LUMEN Research Center Social and Humanistic Studies. http://lumen. international/lumen-nashs2018/program-working-papers/

Antonescu, Madalina Virginia (2018d). "Metropolises in the Global Governance: Towards a 21st Century Neo-Medievalism?" *LUMEN Social Sciences*, vol. 7, no. 1, pp. 29–43. Logos Universality Mentality Education Novelty: Social Sciences ISSN: 2284–5976 | e-ISSN: 2501–0409 | www.lumenpublishing.com/journals/index.php/lumenss/article/view/1142/pdf, doi: https://doi.org/10.18662/lumenss/03

Antonescu, Madalina Virginia (2018e). "New Institutions for the 21st Century Global Order of Peace: The Mediator for Global Peace", vol. 6, no. 1, pp. 1–12. | doi: https://doi.org/10.18662/lumenlaw/01, in Logos Universality Mentality Education Novelty: Law ISSN: 2284–5968, e-ISSN: 2458–1046 http://lumenpublishing.com/journals/index.php/lumenlaw/article/view/752/pdf

Antonescu, Madalina Virginia (2018f). *The Foundation of New Serenissima. Institutional Political Patterns of Mega-Cities Starting from the Second Half of XXIst Century*

World, Participation at the 5th Central and Eastern European Lumen Scientific Conference, Hradec Kralove, Czech Republic, 20–21 September 2018, The LUMEN Research Center Social and Humanistic Studies. http://lumen.international/lumen-nashs2018/program-working-papers/ http://lumen.international/lumen-nashs2018/wp-content/uploads/2018/09/ProgramWorking-Papers_NASHS2018.pdf

Antonescu, Madalina Virginia (2020). "From the Conflict Among Civilizations, to the Global Charter for Peaceful Coexistence of Civilizations. Global Institutions for the Management of Inter-Civilizational Relations, in the 21st Century", *Romanian Review of Political Sciences and International Relations*, tome XVII, no. 1, pp. 192–203. The Publishing House of the Institute of Political Sciences and International Relations "Ion I. C. Brătianu" of the Romanian Academy, ISSN 1841–2300.

Antonescu, Madalina Virginia (2020). "Metropolises and Megalopolises. New Global Actors in the Complex Order of the 21st Century", *Political Sciences & International Relations*, vol. XVII, no. 2, pp. 122–130. Bucharest.

Bonnet, Jacques (2000). *Marile Metropole Mondiale*, translated by Bogdan Geangalau. Iasi: Institutul European.

Cerny, Philip G. (1998). "Neomedievalism, Civil War and the New Security Dilemma: Globalisation as Durable Disorder", *Civil Wars*, vol. 1, no. 1 (Spring), pp. 36–64.

Cerny, Philip G. (2021). "Business and Politics in an Age of Intangibles and Financialization", in Aynsley Kellow, Tony Porter and Karsten Ronit, eds., *Business and Politics*. Edward Elgar Handbook, pp. 193–214.

Cerny, Philip G. and Rosalba Belmonte (2021). "Heterarchy: Toward Paradigm Shift in World Politics", *The Changing Faces of Power*, special issue of the *Journal of Political Power*, vol. 14, no. 1 (February), pp. 235–257.

Giurescu, Constantin C. and Giurescu, Dinu C. (1974). *Istoria românilor*, tome I. Bucharest: Ed. Științifică, pp. 76–125, quoted in Malita, Mircea (1975). *Diplomatia. Scoli si institutii*. Bucharest: Ed. Didactică si Pedagogică, p. 82.

Gorra-Gobin, Cynthia, ed. (2006). *Dictionnaire des mondialisations*. Paris: Ed. Armand Colin.

Griffiths, Martin, ed. (2005). *Encyclopedia of International Relations and Global Politics*. London and NY: Routledge.

Held, David, McGrew, Anthony, Goldblatt, David and Perraton, Jonathan (2004). *Transformări globale. Politică, economie si cultură*, translated by Ramona-Elena Lupascu, Adriana Straub, Mihaela Bordea, Alina-Maria Turcu. Iasi: Polirom.

Incheon Communiqué (2012). *Strengthening Planning and Implementation Capacities for Sustainable Development in the Post-Rio Context*. UNCSD. http://sdg.iisd.org/news/unosd-workshop-calls-for-greater-accountability-on-sustainable-development-targets/

Istanbul+5, Urban Millennium (2001). New York, 6–8 June 2001, United Nations, UNCHS. https://mirror.unhabitat.org/pmss/(X(1)S(lkhmaubcfzwmatevhkfmzzb1))/listItemDetails.aspx?publicationID=1681

Johannesburg Declaration on Sustainable Development (2002). 4 September. www.unescwa.org/johannesburg-declaration-sustainable-development

Lee, Kai N. (2008). "O lume în curs de urbanizare", in The Worldwatch Institute, Molly O'Meara Sheehan, Project Director, Linda Starke, ed., *Starea lumii 2007. Viitorul nostru urban*, translated by Nicolae Damaschin. Bucuresti: Ed. Tehnică, pp. 3–9.

Lévêque, Pierre (1987). *Aventura greacă*, tome II, translated by Constanta Tănăsescu. Bucuresti: Ed. Meridiane.

The Millennium Development Goals Report (2014). *We Can End Poverty 2015*. www.undp.org/content/undp/en

Morris, Jan (2016). *Venetia*, translated by Laura Ciochină. Iasi: Polirom.

Rendina, Claudio (2003). *Dogii Venetiei, istorie si secrete*, translated by Radu Gâdei, Constantin Vlad. Bucuresti: ed. All.

State of the World's Cities, 2012–2013, Prosperity of Cities, Report (2013). "UN-HABITAT", in *For a Better Urban Future*. US, Canada: Routledge. www.unhabitat.org

Toynbee, Arnold (1979). *Orase in Miscare*, col. Idei contemporane. Bucuresti: Ed. Politică.

United Nations Millennium Declaration (2000). 55/2, Resolution adopted by the General Assembly, 6 September.

Vlad, Constantin (2001). *Relatii internationale politico-diplomatice contemporane*. Bucharest: Ed. Fundatiei Romania de maine, Spiru Haret University.

12

HETERARCHY IN AN AGE OF INTANGIBLES AND FINANCIALIZATION

Philip G. Cerny

Introduction

The relationship between business and politics is fundamentally changing in the 21st century. This restructuring is characterized by an uneven *heterarchy* rooted in the 3rd and 4th Industrial Revolutions and dominated technologically by "intangibles"—"capitalism without capital"—and transnational finance— "financialization." In this context, the state is not withering away, but becoming a "reactive state," focused on what is called "firefighting" (Bernanke et al. 2019; Bayoumi 2017), with growing problems of management and control. The main driving force, we argue here, is the disembedding of opaque finance from the "real economy," what is called "financial alchemy," leading to increased inequality and the threat of crises.

1. Beyond State-centrism: The Dialectic of Globalization and Fragmentation

In the 21st century diverse differentiated structures have become more co-dependent and complementary, including multinational firms, financial markets and institutions, as well as a growing transnational division of labor among linked production processes or "supply chains" or "value chains." The integration and differentiation of these structures makes them prone to systemic, rather than localized shocks, as witnessed in the 2008 financial crisis. In the structural environment of the Third (and/or Fourth) Industrial Revolution(s) (Rifkin 2011; Schwab 2016), the core is the shift from the dominance of Fordist economic and political structures, processes and institutions to the rise of what have been called "intangibles" (Haskel and Westlake 2018). These transformations involve a wide and diverse range of economic processes that include information technology,

DOI: 10.4324/9781003352617-14

new forms of research and development, the shift of investment from expensive and hierarchical production processes to profitmaking through distribution and the embedding and deepening of a consumer culture, artificial intelligence, digitalization, the advent of what is called Big Data, including the increasing use of algorithms (Gritsenko and Wood 2020), robotics, the growing flexibility and vulnerability of labor processes and their replacement by flexibilization of diverse kinds (Gratton 2011), including increasing dependence on debt and leverage, or credit (see below).

The increasing complexity of this system raises questions about whether this complexity will lead to endemic conflict or a "durable disorder" in which key actors are increasingly engaged in various forms of "brokerage" to smooth over the underlying dysfunctionality of the system. In fact, in the United States and in the rest of the developed and developing worlds, economic growth may well be slowing down as the Third/Fourth Industrial Revolution runs out of steam (Gordon 2016; Stiglitz 2019), while inequality increases (Piketty 2014; Milanovic 2016; for an authoritative literature review on this issue see Sawyer 2018). Furthermore, austerity and the erosion of the rights of labor are undermining the mid-20th century social contract on which the welfare state and liberal democracy have been based (Blyth 2013). Political leaders in unstable states are either engaged in attempting to restore authoritarian repression, as in Russia, China, Egypt and Turkey, or are ensnared in the breakdown of the political system, as in Brazil, Venezuela and a range of African countries, leading the emergence of quasi-authoritarian populism.

Rationalities of marginal utility have transformed statehood itself into a marketizing, *commodifying* process (Cerny 2013). The regulatory power and effectiveness of the state in a range of sectors is seen as itself eroding through what is called "regulatory arbitrage." Furthermore, the state has become a promoter of financialization rather than welfare or social democracy, replacing decommodifying welfare and public services through austerity and undermining the potential for what has been called the "entrepreneurial state" concerned with providing public goods (Tiberghien 2007; Block and Keller 2011; Mazzuccato 2013; Herman 2012). Nevertheless, the state remains the primary provider of welfare programs, and finance cannot do without it either, for a host of public goods rely on finance for credit. Social democracy has been replaced by the supposed "democratization of finance" and "financial inclusion" (see Litan and Rauch 1998; Shiller 2003). The state has become, through such policies as quantitative easing, a monetary Keynesian rather than a fiscal Keynesian approach.

So, for example, while semi-dematerialized price mechanisms by which markets and institutions relate to each other and to the wider economy, society and polity, shape our interactions, they take place through our interactions with the computers, logistics, and groups of people "next" to us in an increasingly intangible world of "capitalism without capital" (Haskel and Westlake 2018). The process is itself non-linear and causally complex. Actors and political processes can only react to price changes independently produced by market and institutional transactions, many of which are increasingly automated, and certain sectors like communications and social media—symbolized by Facebook, Amazon, Apple, Netflix and Alphabet (formerly Google), known as the FAANGs—require further regulation.

Information and communications technologies that circle the globe also create the potential for backlashes of diverse kinds as awareness of global level. Indeed, business actors are sometimes not only captured by pre-existing state-based structures and practices but paradoxically also see them as valid reactions to globalization and transnationalization—what Bohas and Morley call an "anomic mindset" (this book). Strategically situated actors are able to mobilize and manage material resources, influential contacts, ideologies and mind sets, and knowledge in order to take advantage of the evolving system. This has led to the consolidation of a range of "extra-state authorities" (Belmonte, this book) and "regime complexes" across a range of institutions and processes including "low-capacity states," fragmented global governance, and oligopolistic, sectorally differentiated quasi-corporatist policymaking, regulatory and policy implementation processes. These embed the "privileged position of business" (Lindblom 1977) and transnationally powerful interest groups, including intangible sectors such as information technology, banking and finance, etc., as well as transnational corporations, supply chains and other linkages transcending and undermining state territorial and economic boundaries. States themselves have sought to benefit from these structural transformations by sponsoring the international competitiveness of domestically located firms, leading to transnational oligopolization and rent-seeking. The development of an effective global governance structure as a way to reorganize world politics is increasingly unlikely.

State actors themselves, once said to be "captured" by large, well-organized domestic constituencies, are increasingly captured instead by transnationally-linked sectors. These actors do not merely set state agencies and international regimes against each other—a process sometimes called "venue shopping" (or "forum shopping"; see Kellow 2012; Murphy and Kellow 2013) or "regulatory arbitrage." They also cause them to try to network in an increasingly dense fashion with their peers in other states, including extensive lobbying of political and bureaucratic actors, "revolving doors," etc. Among the major losers are trade unions and other groups with few transnational linkages and where labor has become more "flexible" and, indeed, "commodified," although they are sometimes still in a position to obtain compensatory side payments from national governments and the development of intergovernmental institutions and processes—what often referred to as "soft law" (Newman and Posner 2018).

Transnational corporations have an increasing role in law-making processes that they exercise through lobbying activities. Often they turn to practices of self-regulation, private governance, risk management and alternative dispute resolution (Stringham 2015). Their resources come from private sources—even if governments very often support transnational corporations (TNCs) through public investments and favorable tax conditions (Mazzuccato 2013). At the same time, transnational financial agencies operate in several economic-financial fields, including the insurance, accountancy and risk management sector, affecting the allocation of resources between social groups, national economies, and commercial enterprises (Strange 1996; Stringham 2015).

2. Finance and Politics in the 21st Century

Finance is the ultimate intangible sector, because it links and shapes all the others. However, the creation of financial instruments and the evolution of financial markets in a range of circumstances can permit finance to become independent of and autonomous from the real economy and to develop a dynamic of its own. This dynamic concerns the relationship of diverse financial instruments to *each other* rather than to the real economy. We will examine three distinct but inextricably intertwined trends and variables.

The first is the restructuring of the world political economy around the transnationalization of special financial interests. The second is the structuration of the financial sector itself through the development of a range of complex financial instruments, especially securitization and derivatives. Closely intertwined with this is the restructuring of the financial services industry around what is misleadingly called "shadow banking" and its political ramifications, including "capture" and "reverse capture." The third trend involves the wider political context and impact of government and transnational regulation of finance. In this context we will consider a range of crucial social and political consequences of what has been called "financialization" (Epstein 2005; Gemzik-Salwach and Opolski 2017; Sawyer 2019).

The role of finance in the world economy has been evolving in the general direction of financialization since the 1950s. (This section draws on a wide range of sources, but in particular Epstein 2005; Christophers 2013; Mattli 2019; Faroohar 2016; D'Arista 2018; Nesvetailova 2007; Guttman 2016). There have been several factors driving this process: growing trade and pressures on the international system to reallocate capital across borders as a result, with the postwar financial system becoming more flexible and extensive; domestic budgetary and other pressures on the postwar welfare state, leading to neoliberal economic policies; leveraging—the role of debt—in both the domestic and the international financial systems, including the ideology of "financial inclusion"; and the increasing predominance of new financial instruments and institutions like securitization and "shadow banking," which will be examined more closely in the next section.

With regard to the post-Second World War period, most writers focus on the emergence of the Eurodollar market in the 1950s and 1960s. This process encouraged and reinforced increasing cross-border financial flows in general, augmented politically as well as financially by the tradition of sterling as an international currency and the historical role of the City of London as an international financial center. Indeed, transnational finance has often been identified as the key independent variable driving the globalization process (for example, see Strange

1996; Cerny 1993, 1995). One of the approaches that several important authors have taken is to apply the theories of Hyman Minsky (1982). Minsky argued that financial crises are endemic in capitalism because periods of economic prosperity encouraged borrowers and lenders to be progressively reckless, leading to financial bubbles and the later busts.

3. The Development of Financial Instruments and Institutions

As financial flows expanded in the postwar period and virtually exploded in the 1980s and 1990s and since, financial firms and actors sought to devise new ways of trading on increasingly complex financial markets, moving away from traditional trading processes and structures including established stock and securities markets. This trend required several developments in the nature of the tradable instruments. The first was flexibility. The second involved the scope or "tradability" of those instruments—their widespread acceptance and use in an interconnected range of settings from the local to the global. The third involved widening the range of financial market actors, from financial firms themselves to households and individuals—what has been called "financial inclusion" or "the financialization of daily life" (Martin 2002). The fourth has been the restructuring and concentration of the overarching financial industry itself into fewer and fewer "SIFIs"—systemically important financial institutions (Sorkin 2009).

The fifth, as noted above, required the extremely rapid expansion of leverage—debt—to finance these developments, rather than redistributing profits or assets from the real economy (Graeber 2011; Di Muzio and Robbins 2016). The sixth has been the doctrine of "shareholder value" capitalism, in which the first priority of all firms is the making of profits that are transferred to shareholders rather than reinvested in a real economy firm's production and exchange processes that include labor and other "stakeholders" (Stout 2012). The final development has been said to be the consolidation of a new form of *rentier* capitalism, in which profits are skimmed off by financial elites (Fullbrook and Morgan 2020). This final trend is also sometimes said to enable and entrench illegal activities and the rigging of economic and financial outcomes.

The financial instruments at the core of the process mainly involve "securitization" and "derivatives." Traditional banks, both commercial and investment, operated on the basis of what has been called "originate-to-hold." In contrast, what have been called "non-bank" financial firms and institutions restructure and sell the instruments they originally "own"—design and offer for sale—in a range of formal and informal financial markets. They transform them into new kinds of securities in a process known as "securitization" and the value of those securities comes from the prices they attract as well as their saleability in various formal and informal markets. (This process is widely covered in the literature; this section draws, in particular, on Zandi 2009; Mattli 2019; Helleiner et al. 2018.) This process is called "originate-to-distribute." Derivatives, in turn, are securities the value of which does not derive from the original securities themselves but from their being based on the market value of these securities themselves when bought and sold.

Securitization is a complex process in which the original securities themselves are "sliced and diced" into what are called "tranches," which are bundled into much more complex securities. Tranches are segments created from a pool of securities—usually debt instruments such as bonds or mortgages—that are divided up by risk, time to maturity, or other characteristics in order to be marketable to different investors. Each portion or tranche of a securitized or structured product is one of several related securities offered at the same time, but with varying risks, rewards and maturities to appeal to a diverse range of investors. Different tranches will have different credit ratings, appealing to different buyers—the "liability structure"—with senior tranches for the highest and safest credit ratings, junior tranches for the riskiest ratings, and mezzanine tranches for a generally small intermediate category. Typical investors of senior tranches tend to be conduits, insurance companies, pension funds and other risk averse investors. Junior tranches are more risky investments because they are not secured by specific assets. The natural buyers of these securities tend to be hedge funds and other investors seeking higher risk/return profiles. Tranches allow for the "ability to create one or more classes of securities whose rating is higher than the average rating of the underlying collateral asset pool or to generate rated securities from a pool of unrated assets" (Fender and Mitchell 2005, 129)—i.e., making them *more profitable than "real" investments*. The equity/first-loss or junior tranche absorbs initial losses, followed by the mezzanine tranches which absorb some additional losses, again followed by more senior tranches. Thus "the most senior claims are expected to be insulated—except in particularly adverse circumstances—from default risk of the underlying asset pool through the absorption of losses by the more junior claims" (Committee on the Global Financial System, January 2005). Some tranches are sold and traded separately and some as parts of single, combined securities.

> The most common derivatives instruments are forwards, futures, options and swaps. . . . Unlike forwards, option contracts do not involve a contractual commitment. . . . It is also possible to create more complex instruments by combining these derivatives with each other or with securities and loans.
> *(for details, see Spagna 2018, 28–35)*

Some are traded on regulated exchanges, through "central counterparties" (CCPs) which bear the credit risk, and some bilaterally in what are called "over the counter" (OTC) deals. Exchange-traded contracts have standardized terms and are more liquid (i.e., more easily marketed and tradable). The "notional value" of OTC derivatives in 2008 was U.S. $684 trillion (Spagna 2018, 30), approximately ten times global GDP. The notional—gross—size is an overestimate, as the underlying asset is not always actually exchanged and does not take into account widespread bilateral netting arrangements, but the trend is the same.

However, in the context of the free market, neoliberal and deregulatory ideology of national governments—both bureaucrats and politicians—and transnational regime complexes (Barofsky 2012), such financial instruments and processes are still treated lightly and warily by both policymakers and regulators. The highly institutionalized commercial and investment banks described above have historically been the core of traditional financial systems, and until recently have been highly regulated and insured by governments. This was particularly true of the U.S. Emergency Banking Act of 1933, known as the Glass-Steagall Act, which divided up commercial and investment banking and administered them separately. In particular, the act set up the Federal Deposit Insurance Corporation to underpin the commercial banking sector, insuring deposits originally of $2,500, increased over the years to six deposits in different accounts of $250,000, for a total of $1,500,000 in 2011. While these banks are still propped up by the U.S. Government, they have increasingly had to compete with what have called "shadow banks."

Nesvetailova (2018: 2) provides a useful definition of the difference:

> While, for instance, traditional banks are assumed to be taking in short-term deposits and converting them into long-term loans, shadow banks do the opposite: they take in long-term savings (e.g., pension fund liabilities) and transform them into short-term savings. If traditional banks take in liquid deposits (e.g., cash and similar instruments) and transform them into less liquid securities, shadow banks do the opposite: through a combination of financial and legal operations they transform illiquid assets (such as mortgages or car loans) into apparently liquid financial securities.

The way shadow banks have done business over recent decades have absorbed and forced the reconstruction of traditional banks too, creating "long and opaque chains of credit intermediation" (*ibid.*, pp. 6–7). This is particularly true of what are called "universal banks," which originate consumer and corporate loans, package loans into what are called "asset-backed securities" (one of the major dimensions of the securitization process) and what are called "collateralized debt obligations" (CDOs), create over-the-counter (OTC) derivatives whose value are derived from loans, and distribute the resulting securities and other financial instruments to investors. Furthermore, complex financial institutions have used the OTC strategy to maximize their fee income—their profits increasingly come from fees—to reduce their capital charges and to transfer the risks associated with securitized loans to investors. Other structural shifts include the setting up of Special Purpose Vehicles (SPVs), Structured Investment Vehicles (SIVS) and other non-regulated, quasi-independent institutions in which to park, especially, less profitable or endangered securities the markets for which have slowed or shut down. Regulated banks in effect become shadow banks, because they had to restructure and become more opaque and complex in order to compete (*ibid.*, 6).

A major consequence of the rise and dominance of shadow banking therefore concerns the shift of investing from cash and investment in the real economy to the circulation of the purely financial instruments described above. For example, pension funds have grown dramatically as the result of the shift from defined benefit to defined contribution pensions (the result of the declining power of labor unions in the real economy), along with Money Market Mutual Funds (MMMFs), and hedge funds (Coggan 2010; Lack 2012). In particular, real estate mortgages accelerated the shift, based on the assumption that house prices would continue to rise; thus, household indebtedness increasingly became the core of the financial economy. This process included "subprime" mortgages where borrowers were not required to provide information about their ability to repay—the original trigger of the Global Financial Crisis in 2007–8. Growing demand for profitable investment increasingly creates more and more supply *because of and facilitated by the abstract nature of finance itself* (Gabor 2018).

All national governments and regional organizations such as the European Union have considered and even attempted to implement a range of regulatory changes in the financial sector, and all of these have been critically scrutinized and found wanting. Furthermore, the Dodd-Frank Act of 2010 in the United States has been seen as counterproductive because of (a) maintaining competing regulatory bodies that have different approaches, (b) leaving actual regulation-making to these bodies in the future, resulting in partiality and whipsawing, (c) insufficient transnational convergence (e.g. Helleiner et al. 2018; Gemzik-Salwach and Opolski 2017), and (d) limitations the capacity of the Financial Stability Oversight Council (FSOC) to create policy consistency. Indeed, The Trump Administration engineered a partial rollback of Dodd-Frank in 2018, the Crapo Bill, formally the Economic Growth, Regulatory Relief, and Consumer Protection Act. Finance is the hegemonic sector in the structural transformation of the simultaneously globalizing and fragmenting intangible economy

4. Conclusion

Therefore a central debate in the business and politics issue area is whether the trends discussed here are: (a) crowding out investment in the real economy; (b) strengthening the "intangible" economy, especially the technology sector, which is itself creating new forms of monopolization; (c) leading to greater inequality and political backlashes such as populism (Sawyer 2018); (d) creating a growing level of over-indebtedness and leverage, from real economy firms to financial firms (both shadow banks and commercial banks) that will lead to chronic Minskyian crises; and (e) limiting nation-state governments to "firefighting" and "bailouts" to salvage national financial systems—i.e., the "reactive state" rather than the "proactive state."

D'Arista (2018) argues that financial institutions need stress tests to be based on cash reserves rather than capital requirements (i.e. debt-based financial instruments); Guttman (2016) argues for revising the International Monetary Fund's Special Drawing Rights and giving them a greater international role; and Roos (2019) argues for the greater use of debt default to tackle overleveraging, especially of sovereign debt. Perhaps most interestingly, Nesvetailova and Palan (2020) argue that greater prohibition and even criminalization of market-rigging practices will ultimately be necessary to tame Minskyian tendencies.

Thus finance is the predominant heterarchical structure in the world political economy of the 21st century. It is the ultimate structural—and intangible—link among all other economic sectors. At some levels, therefore, finance itself can be seen to be evolving into a quasi-hierarchical, overarching structure. However, the significance of other heterarchical dimensions and crucial issue areas, from trade to environmental policy and climate change, to the Third (or Fourth) Industrial Revolution, to anomic, nationalist and sub-nationalist populism, will increasingly create a range of regulatory challenges that will require financial support, especially to find an alternative to diminishing growth. The political challenges of a fractionated world may require more regulation, indeed more global governance, to meet those challenges—a new proactive normativity, beyond and above the reactive state. However, as the old proverb goes (variously attributed to at least two dozen people, from Niels Bohr and Yogi Berra to Woody Allen and Confucius): "Prediction is difficult, especially about the future."

References

Albert, Mathias, Barry Buzan and Michael Zürn, eds. (2013). *Bringing Sociology to International Relations: World Politics as Differentiation Theory* (Cambridge: Cambridge University Press).

Alter, Karen J. and Kal Raustiala (2018). "The Rise of International Regime Complexity," *Annual Review of Law and Social Science*, vol. 14 (27 June), pp. 18.2–18.21.

Barofsky, Neil (2012). *Bailout: An Inside Account of How Washington Abandoned Main Street While Rescuing Wall Street* (New York: Free Press).

Bayoumi, Tamim (2017). *Unfinished Business: The Unexplored Causes of the Financial Crisis and the Lessons Yet to be Learned* (New Haven, CT and London: Yale University Press for the International Monetary Fund).

Bernanke, Ben S., Timothy F. Geithner and Henry M. Paulson, Jr. (2019). *Firefighting: The Financial Crisis and its Lessons* (New York: Penguin Books).

Block, Fred and Matthew R. Keller (2011). *State of Innovation: The U.S. Government's Role in Technology Innovation* (Abingdon: Routledge).

Blyth, Mark (2013). *Austerity: The History of a Dangerous Idea* (New York: Oxford University Press).

Cerny, Philip G. (1993). *Finance and World Politics: Markets, Regimes and States in the Post-Hegemonic Era*, editor and co-author (Aldershot, Hants, and Brookfield, VT: Edward Elgar).

Cerny, Philip G. (1995). "Globalization and the Changing Logic of Collective Action," *International Organization*, vol. 49, no. 4 (Autumn), pp. 595–625.

Cerny, Philip G. (2013). "Functional Differentiation, Globalisation and the New Transnational Neopluralism," in Mathias Albert, Barry Buzan and Michael Zurn, eds., *Bringing Sociology into International Relations: World Politics as Differentiation Theory* (Cambridge: Cambridge University Press), pp. 205–227.

Christophers, Brett (2013). *Banking Across Boundaries: Placing Finance in Capitalism* (Chichester: Wiley).

Coggan, Philip (2010). *Guide to Hedge Funds: What They are, What They Do, Their Risks, Their Advantages* (London: Profile Books for The Economist, second edition).

Committee on the Global Financial System (2005). "The Role of Ratings in Structured Finance: Issues and Implications," *Bank for International Settlements*.

D'Arista, Jane (2018). *All Fall Down: Debt, Deregulation and Financial Crises* (Cheltenham, UK and Northampton, MA, USA: Edward Elgar).

Di Muzio, Tim and Richard H. Robbins (2016). *Debt as Power* (Manchester: Manchester University Press).

Epstein, Gerald A., ed. (2005). *Financialization and the World Economy* (Cheltenham, UK and Northampton, MA, USA: Edward Elgar).

Faroohar, Rana (2016). *Makers and Takers: The Rise of Finance and the Fall of American Business* (New York: Crown Business).

Fender, Ingo and Janet Mitchell (2005). "Structured Finance: Complexity, Risk and the Use of Ratings," *Financial Stability Review*, vol. 3, no. 1 (June), pp. 127–135.

Fullbrook, Edward and Jamie Morgan, eds. (2020). *The Inequality Crisis* (Bristol: World Economics Association Books).

Gabor, Daniela (2018). "Shadow Connections: The Hierarchies of Collateral in Shadow Banking," in Nesvetailova, Anastasia, ed., *Shadow Banking: Scope, Origins and Theories* (London: Routledge), pp. 143–162.

Gemzik-Salwach, Agata and Krzysztof Opolski, eds. (2017). *Financialization and the Economy* (London and New York: Routledge).

Gordon, Robert J. (2016). *The Rise and Fall of American Growth: The U.S. Standard of Living Since the Civil War* (Princeton, NJ: Princeton University Press).

Graeber, David (2011). *Debt: The First 5,000 Years* (Brooklyn, NY: Melville House).

Gratton, Lynda (2011). *The Shift: The Future of Work is Already Here* (London: William Collins).

Gritsenko, Daria and Matthew Wood (2020). "Algorithmic Governance: A Modes of Governance Approach," *Regulation and Governance*. doi: 10.1111/rego.1236.

Guttman, Robert (2016). *Finance-Led Capitalism: Shadow Banking, Re-Regulation and the Future of Global Markets* (Basingstoke: Palgrave Macmillan).

Haskel, Jonathan and Stian Westlake (2018). *Capitalism Without Capital: The Rise of the Intangible Economy* (Princeton, NJ: Princeton University Press).

Helleiner, Eric, Stefano Pagliari and Irene Spagna, eds. (2018). *Governing the World's Biggest Market: The Politics of Derivatives Regulation After the 2008 Crisis* (New York and Oxford: Oxford University Press).

Herman, Arthur (2012). *Freedom's Forge: How American Business Produced Victory in World War II* (New York: Random House).

Kellow, Aynsley (2012). "Multi-level and Multi-arena Governance: The Limits of Integration and the Possibilities of Forum Shopping," *International Environmental Agreements*, vol. 12, pp. 327–342.

Lack, Simon (2012). *The Hedge Fund Miracle: The Illusion of Big Money and Why It's Too Good to be True* (Hoboken, NJ: Wiley).

Lindblom, Charles E. (1977). *Politics and Markets: The World's Political-Economic Systems* (New |York: Basic Books).

Litan, Robert E. and Jonathan Rauch (1998). *American Finance for the 21st Century* (Washington, DC: Brookings Institution Press).

Martin, Randy (2002). *Financialization of Daily Life* (Philadelphia: Temple University Press).

Mattli, Walter (2019). *Darkness by Design: The Hidden Power in Global Capital Markets* (Princeton, NJ: Princeton University Press).

Mazzuccato, Mariana (2013). *The Entrepreneurial State: Debunking Public vs. Private Sector Myths* (New York: Anthem Press).

Milanovic, Branko (2016). *Global Inequality: A New Approach for the Age of Globalization* (Cambridge, MA: Harvard University Press).

Minsky, Hyman P. (1982). *Can "It" Happen Again?: Essays on Instability and Finance* (London: Routledge).

Murphy, Hannah and Aynsley Kellow (2013). "Forum Shopping in Global Governance: Understanding States, Business and NGOs in Multiple Arenas," *Global Policy*, vol. 4, no. 2, pp. 139–149.

Nesvetailova, Anastasia (2007). *Fragile Finance: Debt, Speculation and Crisis in the Age of Global Credit* (Basingstoke: Palgrave Macmillan).

Nesvetailova, Anastasia, ed. (2018). *Shadow Banking: Scope, Origins and Theories* (London: Routledge).

Nesvetailova, Anastasia and Ronen Palan (2020). *Sabotage: The Business of Finance* (London: Allen Lane).

Newman, Abraham L. and Elliot Posner (2018). *Voluntary Disruptions: International Soft Law, Finance, and Power* (Oxford: Oxford University Press).

Neyer, Jürgen (2012). *Justification of Europe: A Political Theory of Supranational Integration* (Oxford: Oxford University Press).

Ostrom, Vincent, Charles M. Tiebout and Robert Warren (1961). "The Organization of Government in Metropolitan Areas: A Theoretical Inquiry," *American Political Science Review*, vol. 55, no. 3 (September), pp. 831–842.

Piketty, Thomas (2014). *Capital in the Twenty-First Century* (Cambridge, MA: Harvard University Press).

Rifkin, Jeremy (2011). *The Third Industrial Revolution: How Lateral Power is Transforming Energy, the Economy, and the World* (London and New York: Palgrave Macmillan and St. Martin's Press).

Roos, Jerome (2019). *Why Not Default? The Political Economy of Sovereign Debt* (Princeton, NJ: Princeton University Press).

Sawyer, Malcolm (2017). "Financialization and Economic and Social Performance," in Agata Gemzik-Salwach and Krzysztof Opolski, eds., *Financialization and the Economy* (London and New York: Routledge), pp. 9–25.

Sawyer, Malcolm (2018). "Financialisation, Financial Crisis and Inequality," in Philip Arestis and Malcolm Sawyer, eds., *Inequality: Trends, Causes, Consequences, Relevant Policies* (Houndmills: Palgrave Macmillan), pp. 43–88.

Sawyer, Malcolm (2019). "Financialisation and the Dysfunctional Nature of the Financial System," in Jesper Jespersen and Finn Olesen, eds., *Progressive Post-Keynesian Economics: Dealing with Reality* (Cheltenham, UK and Northampton, MA: Edward Elgar), pp. 69–85.

Schwab, Klaus (2016). *The Fourth Industrial Revolution* (London: Portfolio Penguin).

Shiller, Robert J. (2003). *The New Financial Order: Risk in the 21st Century* (Princeton, NJ: Princeton University Press).

Sorkin, Andrew Ross (2009). *Too Big to Fail: The Inside Story of How Wall Street and Washington Fought to Save the Financial System from Crisis—and Themselves* (New York: Viking).

Spagna, Irene (2018). "Becoming the World's Biggest Market: OTC Derivatives Before the Global Financial Crisis of 2008," in Eric Helleiner, Stefano Pagliari and Irene Spagna, eds., *Governing the World's Biggest Market: The Politics of Derivatives Regulation After the 2008 Crisis* (New York and Oxford: Oxford University Press), pp. 27–53.

Stiglitz, Joseph E. (2019). *People, Power, and Profits: Progressive Capitalism in an Age of Discontent* (London: Allen Lane).

Stout, Lynn (2012). *The Shareholder Value Myth: How Putting Shareholders First Harms Investors, Corporations, and the Public* (San Francisco: Berrett-Koehler).

Strange, Susan (1996). *The Retreat of the State: The Diffusion of Power in the World Economy* (Cambridge: Cambridge University Press).

Stringham, Edward P. (2015). *Private Governance: Creating Order in Economic and Social Life* (Oxford: Oxford University Press).

Tiberghien, Yves (2007). *Entrepreneurial States: Reforming Corporate Governance in France, Japan, and Korea* (Ithaca, NY: Cornell University Press).

Zandi, Mark (2009). *Financial Shock: A 360° Look at the Subprime Mortgage Implosion, and How to Avoid the Next Financial Crisis* (Upper Saddle River, NJ: FT Press).

13

WTO DISPUTE SETTLEMENT AND THE APPELLATE BODY CRISIS AS A CASE STUDY OF HETERARCHY

Judit Fabian

On the 20th of May 2020, the term of Hong Zhao expired as an Appellate Body member of the World Trade Organization (WTO); with it, the Appellate Body (AB) ceased to function. No successor has been approved, and none is currently foreseen. Zhao's was the final expiration in what has come to be called the Appellate Body crisis, by which the AB has been starved of members and thereby negated as an institution.

The AB crisis is undoubtedly a crisis of global trade governance. It is also, however, an example of crisis in the international sphere that accords with ideas of heterarchy concerning the nature of power and institutional capture. As such, the present discussion treats it as a valuable case study of heterarchical power relations in practice.

In so doing, the paper first describes heterarchy, focusing on how a heterarchical understanding of power differs from the theoretical assumptions and presuppositions of traditional international relations (IR) theory. It then describes the Appellate Body crisis, focusing on the intersecting interests at play in its origin and development, and especially the role of the steel industry in the United States. Finally, the paper concludes by reflecting upon the nature and limits of capture if heterarchical power relations operate within complex adaptive systems.

1. Heterarchy and Power

Belmonte and Cerny define heterarchy as "the coexistence and conflict between differently structured micro- and meso- quasi-hierarchies that compete and overlap not only across borders but also across economic-financial sectors and social groupings" (2021, 1). From this definition, important points of similarity to complexity theory and divergence from IR realism and neorealism are already clear. Specifically, in IR realist and neorealist theory, liberal institutionalism, and even

DOI: 10.4324/9781003352617-15

constructivism, power is understood to operate hierarchically (Crumley 2015, 5). By contrast, heterarchical power is networked to the most fundamental degree. It operates horizontally and diagonally (Belmonte and Cerny 2021, 7), meaning that heterarchical power is multidirectional, multinodal, and international across distinctions of class, state, race, social grouping, and jurisdiction.

Second, for heterarchical power to 'compete and overlap' across borders, economic-financial sectors, and social groupings, the state cannot be blackboxed even as a useful theoretical simplification; domestic politics must always be considered. This opposes one of the basic assumptions of IR realism and neorealism: that by ignoring domestic politics, international relations can be simplified and clarified to the extent that predictive generalization becomes possible. In this way, heterarchy also breaks with the state-centrism (ibid. 2021, 1–7) of IR realism and neorealism more extensively than liberal institutionalism.

Finally, the anarchic international realm is neither as necessary to heterarchy as it is to IR realism and neorealism nor as simple as the absence of an overarching authority (ibid. 2021, 3). Rather, in the absence of such an authority, heterarchical anarchy is not the mere absence of power but the presence in international relations of a greater multiplicity of sources of power interacting in a more complex, multidirectional constellation of ways.

To this point, then, heterarchy accords closely with complexity theory in its conception of power in international relations. Where the two diverge is with respect to the epistemology of causality and the possibility of systemic comprehensibility. These in turn lead to divergences in the questions of capture and the possibility of effective global trade governance. Regarding the first, Belmonte and Cerny argue that "it is sociologically and methodologically more productive to consider all social relationships as constituted horizontally and diagonally, always through concrete traceable causation whether material or ideological" (2021, 7–8). Complexity theory would agree concerning social relationships, but causality is much less certain. Specifically, a complex adaptive system displays three key features: self-organization, emergence, and adaptation (Orsini and Le Prestre 2020, 1008–1012; following Kavalski (2007), Lehmann (2012) and others). The first reflects only that a CAS organizes itself; there is no overarching authority regulating its constituent parts. 'Emergence' refers to the "systemic unexpected outcomes" (Orsini and Le Prestre 2020, 1010) that occur in every CAS, while 'adaptation' refers to systemic response to environmental change. 'Emergence' and 'adaptation,' combined with multidirectional and multinodal power relations, make tracing causation extremely difficult. Moreover, they make the system as a whole very difficult to comprehend, to the point that studies of failure in CAS often cite systemic incomprehensibility as a leading cause (Scharre 2016).

As the case study supports, proximate causes and principal agents can, of course, be identified in a complex system; however, if one accepts the nonlinear causality and systemic incomprehensibility suggested by 'emergence' and 'adaptation' in complexity theory, identification of systemic causes and subordinate agents becomes difficult or impossible to achieve. This carries implications for the idea of capture, which Belmonte and Cerny follow Dauvergne and Lebaron (2014) in defining as, essentially, the co-optation of an institution, organization, or movement by private interests.[1] This makes the specific duration, extent and agents of capture and recapture difficult to delineate. Moreover, the high difficulty or impossibility of tracing nonlinear causality, of understanding a CAS in itself, and of knowing precisely how capture operates at any given time greatly increases the importance of planning and developing institutional and systemic resilience. This requires flexible institutions that can evolve to survive 'emergent' change, and flexible systems of international governance, as opposed to government, that decentralize power.

2. The Appellate Body of the World Trade Organization

The play of heterarchical power in a complex adaptive system is evident in the ongoing crisis of the World Trade Organization's Appellate Body. Like the WTO itself, the Dispute Settlement Body (DSB), of which the Appellate Body (AB) is part, evolved from practices normalized under the General Agreement on Trade and Tariffs (GATT) of 1947. Dispute settlement under GATT 1947 was much less formal than the process instituted in 1994 with the WTO's advent. Indeed, one of the major themes of post-WWII global trade governance is the continual juridification of dispute settlement.

Articles XXII and XXIII of GATT 1947 governed dispute settlement originally. Taken together, they provide for the referral of disputes to the Contracting Parties as a body, and require that body to investigate and issue recommendations or rulings as appropriate. The first recorded disputes occurred in 1948 between the Netherlands and Cuba, and between India and Pakistan (Hudec 1975, 66–68; Trebilcock et al. 2013, 173). Both were referred to the GATT Chairman for a ruling, producing a solution to the first but not the second. The 'Chairman's ruling' method was quickly superseded by regular use of Working Parties as specially focused loci of negotiation, comprising the disputants and selected neutral countries. Numerous Working Parties were established between 1948 and 1952; in fact, by the close of the Annecy Round in 1949, Working Parties had entirely supplanted the Chairman's ruling (Hudec 1975, 66–67). Although the period from 1947 through 1952 shows mild formalization of GATT dispute settlement, the clear theme is of dispute settlement as a means to facilitate negotiation between disputants, not to establish a neutral adjudicative authority. This leaves dispute settlement under the early GATT regime far more open to the direct exercise of power, to capture, and therefore to heterarchical power relations than under the WTO. To a significant extent, the developments of the subsequent seven decades of dispute settlement in global trade governance are the process of restricting the direct application of power, of narrowing, redefining, and circumscribing the possibilities for capture and the play of heterarchical power, and of managing or failing to manage the tensions this causes.

A series of six further milestones marks the increasing juridification of GATT dispute settlement between 1952 and 1994. First is the establishment of the earliest dispute settlement panel in 1952 (Trebilcock et al. 2013, 173; Hudec 1975, 74–83), which was the first dispute settlement body under GATT from which authoritative interpretation and application of trade rules would be expected. Then, in 1962, a GATT panel in a case initiated by Uruguay ruled that any breach of GATT was *prima facie* 'nullification and impairment' (Jackson 1998, 166). This placed the burden of proof upon respondents to show that a complaint was without merit or a breach of GATT justified. The report was cited by numerous panels throughout the 1960s and '70s, giving it *de facto* authority as precedent, and the doctrine of *prima facie* nullification and impairment was embodied in GATT following the 1979 Tokyo Round.

Of the four last milestones, the *Decision of 5 April 1966 on Procedures under Article XXIII* requires a Panel and a report when disputes between developed and developing countries cannot be resolved and authorizes retaliatory suspension of trade concessions when justified (Fabian 2015, 190). Second, the 1979 *Understanding regarding Notification, Consultation, Dispute Settlement and Surveillance* was essentially the first formal codification of GATT dispute settlement practices. It also rejects the linking of disputes, authorizes a standing roster of panel members, and requires the establishment of a Panel to follow a Council decision by 30 days or fewer (Hudec 1980, 145). Third, the *Ministerial Declaration of 29 November 1982* affirms the primacy of the 1979 *Understanding* and institutes 10 new reforms, including making the GATT Secretariat responsible for assisting Panels, and several measures to monitor compliance with Panel reports and ensure clear findings of contravention of trade rules where they exist. This last implies prior efforts by some GATT members to capture the dispute settlement process by using terms of reference to preclude specific unfavorable outcomes (Fabian 2015, 192–194). The fourth is the *Action* of 30 November 1984, wherein many GATT members expressed dissatisfaction with the dispute-settlement process and called for its juridification. This included a directive to create a roster of non-government panelists to be drawn from as needed (Trebilcock et al. 2013, 176–178; Hudec et al. 1993, 18).

One sees in these reforms the movement toward a timely, formal, expert-based, and officially disinterested dispute settlement system that would culminate in the creation of the Appellate Body and constitute precisely the source of frustration with the Appellate Body during the Obama and Trump administrations. It is essential to understand this evolution because it gives important indications of the original conditions under which the WTO Dispute Settlement Body (DSB) was agreed, and to which, over the subsequent 27 years, a plenitude of nodes in myriad intersecting networks would refer in increasing frustration as they sought to exert power and gain their ends within the rules of trade governance the WTO represents, or they sought to undermine the institution or to capture it.

3. The DSB

The Dispute Settlement Body of the World Trade Organization was established by the 1994 Dispute Settlement Understanding (DSU). Under the DSU, any WTO member may bring a complaint to the DSB against any other member; should mediation fail to produce a resolution after 60 days, a Panel must be established within 45 days of the complainant's request. The Panel's report must be made within six months, decide upon the complaint and be circulated to the full WTO membership. If no appeal is made, then the DSB adopts the report absent 'reverse consensus' to the contrary (WTO 1994, *Marrakesh Agreement*, Annex 2).

Appeals are made to a panel of three members from the permanent seven-member Appellate Body, which must then issue its own report within 90 days. Appellate Body reports must also be adopted by the DSB unless opposed by reverse consensus including both of the original disputants. If a member is found in violation and does not amend its practices, then the DSB can authorize appropriate compensatory trade sanctions (WTO 1994c, *Marrakesh Agreement*, Annex 2). This enforcement mechanism, together with the shift from requiring positive consensus for a report's adoption to requiring 'reverse' or 'negative' consensus for it not to be adopted, has contributed to making the DSB uniquely effective amongst judicial institutions of global economic governance. This, of course, is the foundation of the concern many American interests, including the Obama and Trump Administrations, have expressed respecting the DSB. It frustrates the exercise of quasi-coercive tactics of power while giving greater scope to other nodes and networks to exercise influence by different means.

4. The Appellate Body Crisis

By the mid-1980s, and until the mid-1990s, chief amongst these quasi-coercive measures were so-called Voluntary Export Restrictions (VERs). and the three primary trade remedies employed most frequently by the United States: antidumping tariffs; countervailing duties; and safeguards against import surges (Bown and Keynes 2020, 12). Of these, VERs and antidumping tariffs caused the greatest resentment amongst US trading partners. As Bown and Keynes describe, VERs were "opaque, government-negotiated, managed trade arrangements that short-circuited markets" (2020, 4) by requiring American trading partners to limit exports artificially and "voluntarily" to the United States. Negotiated under duress, they gave rise to corrupt practices in the distribution of limited export licenses, and made trade policy unduly difficult because of the need to prevent anticompetitive behavior while managing export sales and pricing decisions (ibid. 4). VERs were primarily directed against emerging markets and always to the benefit of domestic interests. For example, by one analysis, the 1981 VER restricting Japanese automobile imports had added USD 2000 to the cost of each Japanese automobile in the United States by 1984 (Lee 1987), thus protecting the American automobile industry. More generally, between 1986 and 1988 VERs covered about 12% of American imports (Bown and Keynes 2020, 4). Indeed, in 1986 there were 99 VERs in force globally of which fully 25 protected American steel interests, and 7 protected automobiles, textiles, electronics and machine tools (Boonekamp 1987, 4). This necessarily benefited myriad specific US domestic interests and incentivized them to undermine or capture the WTO Appellate Body. The same is true of VERs limiting imports of Canadian softwood lumber, which persisted well into the 2000s, and of the 2005–08 VER covering Chinese clothing and textile imports, which was implemented following the scheduled termination of the WTO Agreement on Textiles and Clothing in 2005 (Bown and Keynes 2020, 5). Finally, the strong likelihood that beneficiaries of VERs also resented the WTO is supported by the actions of the Trump Administration, which negotiated VERs on steel and aluminum with South Korea, Brazil and Argentina contemporaneously with its actions to paralyze the WTO Appellate Body (ibid. 5).

Such actions were taken despite VERs having been condemned to be phased out and prohibited under the WTO *Agreement on Safeguards* (WTO 1994a). In the event, although they continued to a degree beyond 1995, their prevalence was greatly reduced and they were generally instituted under alternate names (Bown and Keynes 2020, 4). For American negotiators, this loss of VERs was acceptable because they believed the WTO Agreements had preserved the legality of American antidumping measures. The belief was that antidumping tariffs had been 'ring-fenced' (Kerr 2021, 6) by two guarantees in Article 17.6 of the WTO's *Anti-Dumping Agreement*: first, that a dispute settlement panel would abide by the decision of the relevant national authorities concerning the legitimacy of antidumping measures if it found that those authorities had properly established the facts of the case and evaluated them in an unbiased and objective manner (WTO 1994b, Article 17.6 i); and second, that where the dispute settlement panel found that the *Anti-Dumping Agreement* admitted of "more than one possible interpretation," (ibid. Article 17.6 ii) the panel would adopt the interpretation of the national authorities as long as it rested upon a permissible interpretation. To the American negotiators, and evidently successive US Administrations, this meant that Appellate Body panels would be sufficiently deferential to American government decisions and definitions that only the most obvious factual error or deviation from correct procedure would cause antidumping tariffs to be overturned.

This turned out not to be the case. Fully 141 disputes were brought between 1995 and 2017 against US antidumping tariffs and countervailing duties, the majority of which the US lost (Bown and Keynes 2020, 12). This included complaints brought by the EU and Japan that led to the repeal of the US *Antidumping Act* of 1916 (ibid. 11), numerous cases against the practice of "zeroing" to quantify the amount of 'dumping' taking place, and an important eight-member challenge that invalidated the US "Byrd Amendment" (ibid. 11) giving the proceeds from US antidumping and countervailing duties to the companies that had initiated them. In short, the United States faced, and lost, a vast number of disputes before the WTO Appellate Body upon precisely the measures American negotiators believed they had protected at the WTO's founding. Small wonder that government and business interests in the United States were annoyed.

Yet the United States was not the only developed country using antidumping measures, zeroing and VERs to manage imports. Indeed, it was not even the most prolific. For example, while the US employed 32 VERs in 1986, the EC employed no fewer than 55 of the 99 VERs then in force globally (Boonekamp 1987, 4). More-over, the EC also lost disputes against its zeroing practices, and ceased to employ zeroing after the loss of an antidumping dispute concerning 'cotton-type bed-lined' brought by India in 1998 and decided by the Appellate Body in 2003 (*EC—Bed Linen* 2003, DS141). The obvious question is why the EC did not campaign against the Appellate Body and act to undermine it with even greater ardor than the US. Indeed, the US response was to use its veto as a WTO member to block all appoint-ments to the Appellate Body, making it impossible to achieve the quorum necessary to issue reports and rendering the institution defunct. Why did the EC (and later the EU) do nothing of the sort, given that it seemingly had greater motivation?

The answer, it seems, is heterarchy. That is to say, it is the confluence of Ameri-can private and public "interests" projecting power from intersecting networks behaving in the manner of a complex adaptive system in that together they pro-duced an outcome that was not expected or predicted until the inevitability of the dissolution of the Appellate Body was obvious. First and foremost, the steel industry in the United States was a constant and ardent opponent of the WTO and the Appellate Body from their inception in 1994 until the latter's dissolution in 2019. To return to the 1986 IMF figures concerning VERs, although 25 of 32 American VERs protected the steel industry, the protected part of the industry comprised only 1.1% of US imports at the time (Boonekamp 1987, 4; Bown and Keynes 2020, 4). It follows that actors within the steel industry probably con-sidered they had more to lose by the WTO Agreements phasing out VERs than those in other sectors of the American economy. In 1995, at the instigation of Robert Lighthizer and Adam Wolff, Senator Robert Dole sponsored legislation to allow the United States to withdraw from the WTO after three American losses in dispute settlement rulings (Bown and Keynes 2020, 13). Then, in 2000, Ligh-thizer and Wolff strongly criticized the DSB in testimony during the first sched-uled congressional review of US participation in the WTO (ibid. 13). Both had represented the US steel industry as lawyers in trade remedy cases. Wolff would become deputy director of the WTO, while Lighthizer would be US Trade Repre-sentative (USTR) during the Trump Administration—exactly when the Appellate Body crisis culminated. Indeed, the Bush Administration nominated Lighthizer to the Appellate Body in 2003, although unsuccessfully.

Still further, when coverage of US imports by trade remedies increased between 2013 and 2016, it was largely the result of an increase in disputes involv-ing the importation of steel products (Bown and Keynes 2020, 15). Moreover, "steel" is mentioned 53 times in the USTR's *Report on the Appellate Body of the World Trade Organization* (USTR 2020). Finally, leaving aside complaints about form and procedure, such as the Appellate Body's frequent failure to meet its 90-day deadlines (ibid. 26), the substance of USTR resentment toward the Appel-late Body seems built to a significant degree upon three cases affecting American steel industry protections. The first, *US-Stainless Steel* (2008, DS344), is the only dispute mentioned in the report's table of contents and receives a sub-chapter of its own. It is advanced as the source of a purported new doctrine of precedent in

Appellate Body reasoning whereby similar decisions upon similar facts should be followed unless there are "cogent reasons" not to. In the view of the USTR, this approach is entirely novel in the context of the Appellate Body, unjustified by the WTO Agreements, and essentially the creation of new law (USTR 2020, 58–62). *US-Steel Safeguards* (2003, DS252) is similarly criticized for having created "additional obligations for imposing safeguard measures" (USTR 2020, B-9). Third, the report considers that *US-Hot-Rolled Steel* (2001, DS184) has erroneously interpreted and applied article 17.6 of the *Anti-Dumping Agreement* (WTO 1994b). Specifically, the Appellate Body determined that investigating authorities must "separate and distinguish the amount of injury caused by each potential factor relating to a domestic industry's material injury, rather than simply finding that material injury exists and that dumped imports are among the causes of material injury" (USTR 2020, A-25). To the USTR in 2020, as to the *Senate Report on the Bipartisan Trade Promotion Authority Act of 2002* (S. Rept. 107–139), this amounted to the creation of new law (USTR 2020, A-13, 25).

At the same time, US crude steel production in 2018 totaled only 73% of 1970 production, while employment in US steel mills has fallen from above 700,000 in the 1950s to 83,000 in 2018 (BDO United States, August 2019). Given these declines, it seems clear that the steel industry in the United States has exercised influence concerning the WTO Appellate Body well above its share of US economic activity, employment or imports. Whether this amounts to undue influence is beyond the scope of the present discussion, but certainly Bown and Keynes suggest that Lighthizer's role as USTR gave the steel industry particular 'clout' within the Trump Administration (2020, 17).

It may be said, therefore, that the relationship of the US steel industry and the WTO Appellate Body is likely a case of the capture by private interests of a global public good. Perhaps it is as likely a case as one can reasonably expect to be afforded. More than this, however, cannot be asserted because systemic complexity and nonlinear causality make a rigorous causal chain too difficult to establish. Indeed, this is particularly so because such a large number of disparate interests within the United States converged in opposition to the WTO generally or the Appellate Body in particular over its quarter-century existence. To begin, every US Administration since 2000 has, intentionally or not, acted to undermine the Appellate Body. After Lighthizer's unsuccessful nomination to the Appellate Body, the successful nominee, Merit Janow, was dismissed after a single term. Her successor, Jennifer Hillman, was then dismissed by the Obama Administration after only one term, her reappointment was blocked, and the reappointment of Seung Wha Chang was blocked (Hillman 2020; Bown and Keynes 2020, 14). The Trump Administration therefore did not initiate the Appellate Body crisis, though it brought the crisis swiftly to a culmination. That is to say, what the Trump Administration did was different in degree, but not in kind, to the actions of its predecessors.

Moreover, adherence to economic protectionism has long crossed partisan and ideological divides in the United States. The Obama, Trump and Biden Administrations have all advanced 'Buy American' provisions in legislation, and

Hillary Clinton's 2015–16 presidential campaign stated her intention to renegotiate NAFTA (Wayland, *Detroit News*, 26 July 2016). This extends to antipathy toward the WTO and the Appellate Body. The 2020 USTR report presents voluminous evidence of bipartisan, progressive and conservative, denouncement of WTO jurisprudence. Sherrod Brown, for example, the relatively progressive Democratic senator from Ohio, criticizes Appellate Body reasoning (USTR 2020, A-2) in terms much the same as the more conservative Democratic senator Max Baucus of Montana (ibid. A-13–15), and Republican senator Chuck Grassley of Iowa (ibid. A-1). Indeed, the USTR report includes 10 collective bipartisan statements covering 20 years made by senators and House members criticizing WTO jurisprudential reasoning (ibid. A-1–19). Beyond this, progressive activists in the United States have had an antagonistic relationship toward trade liberalization and the WTO since the 1990s. This was most famously demonstrated at the "Battle of Seattle" outside the 1999 WTO Ministerial. However, it was continued well into the 2010s by environmentalists, feminist activists, anti-racism and anti-globalization activists such as Occupy Wall Street, and other interests.

Finally, the reasoning in the 2020 USTR report, and in the critical statements of senators and House members, strongly resembles that of "originalism," a uniquely American jurisprudential hermeneutic doctrine popularized by United States Supreme Court Justice Antonin Scalia and long the dominant legal philosophy of American conservatism (Whittington 2011). Essentially, it holds that the duty of an interpreter of a legal text is to discover the original intent of the author or authors, a project that much Continental European philosophy has considered misguided, dangerous, or merely impossible for more than half a century. Such an approach necessarily produces an impression of activist judges "making law" where others see reasonable and even unavoidable interpretation. As has taken place with respect to the Appellate Body, the confluence of an approach approximating "originalism" with more flexible hermeneutic approaches cannot fail to produce misunderstanding and conflict.

In short, the US steel industry surely played an outsized role as a more direct agent in causing the Appellate Body crisis, but it did so in a context of numerous other intersecting philosophies, influences, and forces stretching across many networks and at least three decades. This complexity, which accords well with a heterarchical account of power relations, is what makes it so difficult to define the precise terms of "capture" and to understand the play of causality in International Relations and International Political Economy in a verifiable way. Proximate causes and apparent capture can be identified, but further progress toward certainty and precise mapping of complex, nonlinear causality, may rest beyond the ken of human epistemology.

5. Conclusion

If, in fact, this be so, and heterarchy describe the operation of power but complexity render it systemically incomprehensible, what is to be done? At least in part, the answer surely lies in greater intellectual modesty. If nonlinear causality cannot be rigorously traced in depth, and if predictive modelling is therefore largely precluded from the study of the international political economy, then it becomes necessary to theorize and build with these limits clearly in mind.

This in turn requires resilience and therefore flexibility, which makes capture less likely to be of long standing or systemically destabilizing. Thus, in the context of the present discussion, the prospect of decentralized global economic governance must be advanced and the temptation of global government resisted. Internally, within institutions such as the WTO, resilience can be achieved at least in part by the hybridization of soft law and hard law, the former allowing for the innovation and evolution necessary for an institution to survive (including by evading capture), and the latter allowing tried and settled principles and practices to be made binding and enforceable.

In this way, part of the institution, such as the WTO's Appellate Body, can be negated with less danger of compromising the institution as a whole, and with a greater chance that the remainder of the institution can evolve to continue the functions necessary to its effectiveness and credibility. The specifics of such endeavors are well beyond the scope of the present discussion, but if one accepts the limitations upon the comprehensibility of the international political economy implied by heterarchy and complexity, then there can be little reason to question the need for the resilience engineering of global economic governance.

Note

1 For example, Dauvergne and Lebaron (2014) define the corporatization of protest as the "securitization of dissent," the "privatization of social life," and the "institutionalization of activism."

References

BDO United States. August 2019. *The Steel Industry and its Place in the American Economy*, available at www.bdo.com/insights/business-financial-advisory/valuation-business-analytics/the-steel-industry-and-its-place-in-the-american-e, accessed 20 February 2022.

Belmonte, Rosalba, and Philip G. Cerny. 2021. 'Heterarchy: Toward Paradigm Shift in World Politics.' *Journal of Political Power* 14 (1): 235–257.

Boonekamp, Clemens F.J. 1987. 'Voluntary Export Restraints.' *Finance & Development* 0024 (004): 2–5.

Bown, Chad, and Soumaya Keynes. March 2020. 'Why Trump Shot the Sheriffs: The End of WTO Dispute Settlement 1.0.' Working Paper 20–4. Peterson Institute for International Economics.

Crumley, Carole. 2015. 'Heterarchy.' In Scott, Robert A., Marlis C. Buchmann, and Stephen M. Kosslyn, eds. *Emerging Trends in the Social and Behavioral Sciences: An Interdisciplinary, Searchable, and Linkable Resource* (John Wiley & Sons, Inc.), 1–14.

Dauvergne, Peter, and Genevieve LeBaron. 2014. *Protest Inc: The Corporatization of Activism* (Cambridge: Polity Press).

Fabian, Judit. 2015. *Towards a Theory of Democratic Global Economic Governance: Hybridization of Soft and Hard Law in the Case of Gender within the World Trade Organization*. Thesis (Ph.D.) Carleton University.

General Agreement on Tariffs and Trade. 16 November 1962. Panel Report. *Uruguay-Recourse to Article XXIII*. L/1923. (BISD 11S/95).

General Agreement on Tariffs and Trade. 5 April 1966. *Decision of 5 April 1966 on Procedures under Article XXIII*, available at www.wto.org/english/tratop_e/dispu_e/disp_set tlement_cbt_e/a2s1p1_e.htm, accessed 22 February 2022.

General Agreement on Tariffs and Trade. 28 November 1979. *Understanding Regarding Notification, Consultation, Dispute Settlement and Surveillance*. L/4907, available at www.wto.org/english/docs_e/legal_e/tokyo_notif_e.pdf, accessed 22 February 2022.

General Agreement on Tariffs and Trade. 29 November 1982. *Ministerial Declaration Adopted on 29 November 1982*. (BISD 29S/9). 'Dispute Settlement Procedures' (BISD 29S/13).

General Agreement on Tariffs and Trade. 30 November 1984. *Dispute Settlement Procedures: Fortieth Session of the Contracting Parties, Action taken on 30 November 1984*. (BISD 31S/9) I.

Hillman, Jennifer. January 2020. 'A Reset of the World Trade Organization's Appellate Body,' *Council on Foreign Relations: Foreign Affairs*, available at www.cfr.org/report/reset-world-trade-organizations-appellate-body, accessed 20 February 2022.

Hudec, Robert E. 1975. *The GATT Legal System and World Trade Diplomacy* (New York: Praeger Publishers).

Hudec, Robert E. 1980. 'GATT Dispute Settlement after the Tokyo Round: An Unfinished Business.' *Cornell International Law Journal* 13 (2): 145–203.

Hudec, Robert E., Daniel Kennedy, and Mark Sgarbossa. 1993. 'A Statistical Profile of GATT Dispute Settlement Cases: 1948–1989.' *Minnesota Journal of Global Trade* 2 (1): 1–113.

Jackson, John H. 1998. 'Designing and Implementing Effective Dispute Settlement Procedures: WTO Dispute Settlement, Appraisal and Prospects.' In Kreuger, Anne, ed. *The WTO as an International Organization* (Chicago: University of Chicago Press), 161–180.

Kavalski, Emilian. 2007. 'The Fifth Debate and the Emergence of Complex International Relations Theory: Notes on the Application of Complexity Theory to the Study of International Life.' *Cambridge Review of International Affairs* 20 (3): 435–454.

Kerr, William A. 2021. 'Dispute Settlement—Or Not?' *The Estey: Journal of International Law and Trade Policy* 22 (1): 1–14.

Lee, Jin W. 1987. *The Cost of the Voluntary Export Restraint of Japanese Automobile Exports to the United States*. Thesis (M.A.) Virginia Polytechnic Institute and State University.

Lehmann, Kai E. 2012. 'Unfinished Transformation: The Three Phases of Complexity's Emergence into International Relations and Foreign Policy.' *Cooperation and Conflict* 47 (3): 404–413.

Orsini, Amandine, and Philippe Le Prestre. 2020. 'Introduction'. In Amandine Orsini, Philippe Le Prestre, Peter M Haas, Malte Brosig, Philipp Pattberg, Oscar Widerberg, Laura Gomez-Mera, Jean-Frédéric Morin, Neil E Harrison, Robert Geyer, David Chandler, 'Forum: Complex Systems and International Governance.' *International Studies Review* 22 (4): 1008–1038.

Scharre, Paul. February 2016. *Autonomous Weapons and Operational Risk*. Ethical Autonomy Project, Centre for a New American Security.

Trebilcock, Michael, Robert Howse, and Antonia Eliason. 2013. *The Regulation of International Trade*. 4th Ed. (New York: Palgrave Macmillan).

United States Senate. 2002. *S. Rept. 107–139—Bipartisan Trade Promotion Authority Act of 2002*, available at www.congress.gov/congressional-report/107th-congress/senate-report/139, accessed 20 February 2022.

United States Trade Representative. February 2020. *Report on the Appellate Body of the World Trade Organization*, available at https://ustr.gov/sites/default/files/Report_on_the_Appellate_Body_of_the_World_Trade_Organization.pdf, accessed 19 February 2022.

Wayland, Michael. 26 July 2016. 'UAW Leader: Clinton Open to Renegotiating NAFTA.' *The Detroit News: Business*, available at www.detroitnews.com/story/business/autos/2016/07/26/clinton-nafta-uaw-renegotiate/87583506/, accessed 20 February 2022.

Whittington, Keith E. 2011. 'Is Originalism too Conservative?' *Harvard Journal of Law and Public Policy* 34 (1): 29–41.

World Trade Organization. 1994a. *Agreement on Safeguards*, available at www.wto.org/english/docs_e/legal_e/25-safeg.pdf, accessed 19 February 2022.

World Trade Organization. 1994b. *Agreement on Implementation of Article VI of the General Agreement on Tariffs and Trade* (Anti-Dumping Agreement), available at www.wto.org/english/docs_e/legal_e/19-adp.pdf, accessed 19 February 2022.

World Trade Organization. 1994c. *Marrakesh Agreement Establishing the World Trade Organization. Annex 2—Understanding of Rules and Procedures Governing the Settlement of Disputes (Dispute Settlement Understanding (DSU)*, available at https://www.wto.org/english/docs_e/legal_e/04-wto_e.htm.

World Trade Organization. 24 July 2001. *DS184: United States—Anti-Dumping Measures on Certain Hot-Rolled Steel Products from Japan*, available at www.wto.org/english/tratop_e/dispu_e/cases_e/ds184_e.htm, accessed 19 February 2022.

World Trade Organization. 29 April 2003. *DS141: European Communities—Anti-Dumping Duties on Imports of Cotton-type Bed Linen from India (EC—Bed Linen)*, available at www.wto.org/english/tratop_e/dispu_e/cases_e/ds141_e.htm, accessed 19 February 2022.

World Trade Organization. 11 July 2003. *DS252: United States—Definitive Safeguard Measures on Imports of Certain Steel Products*, available at www.wto.org/english/tratop_e/dispu_e/cases_e/ds252_e.htm, accessed 19 February 2022.

World Trade Organization. 30 April 2008. *DS344: United States—Final Anti-Dumping Measures on Stainless Steel from Mexico*, available at www.wto.org/english/tratop_e/dispu_e/cases_e/ds344_e.htm, accessed 29 February 2022.

14

HETERARCHY AND GLOBAL ENVIRONMENTAL CHANGE

Gabriela Kütting

This chapter examines the global environmental crisis and looks at the evolution of global environmental cooperation from the first environmental regimes in the 1970s to the heterarchical patterns of the 21st century. While international/global environmental politics was never situated in the field of "high politics" and therefore not driven by anarchical patterns, historically, it was firmly rooted in state-centric forms of cooperation until the late 1980s.

The IR literature on the environment is heavily centered around the notion of governance, either in its traditional neoliberal institutionalist regime theory form or in its transnational form. In the 1990s, the literature increasingly focused on the rise of new actors in the environmental policy and governance field, which then led to the study of new forms of governance. It is not surprising that the literature focuses on governance, as global environmental change is very dependent on the cooperation of a range of actors at the international and global levels, which by necessity makes governance the natural policy tool. This explains the governance-heavy focus of this chapter, since the transnational nature of pollution flows and global commons problems such as climate change or ocean pollution are almost exclusively approached through forms of cooperation.

The number of global governance institutions has risen dramatically in the past 30 years or so, and with increasing trade and financial regulation, these areas have been opened up for global institutionalization and removed from the domestic arena. As Rosenau and Czempiel (1992: 12) put it:

> Governance is a more encompassing phenomenon than government. It embraces governmental institutions but it also subsumes informal, non-governmental mechanisms, whereby those persons and organizations within its purview move ahead, satisfy their needs, and fulfill their wants. . . . Governance is thus a system of rule that is as dependent on inter-subjective

DOI: 10.4324/9781003352617-16

meanings as on formally sanctioned constitutions and charters. . . . It is possible to conceive of governance without government—of regulatory mechanisms in a sphere of activity which function effectively even though they are not endowed with formal authority.

In the environmental field, the number of international environmental agreements and voluntary arrangements is well in the thousands and covers all sorts of regional and global issues, ranging from the Climate Change Convention to forest stewardship councils, to public-private partnerships, to voluntary codes of conduct. These form the main subject matter of the study of the environment in international politics. However, from an ecological perspective, the heart of the matter is not environmental governance per se but the relationship between economic and environmental governance and the lack of environmental provisions in the economic sphere or the precedence economic institutions and regulations take over environmental ones (Conca 2000; Kuetting 2010; Ford and Kuetting 2020).

Applying the concept of governance bumps up against at least three sorts of limitations. In the first place, in terms of agenda-setting and policy formulation, policy *inputs* lack coherence. Expectations of concerted action, whether by interest groups, social movements and NGOs, or state and intergovernmental actors, are simply not fulfilled. Policy negotiations limp along with space created for behind-the-scenes lobbying and regulatory arbitrage. Second, institutions themselves are fragmented; actors focus predominantly on inter- and intra-institutional games. So-called *withinputs* are concerned with endogenous institutional and managerial (in) stability, coherence, and hierarchical issues, rather than with substantive policy challenges. Third, *outputs* are suboptimal, leading to lowest-common-denominator, often highly compromised outcomes. Watered-down, ineffective agreements are presented as successes, while implementation and enforcement are left until further compromises, while interest group actors regroup and marshal their forces for the next round. This can be seen in the recent UNFCCC negotiations.

One common denominator of the increasingly heterarchical nature of global environmental politics is the commodification of nature. With increasing commodification, the relations between public and private forms of governance have changed quite dramatically, relating to questions of legitimacy. While an increasing plurality of actors and organizing principles has emerged, there has been no real debate on what that means for the legitimacy of these arrangements. What used to be firmly in the domain of the state is now being decided by a myriad of actors, most of whom have entrenched economic interests. There has been no discussion of the consequences of these "power-sharing arrangements." Economic actors are fundamentally global actors operating in localities across the globe. However, political and judicial systems are still very territory-based. While global governance adapts to this heterarchical situation with myriad public, private, and hybrid arrangements, the situation leads to a disconnect for social movements and social/environmental justice actors in terms of the governance and governmental frameworks they can refer to for administrative, political, and judicial support.

Traditionally, in the global and western hegemonic law and policy frameworks, the local is governed by local government and local as well as regional government are bound by national legal and policy frameworks. National legal frameworks are influenced by global governance instruments. Technically, the global does not directly regulate the local, but the relations are mediated through the national level. All of these levels are, in an ideal scenario, democratically determined. However, the waters become murky when power sharing governance arrangements with pride of place given to economic actors become a common model of "doing business." It disregards that social relations are not this linear. And not all local forms of socio-legal organization are philosophically based on the same rationale, or, in other words, are necessarily compatible with the liberal and neoliberal forms of governance and government that are hegemonic at the global level and in the Western world. For example, indigenous communities practice forms of social organization that do not easily fit in with global or national governance. Global companies and transnational consortia often evade the legitimacy of the national and global frameworks. Often, they co-opt national frameworks. By the same token, it is often not clear where responsibility or accountability lie, or it becomes clear that there are loopholes or vacuums in governance and in accountability. To take this one step further, in this system, nature also remains invisible and passive in front of cultural arguments. Nature and stewardship over nature at the local level by local communities are invisible in global governance. This is almost tantamount to making it a normative duty for a heterarchical analysis to account for the uneven nature of the complex web in which states, economic actors, social movements, NGOs, indigenous peoples, and local communities operate.

Likewise, there are a huge range of global governance instruments, from the public to the private, and hybrid forms of both—some of which have legal standing while others are normative self-regulating frameworks such as corporate social responsibility frameworks. These are not frameworks that those who are threatened in their existence, who want to speak for future generations or who protest the commodification of nature can effectively utilize because they have been excluded from participating in a meaningful way. The heterarchical aspect of this problem will be discussed in more detail below.

1. Global Governance

Global governance today is a diverse phenomenon and can be divided into public governance, hybrid governance, and private governance (Bulkeley & Newell 2010)—the typical multi-nodality referred to in the concept of heterarchy. In order to understand this evolution, it is appropriate to provide a historical summary of the evolution of the concept of governance. International cooperation has been and is still widely considered to be the most appropriate and effective method for addressing environmental problems of a transboundary nature (Biermann & Pattberg 2012; Kanie et al. 2013; Trudeau et al. 2013). Environmental problems that cross borders (in a variety of forms) need to be addressed collectively since their scope and remediation go beyond the national. Air pollution, marine pollution, climate change, or ozone layer depletion are beyond control at the national level, and so are problems arising from the operation of the global political economy. Most late-20th-century writings in global environmental politics took it for granted that inter*state* cooperation is the appropriate starting point for effective international action. The first wave of this literature focused on international regimes—established by states but developing their own spheres of bureaucratic quasi-independence (Ruggie 1993). The concept of the regime is generally associated with Ruggie's seminal article (1975), as refined by Krasner (1984) and Keohane (1984). These authors assumed the pre-existence of international anarchy, and therefore the need for an overarching intergovernmental regulatory system to deal with transboundary problems of any nature, not just environmental. The growing global environmental politics (GEP) literature was consequently grounded in "neoliberal institutionalist" thought (Keohane 1984). One of the seminal texts of the early writings contextualizing global/international environmental politics poses the question in the following way:

> Can a fragmented and often highly conflictual political system made up of over 170 sovereign states and numerous other actors achieve the high (and historically unprecedented) levels of co-operation and policy co-ordination needed to manage environmental problems on a global scale?
>
> *(Hurrell & Kingsbury 1992)*

Toward the late 1990s, the focus on regimes tended to be supplanted by the related discourse of global governance, with the growing awareness that states were not the only dominant actors in the global system. Although this approach puts less emphasis on formally established organizations and includes other actors, informal structures, and networks, it is nevertheless still focused on how the interstate system might become more institutionalized to deal with transboundary issues. Thakur and Weiss (2015) define global governance as "the sum of laws, norms, policies, and institutions that define, constitute, and mediate relations between citizens, societies, markets, and states in the international system–the wielders and objects of the exercise of international public power" (27). It is still about top-down policy-making rather than the egalitarian collaboration between multiple actors from the state, business, and civil society fields. While much recent literature has been successful in introducing new policy mechanisms and incorporating a multi-actor approach (Young et al. 2008; Andonova 2010; Biermann & Pattberg 2012; Selin 2012), it has not addressed the question of power and hierarchy in a genuinely critical way, skirting the question of who rules and who benefits.

For example, Pattberg and Widerberg (2015) list the following as the main trends in global environmental governance:

> (a) the proliferation of actors (new actors and new roles); (b) the emergence of new governance mechanisms and instruments (for example multi-stakeholder

partnerships or global city networks to combat climate change); and (c) the resulting proliferation and intensified interaction of governance levels (e.g. sub-national and transnational) and functional arenas (e.g. public and private rule making).

(p 685)

However, there is no discussion of how these changes affect power and hierarchy in the global architecture. In fact, the concept of power and the impacts of the distribution of power are strangely absent in the majority of contributions on global governance. This is where heterarchy can contribute to identifying the uneven power relations.

It has been recognized for the past 25 years that a range of actors participates and has inputs into mainstream governance approaches. Transnational environmental movements and NGOs, as well as transnational corporations (TNCs), are a case in point and are considered vital actors in global environmental politics (Princen & Finger 1994; Wapner 1998; Keck & Sikkink 1998). With this came the recognition of more complex webs of interdependence and a richer diversity of actors involved in policy-making (Lipschutz & Mayer 1996; Paterson et al. 2003). More recent governance modes include indigenous peoples as a viable group of actors, for example, as guardians of 20% of the world's land (Suiseeya et al. 2021). This raises questions about who gets to participate and who actually gets to make the rules.

Arguing for the importance of the role of power in analyzing heterarchical relations, Dimitrov engages with the concept of empty institutions as an exercise in power to deflect meaningful institutions designed to address environmental problems (2020). This is a case in point, showing the coloniality of global environmental governance in action. He defines empty institutions as *social arrangements that consist of relatively stable rules and procedures that exclude regulatory policymaking or policy implementation* (2020: 2). In other words, they are institutions that give the impression of being a purposeful agreement, but their content actually makes no contribution to the resolution of a particular problem. Dimitrov cites the example of the Copenhagen Accord in the UN Framework Convention on Climate Change, signed in 2009. Because of the difficulties in uniting the participating parties around a common goal, the aim was to sign a nonbinding declaration that would postpone more definitive action to the new COP meeting yet keep the door open.

Empty institutions are certainly helpful in legitimizing inaction and can be regarded as a hegemonic tool to avoid policy action. It is impossible to engage with the concept of empty institutions without considering power and hegemony in the international system, and thus this concept makes a very valuable contribution to the literature on global governance and heterarchy. It addresses the elephant in the room. It also leads, inter alia, to another type of hegemonic actor, the corporate actor and business in general as a leader of global governance efforts and often as the driving force for developing empty institutions.

2. Heterarchy and Corporate Actors

One of the seminal dimensions of global governance is the conceptualization of corporate actors in the global system, both from a positive and negative perspective. Ford, for example, identifies that business is often regarded as the leader in research for the future, having a long-range global vision, and developing new concepts of corporate responsibility, as with the Business Council on Sustainable Development (BCSD). Furthermore, the United Nations Commission for Global Governance (UNCGG), in its report *Our Global Neighborhood*, posits that we are entering a new era of democratization, economic transformation, multilateralism, and collective responsibility (Ford 2018), running directly counter to our claim of increasing coloniality and hierarchies. However, Ford argues that despite the growing involvement of a wide range of actors, key decision-making institutions remain intergovernmental in nature. Juridically, the claim to state sovereignty retains its primacy (Paterson 2001) and the political framework of the liberal global political economy has not fundamentally changed despite the apparent undermining of state power per se (Lipschutz 2004). Critics claim that global governance is merely a strategy of "global capitalist hegemony" (Ford 2018: 42), but the construction of new regimes and institutions has nevertheless remained at the core of GEP, unsurprisingly, as neoliberal governance is built on the assumption of more governance equaling more improvement of environmental degradation.

A crucial reason for this shortcoming is complexity. Environmental policy making is intricately connected to trade, economic, agricultural, fisheries, industry, financial, and other policy sectors, and usually takes a back seat in the face of economic challenges. Economic actors are often able to bypass or manipulate policy-making processes, putting environmental action lower on the list of policy priorities because environmental protection is argued to undermine economic health. This exists not only at the level of policy design but also of policy implementation; it is not limited to GEP but can also be found in other sectors, such as finance. Furthermore, actors have to combine and coordinate policymaking at various endogenous and exogenous levels. Thus studying environmental governance, however many actors are included, gives a very incomplete and distorted picture of social relations at the global level because the governance level, or governance levels, are just some among many more. For example, climate change is approached through the Climate Change Convention and its various parts but also through public-private partnerships, industry cooperations, collaborations, cooperatives, industry initiatives, etc. These arrangements overlap and cross-reference.

Some writers suggest that an increasing number of private actors initiate governance institutions, which then become recognized by states and become part of regulatory structures (such as ISO 14000 standards, stewardship councils) (Pattberg 2006; Alcock 2008; Betsill & Corell 2008). For a liberal world view, the notion of a pluralist, inclusive global standard seems to be an ideal basis for harmonized global solutions. However, critics argue that it does not take into account unequal power relations between the various actors in the global political economy (Lipschutz 2004; Kuetting 2010). Looking at the many case studies at the local level shows especially how global governance falls far short of its lofty aims exactly because of its blindness toward inequality and hierarchies. A case in point is the way the relations between extractivist industries, the state, and local communities (indigenous or otherwise) are handled.

Critical scholars find that a critique of capital accumulation provides a meaningful and powerful tool through which to analyze the nature–society relations underlying the friction between environment and economy (Saurin 1996; Kuetting 2000, 2010; Paterson 2001; Chew 2008). In particular, the neo-Gramscian framework has proved to be useful for analyzing state-firm relations in fields such as forestry, biodiversity, or climate change (Levy & Newell 2005; Humphreys 2018) as well as the role of civil society and an analysis of governance reproducing capitalist hegemony (Ford 2018). As Vogler puts it, "market-based globalization is the driver of degradation and states (acting as the agents of capital) are regarded as part of the problem rather than, as in mainstream work, the solution" (Vogler 2005: 235). The logical conclusion from this analysis is that the environmental problems regimes or global governance institutions aim to address cannot be resolved through collective action endeavors alone, since these do not touch upon the underlying operation of the hegemonic economic system.

While most global environmental governance is still concerned with what political science does more generally—establishing institutional frameworks to solve problems identified by political actors—the diversification of the global governance literature in recent years to define governance as inclusive of non-traditional actors and to include a normative desire for more representative and equitable institutions has been one way to address the above critique (Trudeau et al. 2013; Young et al. 2013; Stevenson & Dryzek 2014; Pattberg & Widerberg 2015). While more diverse, equitable, just, inclusive, and representative governance institutions (if they exist) are of course extremely desirable from a legitimacy point of view, it would be even more desirable for these new institutions to achieve more effective policies for environmental improvement as a result of increased diversity. However, that connection is tenuous at best, precisely because of the unaccounted-for hierarchies and power inequalities. While more equitable institutions facilitate burden sharing both in terms of environmental and financial burdens, shared burdens do not, unfortunately, equal a better environmental record (Dobson 2003). Institutions are compromises arrived at through negotiated trade-offs between actors and constrained by the power constellations underlying these trade-offs. While having more actors in the political process has solved some problems, it has not addressed the key problem—the structure of the global economic system that systematically treats nature as an unlimited resource and commodity without intrinsic value or voice. Within this, it does not problematize the notion of economic growth, which is fundamentally taken for granted and embedded in a wide range of institutions, including global governance institutions (Purdey 2010).

This is particularly relevant when it comes to non-traditional participants in global environmental governance. It implies a hegemonic concept of nature as subordinate to the global economy, to which all other actors have to acquiesce by implication. It also implies a hegemonic concept of a Western lifestyle that is non-negotiable and to which all other actors ought to subordinate. Likewise, it assumes the hegemony of human life over all other life and implies that the more a sentient actor is a consuming, contributing member of the global economy, the more worthy this life is. However, indigenous communities in particular do not subscribe to this commoditized view of nature and question its validity. Many communities and individuals whose living space and livelihoods are threatened by global economic projects object to this lifestyle, but their desire to preserve a more local and sustainable life has to give way to the notion of "progress" meaning commoditization.

Likewise, there are a multitude of private governance institutions and instruments that engage with the local–global problematique in a variety of ways. These are obviously not necessarily part of the "linear" structure of global-state-regional/local pathways of norm diffusion and can take a variety of forms. Private governance institutions are not subject to the same legal hierarchies found in public governance, but they are nevertheless based on the processes of commodification found in public governance. Naturally, participation in global private governance institutions implies a high degree of institutionalization itself, which engenders its own hierarchies. For example, corporate social responsibility policies are often based on greenwashing rather than a concern with a fundamental change in business operations. Private initiatives in, for example, indigenous territories, such as investment in rainforests or attempts at biodiversity protection, are usually organized around a mutual profit motive. This leads to a prioritization of "marketable" biodiversity receiving publicity, while ecosystems that are not seen as attractive but fulfill a vital function, such as mangroves, get ignored.

Any corporate policy is necessarily limited by the rationale and operation of the global marketplace. Codes of conduct or corporate social responsibility policies are a response to the demands of civil society organizations and consumer activism, but are not driven by the desire to empower workers in developing countries or steer against rising inequality. These responses are responses to the zeitgeist. Thus, corporate policies will always reflect the dominant, cultural, social, and political role of business in society and be based on the neoliberal principles of the global markets. Yet, as Levy and Kaplan (2009) argue, while such corporate strategies may take off pressure to enact more far-reaching change, they are also a first step toward a second round of negotiations in which civil society can heighten expectations for further change.

The larger question about the role of private governance is how to juxtapose it in relation to public governance. While public governance is accountable through the usual political channels, the accountability of private governance is measured in a different currency. None of these actors are "accountable" in the traditional sense. Yet, the academic, diplomatic, and public discourses have accepted these forms of governance as equal to public governance efforts. Nevertheless, we can see that most of these efforts do not really serve the global public, but tend to serve corporate and state actors better (or only serve corporate and state actors). The global governance literature has not critically engaged with this hierarchization or actors and power discrepancies.

3. Private and Public Environmental Governance

Connecting the takeaway from this look at several public and private governance attempts relating to the global environmental crisis, it becomes clear that the debates around these instruments take place in a power vacuum—that is, there is no emphasis on the "cui bono" question. While there is discussion of accountability and legitimacy, there are no discussions on hierarchy and power among stakeholders. As a result, what we see are the structural inequalities that critical theories such as ecofeminism and decolonial/postcolonial writers critique. The hierarchies of the neoliberal economy are accepted as is, and the hierarchies in the international system are accepted as a "given" rather than as a normative construct to be questioned.

Generally, the diversification of the global governance system to include different types of hybrid governance is seen as a positive development. Public governance can be slow and cumbersome, and private governance can engage in much more direct action, thus acting faster. Of course, in an idealized world, actors rationally admitting environmental challenges and responding to them is a positive development if they were to set aside their self-interest in the face of a threat to humanity and the planet. But when such governance tools are dissected and a critical lens is applied highlighting power, hierarchy, and inequality, it becomes clear that private governance is highly problematic. With its focus on transparency and accountability, these are, of course, two aims that nobody could possibly disagree with. However, oftentimes this emphasis takes away from and diverts attention away from issues of inclusion, equal access, and equal participation. Nevertheless, these are concepts that are more often than not excluded from any discourse or debate on private governance (and, of course, also public governance).

The environmental governance literature is largely descriptive of the evolution of governance without critically engaging with its hierarchical, colonial nature based on commodified nature-society relations and taking for granted the predominant power relations in global architecture. As a result, it cannot conceptually address the neoliberal and industry-centric basis of private governance and fully engage with the underlying issues. This is a debate that takes place in relation to particular governance instruments, but not in relation to the general rise of private governance and its distinction from public governance.

To be clear, this is not a claim that private governance is undesirable or that its impact is negative. From a problem-solving perspective in the Coxian sense, private governance is a very efficient and helpful tool in global cooperation and a supportive mechanism for public governance, being able to develop a mechanism that would not be possible in a public governance setting. This is an achievement.

However, the Coxian critique of problem-solving approaches holds true to this day, and when applying a critical Coxian frame, it is very clear that when we stop unquestioningly accepting the status quo of the current world order as a given that cannot be criticized or changed and we start applying a critical frame with a normative goal of overcoming unequal power relations, then questioning the economic primacy of current hierarchies and the inequalities they generate are urgent and pressing concerns. Since there already is a discourse on transparency, equity, justice, and accountability, there is a general consensus that these are valid concerns. Therefore, it follows easily and naturally that such rhetoric should be followed by the requisite analytical framework. This is a challenge to which heterarchy can and ought to rise.

References

Alcock, F. 2008. 'Conflicts and Coalitions within and Across the ENGO Community.' *Global Environmental Politics*, 8(4): 66–91.

Andonova, L. 2010. 'Public–Private Partnerships for the Earth: Politics and Patterns of Hybrid Authority in the Multilateral System.' *Global Environmental Politics*, 10(2): 25–53.

Betsill, M.M. and E. Corell. 2008. *NGO Diplomacy: The Influence of NGOs in International Environmental Negotiations*. Cambridge, MA: MIT Press.

Biermann, F. and P. Pattberg. 2012. *Global Environmental Governance Reconsidered. New Actors, Mechanisms, and Interlinkage*. Cambridge, MA: MIT Press.

Bulkeley, H. and P. Newell. 2010. *Governing Climate Change*. Routledge. doi: 10.4324/9780203858295

Chew, Sing. 2008. *The Recurring Dark Ages: Ecological Stress, Climate Changes, and System Transformation*. Vol. 2. Lanham, MD: AltaMira Press.

Conca, K. 2000. 'The WTO and the Undermining of Global Environmental Governance.' *Review of International Political Economy : RIPE*, 7(3): 484–494. doi: 10.1080/09692290050174051

Dimitrov, Radoslav S. September 2020. 'Empty Institutions in Global Environmental Politics.' *International Studies Review*, 22(3): 626–650. https://doi.org/10.1093/isr/viz029

Dobson, A. 2003. 'Social Justice and Environmental Sustainability: Ne'er the Twain Shall Meet?' In *Just Sustainabilities: Development in an Unequal World*, edited by Robert Agyeman, R. Bullard and B. Evans, Cambridge, MA: MIT Press, 83–98.

Ford, Lucy. 2018. 'Transnational Actors in Global Environmental Politics.' In *Global Environmental Politics—Concepts, Theories and Case Studies*, edited by Gabriela Kütting, Routledge: London and New York, 2nd edition.

Ford, Lucy and G. Kuetting. 2020. 'Discourses of Degrowth: New Value Systems for Global Environmental Governance?' *Ephemera: Theory and Politics in Organization*, 20(2): 283–306.

Humphreys, D. 2018. 'Forest Politics, Neoliberalism and the Limits of International Environmental Policy.' In *Global Environmental Politics—Concepts, Theories and Case Studies*, edited by Gabriela Kütting, Routledge: London and New York, 2nd edition, 247–268.

Hurrell, A. and B. Kingsbury. 1992. *The International Politics of the Environment, Actors, Interests, and Institutions*. Clarendon Press.

Kanie, N., P. Haas, S. Andresen, G. Auld, B. Cashore, P. Chasek et al. 2013. 'Green Pluralism: Lessons for Improved Environmental Governance in the 21st Century.' *Environment*, 55(5): 14–30.

Keck, M. and K. Sikkink. 1998. *Activists beyond Borders: Advocacy Networks in International Politics*. Ithaca, NY: Cornell University.

Keohane, Robert. 1984. *After Hegemony: Cooperation and Discord in the World Political Economy*. Princeton University Press.

Kimberly, R., Marion Suiseeya, Laura Zanotti and Kate Haapala. 2021. 'Navigating the Spaces between Human Rights and Justice: Cultivating Indigenous Representation in Global Environmental Governance.' *The Journal of Peasant Studies*. doi: 10.1080/03066150.2020.1835869

Krasner, Stephen. 1984. *International Regimes*.

Kuetting, Gabriela. 2000. *Environment, Society and International Relations*. Routledge.

Kuetting, Gabriela. 2010. *The Global Political Economy of Environment and Tourism*. Palgrave Macmillan.

Levy, D. and Peter Newell eds. 2005. *The Business of Global Environmental Governance*. Cambridge, MA: MIT Press.

Levy, D.L. and R. Kaplan. 2009. 'Corporate Social Responsibility and Theories of Global Governance.' In *The Oxford Handbook of Corporate Social Responsibility*, edited by A. Crane, A. McWilliams, D. Matten, J. Moon and D.S. Siegel, Oxford: OUP, 432–451.

Lipschutz, R. 2004. *Global Environmental Politics: Power, Perspectives and Practice*. Washington: QC Press.

Lipschutz, R. and J. Mayer. 1996. *Global Civil Society and Global Environmental Governance: The Politics of Nature from Place to Planet*. Albany, NY: State University of New York Press.

Newell, P. and M. Paterson. 2010. *Climate Capitalism*. Cambridge: Cambridge University Press.

Paterson, M. 2001. *Understanding Global Environmental Politics: Domination, Accumulation, Resistance*. Basingstoke, UK: Palgrave.

Paterson, M., D. Humphreys and L. Pettiford. 2003. 'Conceptualizing Global Environmental Governance: From Interstate Regimes to Counter-Hegemonic Struggles.' *Global Environmental Politics*, 3(2): 1–10.

Pattberg, P. 2006. 'Private Governance and the South: Lessons from Global Forest Politics.' *Third World Quarterly*, 27(4): 579–593.

Pattberg, P. and O. Widerberg. 2015. 'Theorising Global Environmental Governance: Key Findings and Future Questions.' *Millennium*, 43: 484–705.

Princen, T. and M. Finger. 1994. *Environmental NGOs in World Politics*. London: Routledge.

Purdey, S.J. 2010. *Economic Growth, the Environment and International Relations: The Growth Paradigm*, London: Routledge.

Rosenau, J.N. and E.O. Czempiel. 1992. *Governance without Government: Order and Change in World Politics*. Cambridge University Press.

Ruggie, J.G. 1975. 'International Responses to Technology: Concepts and Trends.' *International Organization*, 29(3): 557–583.

Ruggie, J.G. ed. 1993. *Multilateralism Matters: The Theory and Praxis of an Institutional Form*. New York: Columbia University.

Saurin, J. 1996. 'International Relations, Social Ecology and the Globalisation of Environmental Change.' In *The Environment and International Relations*, edited by John Vogler and Mark Imber, London: Routledge.

Selin, H. 2012. 'Global Environmental Governance and Regional Centers.' *Global Environmental Politics*, 12(3): 18–37.

Stevenson, H. and J. Dryzek. 2014. *Democratizing Global Climate Governance*. Cambridge: Cambridge University Press.

Suiseeya, M., L. Zantotti and K. Haapala. 2021. 'Navigating the Spaces between Human Rights and Justice: Cultivating Indigenous Representation in Global Environmental Governance.' *Journal of Peasant Studies.* doi: 1080/03066 150 2020. 1835869.

Thakur, R. and T.G. Weiss. 2015. 'Chapter 2, Framing Global Governance, Five Gaps.' In *The Global Studies Reader*, edited by M. Steger, New York, NY: Oxford University Press, 27–40.

Trudeau, H. et al. 2013. 'Insight from Global Environmental Governance: Forum.' *International Studies Review*, 15(4): 562–589.

Vogler, J. 2005. 'The European Contribution to Global Environmental Governance.' *International Affairs (London)*, 81(4): 835–850. doi: 10.1111/j.1468-2346.2005.00487.x.

Wapner, Paul. 1998. *Politics Beyond the State: Environmental Activism and World Civic Politics.* Albany, NY: SUNY Press.

Young, O., L. King and H. Schroeder eds. 2008. *Institutions and Environmental Change: Principal Findings, Applications and Research Frontiers.* Cambridge, MA: MIT Press.

Young, O., A. Orsini and J.F. Morin. 2013. 'Regime Complexes: A Buzz, a Boom, or a Boost for Global Governance?' *Global Governance*, 19: 27–39.

15

HETERARCHY AND GLOBAL INTERNET GOVERNANCE

The Case of ICANN

Hortense Jongen

Introduction

How do different micro- and meso-hierarchies operate and compete in global Internet governance? And to what extent do these hierarchies limit or transform state capacity? The Internet is a particularly interesting case for studying these questions. What started as a government-sponsored project, run by a small number of engineers and computer scientists, has become a global "network of networks" of widespread social, political, economic, and cultural significance. While it is widely recognized that the Internet needs some form of organization and regulation, states cannot fulfill this role on their own. Instead, due to its decentralized and deterritorialized nature, a transnational network consisting of engineers and other private actors has historically played a leading role in the development of this global technology. This does not mean that states are irrelevant. On the contrary, the US government has been key in the early development of the Internet. Recent academic work additionally demonstrates how states increasingly seek to reassert authority over the Internet or even make normative claims to digital sovereignty within their territorial borders (e.g. Deibert & Crete-Nishihata, 2013; Haggart et al., 2021; Kohl, 2017; Pohle & Thiel, 2020). Hence, states can be best considered among several important actors in the global Internet regime.

So how can we make sense of this complex of state- and non-state actors that collectively governs the Internet? Joseph Nye (2014) describes the management of global cybersecurity (in which Internet governance is situated) as a 'regime complex,' in which a host of different institutions (i.e. regimes) co-exist and overlap in a specific issue area (see also: Alter & Raustiala, 2018). Some of its constitutive elements take more hierarchical forms, while others consist of more loosely organized, informal practices and institutions. While these different actors and institutions might compete for authority, they can also form networks

DOI: 10.4324/9781003352617-17

to coordinate their activities, collaborate, or even engage in *ad hoc* collective problem-solving, what Milton Mueller and his co-authors (2013) refer to as "networked governance." Such networks and connections are formed among institutions operating on different scales and sectors, and are often volatile. Central to this form of "polycentric governance" is the ambiguous hierarchy among the constitutive elements of a regime complex, the dispersion of power among them, and the absence of a central coordinating authority (Scholte, 2017).

This chapter looks at global Internet governance through a different but complementary analytical lens: "heterarchy." Heterarchy is defined as "the coexistence and conflict between differently structured micro- and meso- quasi-hierarchies that compete and overlap not only across borders but also across economic-financial sectors and social groupings" (Belmonte & Cerny, 2021, p. 235). While many institutions involved in global Internet governance can be considered heterarchical in nature, this chapter focuses on one of them: the Internet Corporation for Assigned Names and Numbers (ICANN). ICANN offers an interesting case for studying heterarchy. First, in contrast to traditional multilateralism in which authority is located in states, ICANN makes policy using a multistakeholder approach, involving a range of private, public, and civil society actors (Antonova, 2008; Flyverbom, 2011; Jongen & Scholte, 2021). As such, ICANN is a prime example of how states become networked with other stakeholders in transnational policymaking processes. Second, ICANN, a *private* organization, performs several technical functions that are crucial for the proper functioning of the global *public* good: the Internet. Specifically, ICANN develops policy for the global Domain Name System (DNS) and manages the Internet Assigned Numbers Authority (IANA) functions, which, in addition to the DNS, concern Internet Protocol (IP) numbers and protocol parameters (i.e., standards that enable the transmission of data on the Internet). While at first sight ICANN's responsibilities might appear largely technical, the administration and management of the DNS is inherently political and raises a number of public policy challenges related to free speech, privacy, and (cyber)security, among others (Bradshaw & DeNardis, 2018). Third, ICANN is emblematic of how state capacity in global Internet regulation has been transformed. Particularly relevant in this regard is the IANA stewardship transition, which transferred oversight of the IANA functions from the United States National Telecommunications and Information Administration (an agency of the US Department of Commerce) to the multistakeholder community in ICANN, a process described by the US government as the "culmination of a nearly 20-year effort to privatize the Internet domain name system (DNS)."[1] As such, ICANN is characteristic of the global shift in decision-making authority from public to private actors, the latter of which carry increasing autonomy in global affairs (Cutler et al., 1999; Hall & Biersteker, 2002).

To study heterarchy in ICANN, this chapter first introduces its multistakeholder governance model. It subsequently sheds light on the different micro- and meso-quasi-hierarchies that operate within ICANN's multistakeholder regime. Next, the chapter discusses how ICANN is situated within global Internet governance, paying specific attention to the varying social structures (discourses, narratives, and norms) that define what actors should have authority in global Internet governance and what institutional forms they should take.

1. Multistakeholderism in ICANN

In order to identify how different hierarchies operate within ICANN, we need to understand its multistakeholder model. While the multistakeholder principle has been central to ICANN's policymaking activities since its establishment in 1998, the organization remained strongly tied to a state actor, the US Department of Commerce, for most of its existence. Only by 2016, nearly two decades after its creation and following a lengthy transition process, was full oversight over ICANN and the IANA functions transferred from the US government to the global multistakeholder community.

Multistakeholderism can be best described as a mode of global regulation that seeks to tackle a policy problem by bringing together different actors that have an interest in this issue. Thus, unlike traditional multilateralism, policy-making authority is not solely (or at times not even at all) located in states, but shared between at least two different types of actors, such as academe, businesses, civil society, governments, intergovernmental organizations, or technical experts. This mode of global governance is not unique to ICANN. From the early days of the Internet, many key institutions have made policies or taken decisions using the multistakeholder principle. Examples include the Internet Engineering Task Force (IETF), the Regional Internet Registries (RIRs), and the United Nations-led Internet Governance Forum (IGF). Global multistakeholder arrangements can also be found in other policy areas, such as sustainable forestry (the Forest Stewardship Council), corporate social responsibility (the Global Compact), and the regulation of conflict diamonds (the Kimberley Process), amongst others. These global initiatives do show substantial variation, however, in terms of the institutional forms they take, the types of actors that they involve, as well as the authority relations that exist amongst these actors (Gleckman, 2018; Raymond & DeNardis, 2015; Scholte, 2020a). For example, state actors have comparably more influence in the United Nations-led IGF than in ICANN, although the IGF does not produce binding policy outcomes. The more technically oriented IETF, in contrast, assigns no formal role or responsibilities to state actors and primarily involves technical experts and corporate actors in its operations. The limited role assigned to governments in multistakeholder arrangements is particularly interesting, as states are traditionally seen as the holders of legitimate authority.

Different stakeholders are represented at ICANN: academe, businesses, civil society, governments, technical experts, and the regular Internet user. These stakeholders, in turn, are organized in various supporting organizations (SOs) and advisory committees (ACs): (1) the Address Supporting Organization (ASO), (2) the At-Large Advisory Committee (ALAC), (3) the Country-Code Names Supporting Organization (ccNSO), (4) the Governmental Advisory Committee (GAC),

(5) the Generic Names Supporting Organization (GNSO), (6) the Root Server Security and Stability Advisory Committee (RSSAC), and (7) the Security and Stability Advisory Committee (SSAC). The GNSO, which is the largest SO, consists of different constituency and stakeholder groups, some of which represent commercial interests (e.g., registrars, registries, business users, intellectual property, and internet service providers etc.), while the Non-Commercial Stakeholder Group gives voice to non-commercial interests.

It goes beyond the scope of this chapter to discuss each of these ACs and SOs in detail. Noteworthy, however, is the representation of different public and private interests at ICANN (see also Jongen & Scholte, 2021). Governmental interests are represented in the GAC and—together with academe, business, and civil society—in the ccNSO, which is responsible for developing policy around country code Top Level Domains such as .in or. de. As mentioned before, private actors are primarily active in the Commercial Stakeholder Group of the GNSO, while academe and civil society are represented in the Non-Commercial Stakeholder Group. Further, technical experts participate in ASO, RSSAC, and SSAC, and individual internet users participate through At-Large. Final decision-making authority rests with the ICANN board, which consists of sixteen voting members and four non-voting liaisons, from all constituency groups.

Due to the involvement of a variety of state- and non-state actors in policy-making, multistakeholderism in ICANN is often framed as a bottom-up, pluralist, consensus-based approach. At the same time, it is not without its critics. Jeanette Hofmann (2016) refers to multistakeholderism as a fiction, "a discursive artefact that aims to smooth contradictory and messy practices into a coherent story about collaborative transnational policymaking" (p. 44). Others argue that, rather than dispersing power globally among different stakeholders, multistakeholderism empowers already powerful actors in global Internet governance, such as the US and the private sector (Carr, 2015; see also Glen, 2014; Palladino & Santaniello, 2021). This criticism raises questions about the authority relations that exist between the different actors and stakeholder groups within ICANN, which will be explored in the next section.

2. Heterarchy in ICANN

One of the key defining features of heterarchy is the co-existence, competition and collaboration amongst different micro- and meso-hierarchies that operate on, and cut across, different scales and sectors. This chapter understands hierarchies as "any system through which actors are organized into vertical relations of super- and subordination" (Bially Mattern & Zarakol, 2016, p. 624). While these vertical relationships can be rooted in the distribution of formal authority between different actors, they can also be of an informal character. Consider, for example, inequalities based on age, class (e.g., social capital, wealth, education), ethnicity/race, geography, or gender.

Let's start with a more narrow understanding of hierarchy, conceived as the vertical distribution of political authority between actors. As mentioned before, historically a state actor (the US) maintained a privileged position vis-à-vis ICANN, as the IANA functions were under direct oversight of the US government. Amidst growing pressure from state- and non-state actors who questioned whether a single state should have disproportionate power over this global technology, the US agreed to give up unilateral oversight of the DNS infrastructure (Becker, 2019). However, it did have a say over the conditions under which it was up to give this authority. With backing from several other governments, including Canada and many European states, it staunchly resisted the transfer of the IANA functions to a governmental- or intergovernmental body, such as the UN. Instead, it advocated for these responsibilities to be passed on to the multistakeholder community, thereby promoting the privatization and transnationalization of the global Internet infrastructure.

As mentioned before, ICANN assembles different types of stakeholders, which are organized in trans-sectoral advisory committees and supporting organizations. In principle there exists no formal hierarchy among different stakeholder groups. However, governments are assigned remarkably limited competences and fulfill only an advisory role. While all community groups are represented in the ICANN board, not all members have voting power. Specifically, the board member appointed by the GAC, which represents governmental interests, has a non-voting seat.[2] Further, while the GAC can issue advice to the ICANN board, the board is in the position to reject this advice—although in practice this has never happened (Cavalli & Scholte, 2021). The restricted role of governments in ICANN fits a broader trend of resistance to government involvement in global Internet governance. However, it also raises some concerns. In contrast to multilateralism, most global multistakeholder initiatives place no or only limited restrictions on participation and have no built-in geographical balance (Gleckman, 2018). As a result, the majority of ICANN participants hail from businesses and technical circles in Europe and North America. The marginalization of governments raises the question whether private actors can adequately represent the public interest (Cavalli & Scholte, 2021), and raises concerns about regional inequalities, as most Internet businesses—or at least Internet businesses represented at ICANN—are located in the global north.

Moving beyond a narrow conception of hierarchy, what other hierarchies can we observe in ICANN? While participation in ICANN is in principle open to everyone, not everyone is in the position to participate in its policy-making processes. Aspiring ICANN community members need time and resources to attend ICANN's triannual meetings around the world, which are often held in expensive locations. This disadvantages stakeholders from lower-income countries or those representing less financially endowed organizations or interests. Further, substantial technical expertise and advanced English are required to participate in ICANN, as discussions tend to be highly specialized and are predominantly held in English (Jongen & Scholte, 2022). As such, ICANN has witnessed the formation of a transnational elite network that has a lot of influence in policy-making and standard-setting activities related to the Internet (Scholte, 2020b), but which can be hard to penetrate for outsiders or newcomers.

ICANN is not unaware of this issue. For several years, the organization has operated programs to encourage participation from underrepresented groups, offering travel support and mentoring under the ICANN Fellowship program[3] and the NextGen program.[4] ICANN additionally provides translation services at its meetings, and offers opportunities for community members to attend meetings online. Yet, even if in theory everyone can participate in ICANN, this does not mean that everyone has equal influence in its policymaking processes. Empirical research shows that participants in ICANN perceive inequalities in influence between different social categories, which cut across different scales and sectors (Jongen & Scholte, 2022). Notably, white, older-aged men from the Global North with strong English language skills are not only more numerous at ICANN meetings, but are also viewed as more influential in this multistakeholder model.

3. ICANN as a Heterarchical Institution in Global Internet Governance

Having shown how different hierarchies operate within ICANN, how is ICANN situated within global Internet governance? Looking at global Internet governance through an institutionalist lens, ICANN co-exists, collaborates, and competes with numerous private and public actors at, and across, different scales and sectors. The Internet Society (ISOC), a private, not-for-profit organization that provides an institutional home to the IETF, speaks of an "Internet ecosystem," rather than a single system governing the Internet.[5] These different actors and institutions include nationally- and transnationally-operating firms (Internet service providers, intellectual property firms, registries, registrars, etc.), civil society organizations, universities, national governments, other global and regional multistakeholder initiatives (e.g. the IETF, the IGF, the RIRs, and the World Wide Web Consortium, W3C), and intergovernmental organizations (e.g. the UN International Telecommunication Union, ITU, and the World Intellectual Property Organization, WIPO).

Many of the above institutions and organizations have overlapping memberships and mandates, and participate in or observe multiple transnational and intergovernmental policy-making bodies and standard-setting processes. Hence, the boundaries between these actors and institutions become blurred. For example, the IETF, which plays a key role in developing Internet standards, has a liaison on the ICANN board. The five RIRs, which are responsible for allocating IP numbers, are represented in the ASO constituency group at ICANN. Moreover, many members of the ICANN community also participate in the IETF and the RIRs. While this activity helps to forge cross-border, trans-sectoral, and trans-scalar networks, it also puts in a strategic position those individuals and actors who have the time, resources and technical expertise to participate in multiple global sites of policy-making and standard-setting. Scholte (2020b), in this regard, speaks of a global elite network, composed of affluent institutions and organizations in the Internet ecosystem that have substantial influence in this area.

The abovementioned actors and organizations do not exist in a vacuum, but are situated in a social environment. In line with constructivist theories, global social structures (e.g. certain discourses, narratives and norms) define what types of actors or institutions (public/private/hybrid) should, or should not, have authority in a specific issue area, and what forms these institutions should take (Bernstein, 2011; Bernstein & Cashore, 2007; Scholte, 2018). Likewise, these discourses and norms might legitimize collaborations, interactions, and hierarchies amongst certain actors and institutions, whilst delegitimizing others. The prominent position of multistakeholderism in Internet governance today therefore perhaps does not come as a surprise. It corresponds to (or at least is discursively framed so as to correspond to) global norms of democratizing global governance and "stakeholder democracy" (Bernstein 2011, p. 27; also *Bäckstrand, 2006*). Multistakeholderism is additionally central to legitimizing discourses and narratives promoted by several powerful state- and non-state actors in global Internet governance. These claims include the notions that multistakeholderism (as opposed to government-led modes of regulation) is crucial for preserving Internet freedom and openness;[6] that multistakeholderism "has grown from the Internet's own DNA"[7] and reflects the key architectural principles of the Internet;[8] and that privatization is good for business and therefore for society at large. With regards to the latter, multistakeholderism in ICANN not only speaks to norms and discourses around global democracy, but also fits a broader neoliberal discourse (Chenou, 2014).

While some norms are widely accepted today, others are contested. Likewise, prevailing norms can change over time. Such normative contestation is widespread in Internet governance, where different types of actors seek to create, legitimize, and challenge a variety of norms. A recent special issue even speaks of "normfare" in global Internet governance today (Radu et al., 2021). Of specific interest for this chapter are the tensions between norms related to the privatization and transnationalization of the Internet, on the one hand, and the norm of sovereignty (i.e., the notion that governments are the legitimate holders of authority), on the other, which reflects the dialectic between global integration and territorial fragmentation. Political discourse increasingly speaks of "digital sovereignty," portraying state involvement as crucial for the protection of citizens' interests, for example, in relation to security threats and privacy-related matters (Pohle & Thiel, 2020). These calls for greater government involvement in Internet governance are not exclusive to authoritarian states (Deibert & Crete-Nishihata, 2013; Haggart et al., 2021). Also liberal democracies progressively seek to control the flow of information on the Internet, reportedly to preserve democratic values and to protect citizens against the spread of disinformation.[9] In addition to attempts to reassert control over content on the Internet, several state and non-state actors seek to exert power over the technical infrastructure of the Internet. Bradshaw and DeNardis (2018), for instance, show how the DNS infrastructure is increasingly politicized and at risk of being co-opted by different state- and non-state actors. As the management of the DNS has significant socioeconomic and political significance, it has transformed into a site of (geopolitical) power struggles between different types of actors (Bradshaw & DeNardis, 2018).

As mentioned before, multistakeholderism does not reject the importance of states in Internet governance *per se*. However, it does offer a fundamentally different outlook on their role. After all, states are just one among several stakeholders in ICANN, and some multistakeholder arrangements do not formally involve governments in the first place. The multistakeholder norm has not remained unchallenged. Over time, several states, including the Russian and Saudi Arabian governments, have called for state-led modes of Internet governance, such as the intergovernmental ITU, to assume more responsibilities in the Internet infrastructure (Glen, 2014; Cavalli & Scholte 2021). As mentioned before, normative claims to digital sovereignty are on the rise. Even though the multistakeholder community at ICANN has been mandated to manage the IANA functions and develop policy for the DNS, its authority cannot be taken for granted. In principle, any actor or institution with similar capacity and resources (including the ITU) could take over these tasks.

It remains, however, to be seen whether we will observe a normative shift from multistakeholderism to multilateralism. First of all, despite several governments' outspoken preference for the ITU as the main site for global decision-making on Internet-related matters, multistakeholderism receives backing from many powerful state- and non-state actors. Even governments that were initially skeptical of this governance model, such as the Chinese and Indian governments, now actively participate in ICANN (Cavalli & Scholte, 2021). This has helped solidify multistakeholderism as a governance framework. Second, and relatedly, also the intergovernmental UN has endorsed multistakeholderism as the prevailing framework for global Internet governance.[10] This underscores the notion that multilateralism and multistakeholderism are not necessarily adversarial, opposite ends of the regulatory spectrum, but can co-exist or even collaborate. In fact, as mentioned before, several multistakeholder initiatives, such as the IGF, operate under the auspices of an intergovernmental organization. Third, a recent, large-scale survey of elite perceptions toward different global governance institutions finds that multistakeholderism in ICANN stands its ground among several multilateral arrangements in terms of its perceived legitimacy, including among Russian elites (Scholte et al., 2021; Jongen & Scholte, 2021). It should be acknowledged, however, that a large share of survey respondents indicates to be unaware of, or insufficiently informed about, ICANN to be able to assess its legitimacy.

4. Conclusion

What does this case study of ICANN tell us about heterarchy in global Internet governance? This chapter has shown that, despite the continued privatization and transnationalization of the Internet over the past decades, state capacity has not necessarily *eroded*. Rather, it has been *transformed*. States have become increasingly networked with other stakeholders in transnational policymaking arrangements, including multistakeholder initiatives. To some extent this has constrained them, as some multistakeholder initiatives only allow for limited participation from governments, and are considered to privilege private interests. However, this chapter has also shown that multistakeholderism in ICANN receives backing not just from the private sector, but also from many powerful states, including from governments that were initially skeptical of this governance arrangement. Moreover, the US, supported by several other states, actively advocated for the transfer of the IANA functions to the multistakeholder community in ICANN rather than to the intergovernmental ITU. Thus, (some) state actors have played an important role in defining what types of actors should have authority in global Internet governance and what institutional forms (e.g., multistakeholderism as opposed to multilateralism) they should take, even when their own role in these arrangements might be more limited. Time will therefore tell whether, and if so how, recent calls from some governments for more "digital sovereignty" will affect the regulatory landscape in the global Internet ecosystem.

Notes

1 www.ntia.doc.gov/other-publication/2016/fact-sheet-iana-stewardship-transition-explained Accessed 14–6–2021.
2 Other non-voting seats on the ICANN board are held by the IETF liaison to the ICANN board, as well as two supporting organizations that bring together primarily representatives from technical circles: RSSAC and SSAC.
3 www.icann.org/fellowshipprogram Accessed 10–6–2021.
4 www.icann.org/public-responsibility-support/nextgen Accessed 10–6–2021
5 www.internetsociety.org/wp-content/uploads/2017/09/factsheet_ecosystem.pdf Accessed 24–6–2021.
6 See for example the fact sheet about the IANA transition, provided by the NTIA: Fact Sheet: The IANA Stewardship Transition Explained | National Telecommunications and Information Administration (doc.gov) Accessed 27–7–2021.
7 www.internetsociety.org/resources/doc/2016/internet-governance-why-the-multi stakeholder-approach-works/ Accessed 30–6–2021.
8 Ziewitz and Brown (2013) identify four principles: 'openness, interoperability, redundancy, and end-to-end' (p. 15).
9 An example of the latter is the speech delivered by French President Emmanuel Macron at the 13th annual meeting of the IGF, calling for more state involvement in global Internet regulation (Macron, 2018).
10 Specifically, at the second phase of the UN-sponsored World Summit on the Information Society (WSIS), held in Tunis in 2005, multistakeholderism was recognized as the main governance approach for global Internet regulation (ITU, 2005). The ITU has additionally recognized the importance of the WSIS principles and multistakeholderism in various resolutions adopted at the 2010 plenipotentiary conference in Guadalajara, amongst others (ITU, 2010).

References

Alter, Karen J. & Kal Raustiala (2018) The Rise of International Regime Complexity, *Annual Review of Law and Social Science*, 14 (1), pp. 18.2–18.21.
Antonova, Slavka (2008) *Powerscape of Internet Governance: How was Global Multistakeholderism Invented in ICANN?* Saarbrücken: VDM.

Bäckstrand, Karin (2006) Democratizing Global Environmental Governance? Stakeholder Democracy After the World Summit on Sustainable Development, *European Journal of International Relations*, 12 (4), pp. 467–498.

Becker, Manuel (2019) When Public Principals Give Up Control over Private Agents: The New Independence of ICANN in Internet Governance, *Regulation & Governance*, 13 (4), pp. 561–576.

Belmonte, Rosalba & Philip G. Cerny (2021) Heterarchy: Toward Paradigm Shift in World Politics, *Journal of Political Power*, 14 (1), pp. 235–257.

Bernstein, Steven (2011) Legitimacy in Intergovernmental and Non-State Global Governance, *Review of International Political Economy*, 18 (1), pp. 17–51.

Bernstein, Steven & Benjamin Cashore (2007) Can Non-State Global Governance be Legitimate? An Analytical Framework, *Regulation & Governance*, 1, pp. 347–371.

Bially Mattern, Janice & Ayşe Zarakol (2016) Hierarchies in World Politics, *International Organization*, 70 (3), pp. 623–654.

Bradshaw, Samantha & Laura DeNardis (2018) The Politicization of the Internet's Domain Name System: Implications for Internet Security, Universality, and Freedom, *New Media and Society*, 20 (1), pp. 332–350.

Carr, Madeline (2015) Power Plays in Global Internet Governance, *Millennium: Journal of International Studies*, 43 (2), pp. 640–659.

Cavalli, Olga & Jan Aart Scholte (2021) The Role of States in Internet Governance in ICANN. In: Haggart, Blayne, Tusikov, Natasha & Jan Aart Scholte (eds.), *Power and Authority in Internet Governance. Return of the State?* London: Routledge.

Chenou, Jean-Marie (2014) From Cyber-Libertarianism to Neoliberalism: Internet Exceptionalism, and the Institutionalisation of Internet Governance in the 1990s, *Globalizations*, 11 (2), pp. 205–223.

Cutler, Claire, Haufler, Virginia & Tony Porter (eds) (1999) *Private Authority and International Affairs*, Albany: State University of New York Press.

Deibert, Ronald J. & Masashi Crete-Nishihata (2013) Global Governance and the Spread of Cyberspace Controls, *Global Governance*, 18 (3), pp. 339–361.

Flyverbom, Mikkel (2011) *The Power of Networks: Organizing the Global Politics of the Internet*, Cheltenham: Elgar.

Gleckman, Harris (2018) *Multistakeholder Governance and Democracy: A Global Challenge*, New York: Routledge.

Glen, Carol (2014) Internet Governance: Territorializing Cyberspace? *Politics and Policy*, 5 (42), pp. 635–657.

Haggart, Blayne, Tusikov, Natasha & Jan Aart Scholte (eds) (2021) *Power and Authority in Internet Governance. Return of the State?* Routledge: London.

Hall, Rodney Bruce & Thomas J. Biersteker (eds) (2002) *The Emergence of Private Authority in Global Governance*, Cambridge: Cambridge University Press.

Hofmann, Jeanette (2016) Multi-stakeholderism in Internet Governance: Putting a Fiction into Practice, *Journal of Cyber Policy*, 1 (1), pp. 29–49.

ITU (2005) *World Summit on the Information Society Outcome Documents Geneva 2003— Tunis 2005*. Available at: www.itu.int/net/wsis/outcome/booklet.pdf

ITU (2010) *Final Acts of the Plenipotentiary Conference (Guadalajara, 2010)*. Available at: www.itu.int/en/ITU-D/Regional-Presence/Europe/Documents/Resolution%20 126%20(Rev.%20Guadalajara,%202010).pdf

Jongen, Hortense & Jan Aart Scholte (2021) Legitimacy in Multistakeholder Global Governance at ICANN, *Global Governance*, 27 (2), pp. 298–324.

Jongen, Hortense & Jan Aart Scholte (2022) Inequality and Legitimacy in Global Governance: An Empirical Study, *European Journal of International Relations*, e-pub ahead of print. doi: 10.1177/13540661221098218

Kohl, Uta (ed) (2017) *The Net and the Nation State. Multidisciplinary Perspectives on Internet Governance*, Cambridge: Cambridge University Press.

Macron, Emmanuel (2018) *IGF Speech by Emmanuel Macron*. Available at www.intgovfo rum.org/multilingual/content/igf-2018-speech-by-french-president-emmanuel-macron

Mueller, Milton, Andreas Schmidt & Brenden Kuerbis (2013) Internet Security and Networked Governance in International Relations, *International Studies Review*, 15, pp. 86–104.

Negro, Gianluigi (2020) A History of Chinese Global Internet Governance and Its Relations with ITU and ICANN, *Chinese Journal of Communication*, 13 (1), pp. 104–212.

Nye, Joseph S. (2014) The Regime Complex for Managing Global Cyber Activities, *The Centre for International Governance; Global Commission on Internet Governance: Paper Series*. Accessed 7-6-2021.

Palladino, Nicola & Mauro Santaniello (2021) *Legitimacy, Power, and Inequalities in the Multistakeholder Internet Governance. Analyzing IANA Transition*, Cham: Palgrave Macmillan.

Pohle, Julia & Thorsten Thiel (2020) Digital Sovereignty, *Internet Policy Review*, 9 (4), published online first.

Radu, Roxana, Matthias C. Kettemann, Trisha Meyer & Jamal Shahin (2021) Normfare: Norm Entrepreneurship in Internet Governance, *Telecommunications Policy*, 45 (6), published online first.

Raymond, Mark & Laura DeNardis (2015) Multistakeholderism: Anatomy of an Inchoate Global Institution, *International Theory*, 7 (3), pp. 572–616.

Scholte, Jan Aart (2017) Polycentrism and Democracy in Internet Governance. In: Uta Kohl (ed.), *The Net and the Nation State. Multidisciplinary Perspectives on Internet Governance*, Cambridge: Cambridge University Press.

Scholte, Jan Aart (2018) Social Structure and Global Governance. In: Tallberg, Jonas, Bäckstrand, Karin & Jan Aart Scholte (eds.), *Legitimacy in Global Governance: Sources, Processes, and Consequences*, Oxford: Oxford University Press, pp. 75–100.

Scholte, Jan Aart (2020a) *Multistakeholderism. Filling the Global Governance Gap? Research Overview for the Global Challenges Foundation*. Available at: https://global challenges.org/wp-content/uploads/Research-review-global-multistakeholderism-scholte-2020.04.06.pdf

Scholte, Jan Aart (2020b) Rethinking Hegemony as Complexity. In: Dutkiewicz, Piotr, Tom Casier & Jan Aart Scholte (eds.), *Hegemony and World Order. Reimagining Power in Global Politics*. Abingdon: Routledge, pp. 78–97.

Scholte, Jan Aart, Verhaegen, Soetkin & Jonas Tallberg (2021) Elite Attitudes and the Future of Global Governance, *International Affairs*, 97 (3), pp. 861–886.

Ten Oever, Niels (2019) Productive Contestation, Civil Society, and Global Governance: Human Rights as a Boundary Object in ICANN, *Policy & Internet*, 11 (1), pp. 37–60.

Ziewitz, Malte & Ian Brown (2013) A Pre-History of Internet Governance. In: Ian Brown (ed.), *Research Handbook on Governance of the Internet*, Cheltenham: Edward Elgar, pp. 3–26.

16

HETERARCHY IN THE MEXICAN COMPETITION NETWORK

The Case of COFECE and IFC

Alejandra Salas Porras

Introduction

The superiority of a society centered in the market, competition and the individual is the main idea underlying all the policies that reached consensus in the 1980s around the neoliberal project which validates the commodification and appropriation of collective and state property and naturalizes the conviction that—as Margaret Thatcher contended—there is nothing else to society than the sum of individual interests, preferences and desires (Springer, 2016; Jessop, 2012; Crouch, 2011). Regulation of competition constitutes, as a result, one of the most important areas of neoliberal economic governance, whose basic assumption is that competition is good for the economy and consumers alike, and the most efficient mechanism of the market. But neoliberal currents of thought view competition in a different way: while the Austrian School thinks competition is the natural outcome of a free market, ignoring or belittling the contradictory trends it unleashes—i.e., concentration of markets, mergers and acquisitions (M&A), entry barriers, cartels and other forms of collusion—that paradoxically end up hindering or distorting competition; in contrast, the Freiburg School (known as Ordoliberalism) contends the state has to create, or support, a set of institutions in order to balance these contradictory trends (Cerny, 2016, 2019). In addition, the Chicago School justifies concentration and anticompetitive practices when they lead to lower prices making large corporations not liable to antitrust legislation even if they entail market dominance and predatory prices. Thus, 'consumer welfare' becomes the most important objective of antitrust law (Crane, 2014), and not curbing the market power of large corporations as was originally intended in anti-monopoly traditional institutions (Khan, 2017).

These schools "agree that competition cannot be taken for granted, but effectively needs to be enforced upon the market and its agents by regulation"

DOI: 10.4324/9781003352617-18

(Buch-Hansen and Wigger, 2011, p. 3) and that politically independent agencies should be responsible for this task, to avoid making decisions following social, political or protectionist considerations. But while some anti-competitive practices are considered unacceptable (for example, cartels and state aid) because they interfere with the price mechanism, those involving greater concentration are often tolerated to a greater extent as they are regarded as essential for economies of scale and scope which, in turn, bring about efficiency gains that benefit consumers with lower prices and higher quality products. Consequently, merger and acquisitions are allowed, though the ordoliberal version opposes them if they entail an uncontrolled "dominant" position in the market. However, the point at which concentration reduces the number of competitors, encouraging anti-competitive behavior and affecting competition can be the object of discretionary practices, such as defining when to curb dominant positions in the market. Thus, the difference between ordoliberal and outward neoliberal policies regarding competition is subtle and ambiguous and stems from the fundamental tensions in the process of accumulation. For this reason, ordoliberal regulation has been considered a myth in the literature on competition (Akman and Kassim, 2010; Buch-Hansen and Wigger, 2011, p. 3).

On these contradictory ideological and shaky grounds, a network of organizations has expanded throughout the world involving national and transnational technocracies across regions and countries to push forward a heterarchic form of competition governance.[1] Accordingly, the network of organizations governing competition has become increasingly complex displaying a heterarchic structure, and the technocratic arguments they brandish tend to obscure the relations of power underlying the set of nodes which realign across time, countries, and particular issues.

The purpose of this chapter is to discover the relations of power characteristic of competition policy networks, which in Mexico show a predominantly heterarchic structure, involving functionally diversified and complementary organizations which nonetheless share a similar vision of neoliberalism, that is one in which the market, and competition in particular, require a set of specialized and autonomous regulatory institutions. It is argued that in the absence of a hierarchic structure, this common neoliberal vision is the main source of coherence in a complex, multi-level, network where technocratic and corporate elites intertwine, uphold and elaborate pro-competition preferences. Within this network communities of experts theorize on the significance of competition for the economy intertwining state and corporate elites with lawyers, consultants and academics together shaping and sustaining a complex heterarchic structure. In the context of conferences and discussions, they reach common views around basic ideas and concepts regarding competition in general, but also in particular sectors. They weave in this way sets of

> heterarchical institutions and processes [that] are characterized by increasing autonomy and special interest capture . . . between a range of private

actors and meso- and micro-hierarchies, institutions and processes. The result is the decreasing capacity of macro-states to control both domestic and transnational political/economic processes.

(Cerny 2021, p. 2)

Thus, organizations belonging to this pro-competition network "compete with the state's ability to establish rules, control borders, formulate and implement public policies autonomously, and go beyond states' boundaries and create their own sovereign system" (Belmonte and Cerny, 2021, p. 13). They become, in this way, "extra-state authorities," complementing regulatory functions that institutionalize large corporate interests and paradoxically undermine the neoliberal ideology they espouse. They make it incoherent and contradictory revealing the narrow margin of autonomy of the new regulatory authorities as they find ways to justify the monopoly practices and interests they defend.

To pursue the previous argument, this chapter is structured around the following sections: First, I outline the historical background of competition institutions in Mexico, and the relevance they gained when neoliberal, market-led, strategies became dominant in the country; in the second section I sketch the heterarchic structure of competition networks as they realign around several compelling cases regarding trusts, state aid, mergers and dominant positions; and in the last section, I analyze the origins, preferences and main connections of the elites controlling the most central nodes of the Mexican competition network, particularly those cutting across different issues (i.e., Cofece and IMCO). Following a critical perspective (Harrod, 2001), I aim to discover throughout these sections how the organizations that are part of the Mexican competition network (think tanks, professional and interest associations, consultants, among the most important) strengthen an ideological view of competition that supports large corporate interests and weakens the developmental role of the state.

1. Background of Competition Institutions in Mexico

Efforts to control monopoly practices date back to the 1857 Mexican Constitution, and since then anti-monopoly language was reiterated in most economic reforms (the 1917 Mexican Constitution, the 1934 Monopolies Law, and the 1950 Law on Economic Powers) (Slottje and Prowse, 2001). In practice, however, large influential business groups or cartels and state-owned monopolies were protected from competition with price controls, barriers to entry into several industries, and strong state supervision. Consequently, high levels of concentration prevailed in almost all areas of the economy and most regulatory intentions were offset by politically powerful interests (Salas Porras, 2017; Ros, 1993).

It is in the context of neoliberal reforms and, particularly, the negotiations for the North American Trade Agreement (NAFTA) when in 1993 a new Federal Law of Economic Competition (LFCE, by its Spanish initials) was drafted and the main regulatory bodies to enforce it were created.[2] The law prohibited cartels and abuses of dominance, and merger reviews were required, as well as a specialized agency to act as a watchdog (Comisión Federal de Competencia, CFC). As the law followed the guidelines of antitrust agencies in other countries and antimonopoly overseeing was not a deep-rooted tradition in Mexico's civic society, many of CFC decisions were overturned by courts and there was very little progress in controlling monopoly practices. The reforms of 2006 and 2011 increased substantially the powers of the CFC to investigate and fine monopoly practices (Aydin, 2016).

However, until 2013 regulatory agencies were reformed to make them autonomous from the government, giving way to the Federal Competition Commission (Cofece) and the Federal Institute of Communications (IFC), an independent regulator responsible for enforcing competition in telecommunications and broadcasting. In addition, antitrust courts were introduced and as a consequence multiple law firms specialized in antitrust legislation mushroomed interpretating and further elaborating on competition regulation. In 2014, a new competition law increased Cofece's powers (Aydin, 2016).

Competition regulation became since then a central piece of the market-led reforms and several private, public and quasi-public organizations became part of a pro-competition network—the Alliance in Favor of Competition (Alianza por la Competencia),—created in 2014 with the purpose of promoting the principles and culture of competition in the economy, developing best economic practices among the business community, government and civil society. This Alliance involved national and international organizations, including among the former several think tanks (such as IMCO and CIDAC), academic institutions (CIDE and Instituto de la Judicatura Federal, IJF), professional associations (particularly lawyers associations), judges, magistrates and specialized courts; and among the latter, the Latin American Competition Forum, the USAID, OECD, IDB, and the WB (IMCO, 2014).[3]

All of them have articulated increasingly sophisticated competition rules, the great majority of which require technocratic knowledge that has been transferred and adapted from international organizations, including the International Competition Network (ICN), the American Bar Association Section of Antitrust Law and the International Competition Policy Advisory Committee (ICPAC).[4] The main idea put forward throughout this network is competition as the natural and apolitical consequence of, and condition for, the free market.

2. Heterarchic Structures in Competition Networks

As Crumley (2015) contends, heterarchy stands in a dialectical relationship with hierarchy. While hierarchy is associated with order and stability, heterarchy is associated with disorder and chaos. The former is constructed by national state elites while the latter is assembled by a network of national and transnational technocracies who together with corporate elites, lawyers and other professionals wield scientific and abstract arguments that conceal relations of power, and "serve different social purposes that benefit certain societal groups more than others" (Buch-Hansen and Wigger, 2011, p. 17). In the context of globalization and neo-liberalism, heterarchic structures prosper, as states retreat and delegate authority functions in most regulatory spheres of the economy (particularly, banking and securities), although hierarchic and heterarchic structures coexist and combine in different ways as can be seen in the sphere of competition governed by a dynamic network of public and private, national and transnational, organizations.

To show the predominantly heterarchic structure of the competition network in Mexico, which realigns according to the particular issues being regulated, several controversial cases involving the main regulatory competition agency, Cofece, will be examined in this chapter: (1) the cartel created in 2013 by several banks and traders to manipulate the interest rates of Mexican sovereign debt bonds; (2) the reaction of the pro-competition network to public strategies and reforms to protect the electric state company (CFE) and counteract the process of privatization which has drained it to the point of bankruptcy; (3) multiple attempts to curb the monopoly power of several transnationals, particularly, Walmart, Bimbo and Cinemex. These cases not only involve the different objects of regulation that Buch-Hansen and Wigger (2011, p. 16) identify (concentration, mergers and acquisitions, cartels and state aid), but they reveal a predisposition of Cofece and the pro-competition network that, on the one hand, tend to disallow state aid schemes reducing the developmental capacities of the state who can no longer protect state companies considered strategic, while on the other hand, they tend to favor TNCs, private companies and banking interests. In these cases, the pro-competition network clearly shows more interest in checking government actions affecting competition than in curbing anti-competitive behavior of Mexican and foreign TNCs.

3. Banks and Traders' Cartel for Manipulating Interest Rates

From 2011 to 2013 a group of banks and traders (considered market makers) manipulated the interest rates of Mexican government bonds. The South District Tribunal of New York documented these manipulations effected in chat rooms, that discovered a bank cartel created by Barclays, Deutsche Bank, Santander México, Citi, Bank of America, BBVA México and JP Morgan and, like in other cases, at least one bank sought protection as a whistleblower. These banks colluded to manipulate prices first during Banxico's (the Mexican central bank) bond auctions and later when selling the bonds to pension funds. The texts showing Banxico was involved in the maneuvers were disclosed to Cofece. Three years after scrutinizing the data, Cofece found strong evidence of cartel-practices to manipulate the prices of government bonds.[5]

At the beginning of the investigation, Cofece —presided over by Alejandra Palacios—was criticized by the banking and securities supervising regulator (CNBV) for targeting the banks, although when doing its own investigation in late 2018 the Banking Commission fined these six global banks and traders a total of a little over $US 1 million for manipulating bond-trading volumes. Barclays and JPMorgan have agreed since 2018 to pay a combined $20.7 million to settle charges in New York that their Mexican affiliates conspired with other banks to sell Mexican bonds at inflated prices to U.S. pension funds. This case stemmed from information gathered in the Cofece probe but the charges were later dismissed because the case against the rest of the banks was considered out of jurisdiction.[6]

After judging that the seven banks had indeed conspired to manipulate prices for government bonds, in January 2021 Cofece fined them a total of $1.5 million. Lawmakers were outraged because the fines were tiny compared to the billions of dollars Barclays and Deutsche paid back in 2015 to settle charges with U.S., U.K. and European regulators for precisely the same types of alleged collusion.[7] According to Bloomberg News, "While COFECE can fine companies as much as 10% of their revenues when they engage in cartel-like behavior, banks and traders were fined under a less-harsh statute that set maximums at 200,000 times the country's daily minimum wage."[8] However, when summoned by Congress to account for this decision, Alejandra Palacios argued this was the only legal option.

Although cartels are considered an unacceptable form of collusion by all schools of neoliberalism, the settlements and ruling in the Mexican case of the banks and traders cartel examined above clearly show that the allegedly independent antitrust regulator, Cofece, favored the banks' interests fueling a sentiment against autonomous regulating entities that in Mexico are considered part and parcel of the neoliberal legacy from the past decades.[9]

In this contentious case, Cofece was then part of a network that included several public and private agencies, none of which openly condemned the cartel practices: the Central Bank (Banxico), an autonomous entity that allegedly participated in the collusion; the banking and securities supervising regulator (CNBV), a semi-autonomous entity whose role in the process was rather ambiguous; and the Mexican Banking Association, who openly defended the banks involved in the cartel. Surprisingly, think tanks and professional associations belonging to the pro-competition network (like IMCO, CIDE, the American Bar Association Section of Antitrust Law, and the national lawyer's associations) did not denounce the collusion.

4. No Tolerance to State Aid: Energy Sector Reforms

Privatizing the energy sector was a very difficult task for historical reasons. The nationalization of the most important companies in oil and electricity was considered a sovereign decision that required great popular support, becoming a symbol of independence among large sectors of the population (Hamilton, 1982). In addition, these two companies played a very important role in the development strategies of the import substitution industrialization period (from the 1950s to the 1970s). A nationalistic rhetoric was difficult to surmount, making privatization a slow and arduous process that ended up with constitutional reforms during the administration of Enrique Peña Nieto (2012–2018). Intense ideological debates and a coalition between different parties and lawmakers (not free of corruption and bribery) were required to advance these reforms.[10]

The most important argument to justify privatization was to open the sector to competition, eliminating subsidies and other forms of state aid that these two state monopolies enjoyed over several decades. The privatizing reforms, however, have entailed great advantages for national and foreign companies (including subsidies and lucrative contracts). In its effort to introduce new reforms and reverse some of the most harmful disadvantages for the state company (CFE), improve energy security and make the sector self-sufficient (Sandoval Cervantes, 2021), the current left-wing government has faced a ferocious response from big business, national and transnational, and most members involved in the pro-competition network, including: business associations (among others, CCE, Canacintra, International Chamber of Commerce México, ICC), think tanks (IMCO, CIDAC and CIDE), scholars, lawyers, lawmakers, all of whom have defended private interests against the state. Even the Supreme Court has championed competition, disallowing state plans.

Cofece filed a constitutional complaint claiming that the counter-reforms proposed by the current administration were unconstitutional. In addition to violating the rule of law, members of the pro-competition network contend that giving priority to the state company was going to affect consumers with price increases, squandering of public resources, and infringing international agreements (particularly, the United States–Mexico–Canada Agreement). As a consequence, they warn that uncertainty in this key economic sector would follow suit, discouraging new investments and slowing growth. Economic forecasts for and against the ongoing reforms have thrived.

Neoliberal regulation theory argues that when a company receives government support, it has an advantage over its competitors, which does not stem from productivity gains and hence entails an inefficient allocation of public resources. However, state companies have been one of the main mechanisms used by both advanced and backward countries to diversify the economy toward more advanced activities. To gain a position in markets with great developmental potential, these companies (often called national champions) receive state aid of different sorts, fostering technological upgrades.

5. Efforts to Curb the Power of Dominant Players

The levels of concentration in the Mexican economy have historically been very high, but they have increased substantially with the wave of M&A greatly intensified with the process of globalization (Salas Porras and Medina, 2021). Today there is one dominant player in virtually every sector, but three in particular have been the object of increasing concern among competition watchdogs: Bimbo, Walmart, and Cinemex. All of them are transnational corporations with investments in several countries and regions, but while Bimbo and Cinemex originated in Mexico, Walmart comes from the United States.

In 2020, Bimbo reached annual sales of more than $US 15 billion on a global scale with more than 100 brands and ten thousand products.[11] It has an overwhelming participation in most segments of the bread market. All this notwithstanding, Bimbo has not been the object of any serious investigation by Cofece, while in the US and Canada competition authorities have closely followed its expansion plans and have forced the company to disinvest. In the US, in particular, when Bimbo acquired Sara Lee, the Department of Justice forced Bimbo to sell some assets in order to give consumers more options. It took Bimbo more than a year to meet the requirements. Xavier Ginebra, an expert in competition law, member of a law firm, and ex-official of the antimonopoly agency, declared that Bimbo has never been sanctioned, despite finding barriers that closed entry to competitors. Two complaints were presented to Cofece, but according to one of the officials, they were discarded because no monopoly practices were proven.[12]

In the case of the retail market, there are only three chains with a national presence (Walmart, Soriana, and Chedraui), but Walmart faces no competition whatsoever in 21% of the localities where it operates. It has almost 2,600 establishments in 524 Mexican cities. This North American corporation controls 87% of the retail market according to Cofece, and although the antimonopoly agency has undertaken several investigations to limit Walmart's monopsony power, only in marginal cases has it been able to stop an acquisition or fine the company. This is despite the widely known predatory practices toward suppliers, who have to accept very low prices for their produce, longer-than-agreed terms for payment, and even returns of merchandise without previous notification, making them in this way absorb the risks of the market cycles. These practices have been the object of criticism in Mexico and other countries, but the company argues that they benefit consumers. In 2019, the Securities and Exchange Commission (one of the most important antimonopoly agencies in the United States) fined the company 282 million USD for paying bribes to officials in Mexico, Brazil, and India in order to get authorization to open new establishments.[13]

Another interesting paradigmatic case is the merger between Cinemex and Cinemark, which was authorized by Cofece in 2015, consolidating movie theaters in the hands of two players, Cinemex and Cinepolis. The latter is controlled by Alejandro Ramírez Magaña, one of the main sponsors of IMCO, which is a think tank at the center of the pro-competition network. According to Alejandra Palacios, President Commissioner of Cofece, after the merger, these two corporations would concentrate 90% of the market, but Cinemark did not represent competitive pressure, the main criterion in her view when deciding whether to authorize mergers. However, the merger has not only increased concentration and prices but has also made the existence of independent theaters increasingly difficult.[14]

All of the cases examined above show that Cofece has not been able to curb monopoly practices. Specialists accept that the reforms have not been able to restrain economic concentration in the hands of the largest corporations. They argue Cofece does not live up to the expectations that the competition reforms elicited in 2013 and allege that although the Mexican Anti-monopoly Law prohibits monopoly practices, in order to demonstrate them it is necessary to prove that the negative effects of the practices surpass the positive effects. However, they contend this is practically impossible because the criteria to assess such effects are vague, abstract, and even obscure, all of which facilitate discretionary decisions on the part of competition authorities.[15] These are by and large technocrats that have revolved through organizations and agencies whose preferences favor—or are captured by—the same large corporations they are supposed to control. As in the European case analyzed by Buch-Hansen and Wigger (2011, p. 23), autonomous institutions like Cofece and IFC have been entrusted with discretionary powers when making decisions that affect particular interests, although they act in the context of far-reaching networks.

6. Technocracies and Pro-competition Networks

Two autonomous organizations—Cofece and IFC—and the technocrats who design, interpret, and enforce the rules occupy a center position in the Mexican pro-competition network. Cofece is no doubt the most important node in the network, and its main obligation is securing competition that prevails in most economic areas. The IFC is only responsible for procuring competition in the area of telecommunications (TV, internet, landline and mobile phones). The technocrats presiding over these organizations have shown throughout their trajectories a neoliberal understanding of competition, that is, one that favors low prices and consumer welfare instead of controlling monopoly power.

Alejandra Palacios Prieto—who was appointed to Cofece by the Senate after the constitutional reforms of 2013 and re-elected in 2017 for a second term—is the most important official in the pro-competition network. She has revolved through several pro-competition think tanks. Among the most important positions, she has held a directorship for Project Regulation and Good Governance at the Mexican Institute for Competitiveness (IMCO), where she led research projects in economic regulation; she has been since 2016 the Vice President of the International Competition Network (ICN), an association gathering 130 national competition regulators and member of the OECD's Competition Committee Bureau, and she remains closely linked to several think tanks in the network, particularly IMCO and México Evalúa.

IMCO is the most important think tank in the network and has been highly influential in the area of competition since the reforms introduced in 2013. This think tank was created and financed by big business, including Bimbo and Cinepolis (Salas Porras, 2018), which have been favored in the competition disputes examined above. IMCO and Mexico Evalúa are connected in different ways: they share sponsors, donors, and directors, but in particular they share a common neoliberal view on competition. The experts affiliated with these think tanks have made competition one of their most important lines of work, and they disseminate their views not only on their websites but throughout the media. Although both of them claim to oppose concentration, up to now there has been no pronouncement or pressure on Cofece to contain the monopoly practices and curb concentration in the cases examined above (Bimbo, Walmart, and Cinemax). In contrast, in the case of the recent energy reforms, the experts of both think tanks have been very vocal and proactive, energizing multiple nodes of the network to stop and reverse the state's intentions to support the state company in several ways.

Clearly, these two think tanks strengthen an ideological view of competition that supports large corporate interests and weakens the developmental role of the state. To this end, they assemble research teams with financial support from business associations and large corporations, propagate multiple reports that show the inefficiency of state companies, and carry out activism in the media to influence public opinion, lawyers, and lawmakers, as well as court decisions on the most controversial cases.

7. Conclusion

The pro-competition stance that circulates throughout the heterarchic network has motivated the creation of autonomous regulatory bodies to prevent the formation of cartels, mergers, manipulation of prices, entry barriers, and other monopoly practices. However, as several authors contend (Crouch, 2011; Buch-Hansen and Wigger, 2011; Wigger and Buch-Hansen, 2012, 2013; Buch-Hansen, 2012), most of these regulatory bodies have been captured by TNCs and powerful technocracies—that is, by the same interests advocating competition. Consequently, the degree to which regulatory agencies have succeeded in curbing monopoly practices is seriously questioned.

The cases examined in this chapter reveal how the institutions and elites belonging to the Mexican competition network organize heterarchically in order to aggregate political power and check government actions affecting competition, and not to contain the anti-competitive behavior of Mexican and foreign TNCs. In this way, they strengthen a neoliberal view of competition, but more importantly, as Cerny (2021) points out, they destructure the state apparatus. Autonomous regulatory bodies, which are key nodes of these heterarchic structures, play an important role in this process of destructuring and fragmentation of the state and its hierarchical structures. And, as in other spheres of regulation (particularly, banking, and securities), in the sphere of competition, these heterarchic structures act as centrifugal forces linked with international regulatory bodies while fragmented from the national state apparatus. Integration into global policy networks leads to the adoption of standards in the area of competition and meeting the requirements of transnational technocracies, eroding state capacities to carry out national development strategies since the state can no longer protect public companies considered strategic.

Notes

1 According to Jessop, heterarchy as a "form of governance involves the coordination of differentiated institutional orders or functional systems (such as the economic, political, legal, scientific, or educational systems), each of which has its own complex operational logic such that it is impossible to exercise effective overall control of its development from outside that system." (Jessop, 1998, p. 2).

2 This Law was drafted following the guidelines of antitrust agencies in other regions to respond to NAFTA that required Canada, Mexico, and the U.S. to prohibit anti-competitive conduct (Aydin, 2016; Slottje and Prowse, 2001).

3 See: https://imco.org.mx/na ce-alianza-por-la-competencia/.

4 Dolowitz and Marsh (1996) define policy transfer as the process whereby policies move across countries and jurisdictions.

5 www.bloomberg.com/news/articles/2021-01-24/seven-big-banks-escape-with-minor-fines-in-mexico-antitrust-case. Accessed 20 February 2021

6 www.competitionpolicyinternational.com/7-banks-receive-only-minor-antitrust-fines-in-mexico/. Accessed 15 February 2021.

7 https://ec.europa.eu/commission/presscorner/detail/en/IP_19_2568. Accessed 11 February 2021.

8 www.bloomberg.com/news/articles/2021-01-24/seven-big-banks-escape-with-minor-fines-in-mexico-antitrust-case. Accessed 18 February 2021.

9 Mexican President Andrés Manuel López Obrador has suggested autonomous regulators should be reintegrated into federal ministries because they are not autonomous and have produced expensive and powerful bureaucracies.

10 Emilio Losoya Austin, Pemex Director during the administration of Enrique Peña Nieto, declared to the Attorney General that bribes and blackmail were used to convince lawmakers to vote in favor of the energy reforms. See: www.reforma.com/aplica cioneslibre/preacceso/articulo/default.aspx?__rval=1&urlredirect=www.reforma.com/una-cena-de-moches-y-pleito-de-cantina/ar2069327?referer=-7d616165662f3a3a626 2623b727a7a7279703b767a783a–. Accessed 12 January 2021.

11 See: www.grupobimbo.com/en/investors/financial-information/annual-information

12 For this case see: www.dineroenimagen.com/2014-03-11/33919. Accessed 15 December 2020.

13 For this case, see: www.america-retail.com/mexico/walmart-concentra-el-87-del-mercado-en-mexico-cofece/ and www.forbes.com.mx/negocios-cofece-investigacion-supermerca dos-posibles-practicas-monopolicas/. Both accessed 27 February 2021.

14 See: https://deadline.com/2020/05/cinepolis-of-mexico-takes-stake-cinemark-1202939667/. Accessed 20 February 2021. See also www.sinembargo.mx/23-02-2015/1254714. Accessed 13 February 2021.

15 See: www.sinembargo.mx/23-02-2015/1254714. Accessed 13 February 2021.

References

Akman, P. and H. Kassim (2010) "Myths and Myth-Making in the European Union: The Institutionalization and Interpretation of EU Competition Policy." *Journal of Common Market Studies*, Vol. 48, No. 1, pp. 111–132.

Aydin, U. (2016) "Competition Law and Policy in Mexico: Successes and Challenges." *Law and Contemporary Problems*, Vol. 79, pp. 155–186. http://scholarship.law.duke.edu/lcp/vol79/iss4/6

Belmonte, R. and P. Cerny (2021) "Heterarchy: Toward Paradigm Shift in World Politics. In Giulio Gallarotti, ed., *The Changing Faces of Power*." Special issue of the *Journal of Political Power*, Vol. 14, No. 1.

Buch-Hansen, H. (2012) "Freedom to Compete? The Cartelization of European Transnational Corporations." *Competition and Change*, Vol. 16, No. 1, February, pp. 20–36.

Buch-Hansen, H. and A. Wigger (2010) *The Politics of European Competition Regulation: A Critical Political Economy Perspective*. London and New York: Routledge.

Buch-Hansen, H. and A. Wigger (2011) *The Politics of European Competition Regulation. A Critical Political Economy Perspective*. London: Routledge.

Cerny, P. (2016) "In the Shadow of Ordoliberalism: The Paradox of Neoliberalism in the 21st Century." *ERIS*, Vol. 3, No. 1, pp. 78–91.

Cerny, P. (2019) "From Theory to Practice: The Paradox of Neoliberal Hegemony in 21st Century World Politics." In Benjamin Martill and Sebastian Schindler, eds., *Theory as Ideology in International Relations: The Politics of Knowledge*, London: Routledge, pp. 140–164.

Cerny, P. (2021) "Business and Politics in an Age of Intangibles and Financialization." In Aynsley Kellow, Tony Porter and Karsten Ronit, eds., *Business and Politics*. Edward Elgar Handbook.

Crane, D. A. (2014) "The Tempting of Antitrust: Robert Bork and the Goals of Antitrust Policy." *Antitrust Law Journal*, Vol. 79, No. 3, pp. 835–853.

Crouch, C. (2011) *The Strange Non-Death of Neoliberalism*. Cambridge: Polity.

Crumley, C. (2015) *Emerging Trends in Social and Behavioral Sciences. An Interdisciplinary, Searchable, and Linkable Resource*. John Wiley. doi: 10.1002/9781118900772. etrds0158

Dolowitz, D. and D. Marsh (1996) "Who Learns What from Whom: A Review of the Policy Transfer Literature." *Political Studies*, Vol. XLIV, pp. 343–357.

Hamilton, N. (1982) *The Limits of State Autonomy. Post-Revolutionary Mexico*. New Jersey: Princeton.

Harrod, J. (2001) "Global Realism: Unmasking Power in the International Political Economy." In Richard Wyn Jones, ed., *Critical Theory and World Politics*. London: Lynne Rienner, pp. 111–125.

IMCO (2014) "Nace Alianza por la Competencia." https://imco.org.mx/nace-alianza-por-la-competencia/ March 12, 2021.

Jessop, B. (1998) "The Rise of Governance and the Risks of Failure." *International Social Science Journal*, No. 155, pp. 29–46.

Jessop, B. (2012) "Neoliberalism." In George Ritzer, ed., *The Wiley-Blackwell Encyclopedia of Globalization*, 1st edn, vol. 3. pp. 1513–1521.

Khan, L. (2017) "Amazon's Antitrust Paradox." *Yale Law Journal*, Vol. 126.

Ros, J. (1993) "Mexico's Trade Industrialization Experience Since 1960: A Reconsideration of Past Policies and Assessment of Current Reforms." Working Paper #186 — January. Kellogg Institute. http://kellogg.nd.edu/publications/workingpapers/WPS/186. pdf. July 9, 2013.

Salas Porras (2017) *La Economía Política Neoliberal en México. ¿Quién la diseñó y Cómo lo Hizo?* México: AKAL.

Salas Porras (2018) *Conocimiento y Poder. Las Ideas los Expertos y los Centros de Pensamiento*. México: AKAL.

Salas Porras and Medina (2021) "Transnationalization of the Mexican Corporate Elite: Looking Beyond Cross-Border Corporate Networks." *Review of International Political Economy*. doi: 10.1080/09692290.2021.1961841

Sandoval Cervantes, D. (2021) "Política energética en México. Integración desigual, seguridad y transición energética." In *Energía y Desarrollo Sustentable. Problemas de Integración Energética Regional. Boletín del Grupo de Trabajo Energía y Desarrollo sustentable*. Buenos Aires: CLACSO.

Slottje, D.J. and Stephen D. Prowse (2001) "Antitrust Policy in Mexico Daniel J. Slottje et al., Antitrust Policy in Mexico." *Law and Business Review of the Americas*, Vol. 7, p. 405. https://scholar.smu.edu/lbra/vol7/iss3/6

Springer, S. (2016) *The Discourse of Neoliberalism. An Anatomy of a Powerful Idea.* New York: Rowman & Littlefield International.

Wigger, A. and H. Buch-Hansen (2012) "The Unfolding Contradictions of Neoliberal Competition Regulation and the Global Economic Crisis: A Missed Opportunity for Change?" In H. Overbeek and B. van Apeldorn, eds., *Neoliberalism in Crisis*. International Political Economy Series. London: Palgrave Macmillan, pp. 23–44.

Wigger, A. and H. Buch-Hansen (2013) "Explaining (Missing) Regulatory Paradigm Shifts: EU Competition Regulation in Times of Economic Crisis." *New Political Economy.* doi: 10.1080/13563467.2013.768612

17

HETERARCHY IN RUSSIA

Paradoxes of Power

Richard Sakwa

The paradox of the relative powerlessness of a powerful system has been an enduring feature of Russian governance (Mendras 2012).[1] Russian studies have traditionally focused on hierarchy and control, although the chaotic elements have also been analyzed (Hale 2015; Zygar' 2016; Taylor 2018). However, a theoretical explanation for this apparent contradiction has typically been lacking. The concept of heterarchy provides a framework to analyze exaggerated control amid the underlying condition of anarchy. This is more than the typical post-communist condition of hybridity but points to a foundational characteristic of the polity. This fluidity is the thread that combines power and powerlessness (Frye 2021). It provides the social and political context for the emergence of the dual state, in which two principles of order-making operate simultaneously, but allows neither to consolidate, generating flux and fluidity amid rigidity. The constitutional state, encompassing the presidency, parliament, parties, and legal bodies together with processes such as elections, a competitive public sphere, and rule of law, is balanced and to a degree controlled by an administrative regime, standing above the constitutional state yet drawing its legitimacy from claimed adherence to the principles of constitutionality (Sakwa 2010). The concept of heterarchy identifies the constellation of forces shaping a polity and conceptualizes the dynamics of interaction. The Putin system prided itself on restoring the managerial capacity of the state but it was unable to overcome inertia and remained prey to societal interests.

A heterarchy is a system where the elements of organization are unranked (non-hierarchical) or where they possess the potential to be ranked in a number of different ways (Crumley 1995). Heterarchies are networks in which elements share the same "horizontal" position of power and authority, with each hypothetically playing an equal role. The existence of heterarchy is not incompatible with the existence of hierarchy; indeed, hierarchies are usually composed

DOI: 10.4324/9781003352617-19

of quasi-independent heterarchic sub-units, and vice versa. In ontological terms, the idea that any pair of items can be related in two or more ways means that the inherent pluralism of any given social system is accentuated. Instead of reducing a state or social system to certain predominant features, characteristics, or linear developmental patterns, the social subject becomes multivalent and complex. In epistemological terms, the hierarchical approach sorts the material in terms of the greater (more powerful) at the top reducing to something smaller (less powerful) at the bottom, whereas heterarchy assesses multiple factors and concerns, and thus gives greater valence to the subjectivity of elements whose agency fluctuates as the relationship with the power system and other actors changes. The heterarchy model rejects totalizing and teleological approaches and instead emphasizes the partiality of particular viewpoints and privileges complexity and contradiction.

Russian governance operates amid complex and shifting patterns of influence and interactions. As in the late Soviet years, Russia under Putin once again became a "stabilocracy" (*stabilokratiya*), a system designed to maintain stability by manual or mechanical means. Instead of organic forms of stability based on the balance of political forces expressed through competitive politics and the relatively free exercise of the institutions of representative democracy, which sustain the pluralism that Robert Dahl (1971) described in his classic work on polyarchy, late Soviet patterns were reproduced. Once considered the core of pluralist democracies, traditional interest groups in late modern neoliberal states have undergone a qualitative transformation, described by Philip G. Cerny (2010) as "neopluralism." The polity is shaped by the three-fold tension between the hierarchy and control imposed by the administrative regime, the stymied development of polyarchy derived from the constitutional state, and the heterarchy of the sociopolitical order.

Russian heterarchy is shaped by the complex interaction between the power vertical (*vertikal'*), with the Kremlin at the top, and the horizontalism of the regions and special interests. Statist centralization is tempered by the persistence of horizontal structures. This is more than the informal practices of the network state (Kononenko and Moshes 2010), and less than the *sistema*, an informal set of informal practices that subvert or bypass formal institutions (Ledeneva 2013). Heterarchy tempers the traditional institutions of the nation-state, transforming the character of agency (Brenner et al. 2003). The Russian power hierarchy is better theorized as part of a conglomeration of power systems. The classic Weberian conception of the modern state is modified. However, in a paradoxical turn, the prevalence of heterarchy in a weakly institutionalized state order accentuated the order-making properties of centralized leadership, and *in extremis* ultimately threatened the stability of the system in its entirety. The potential for runaway heterarchy remained. In Russian history, repeated heterarchical crises have triggered new cycles of hierarchical imposition. The balance was disrupted in Putin's fourth presidential term starting in 2018, with the predominance of the security bloc and, most recently, the invasion of Ukraine in 2022.

1. Heterarchy in Russia

Vladimir Putin's rule is a specific form of Hobbesian statecraft, standing at the origins of liberalism but fearing to embrace its pluralistic elements while strengthening the Leviathan (Medvedev 2019). It manages complexity but remains torn between polyarchy, hierarchy, and heterarchy. Polyarchy entails the political representation of societal interests, hierarchy the management of decision-making, while heterarchy denotes neopluralism—the unmediated existence of societal and political blocs.

Russian heterarchy comprises three levels: the macro, comprising the four major ideological-interest groups of Russian modernity; the meso, encompassing institutional actors and social organizations, including the "third state" of organized crime and corrupt networks; and the micro, the personalities and networks in the constellation of power. Vertical networks cut across the three horizontal levels, and individuals can be located simultaneously in more than one horizontal or vertical matrix. This interlocking co-location endows the Russian polity with its extraordinary stability, although by the same token rendered the system vulnerable to systemic shocks. Stability, as the collapse of previous regimes attests, is fragile. The absence of what Antonio Gramsci would call the hegemony of a "historical bloc," in which its world view becomes the common sense of the epoch, allows the administrative regime to rise above a divided society and a fragmented party-representative system (Sakwa 2020). The logic of administrative order takes technocratic managerialism to the extreme, operating effectively outside of politics. This attenuates the constitutional foundations of the system and ultimately erodes even the vestigial checks and balances and instruments of accountability. The pursuit of stability ultimately generated instability.

The Macro-level: The Ideational-factional Blocs of Russian Modernity

Four major ideational-factional blocs shape Russian political society, each with its perspective on how Russia should be governed. Michel Foucault called such constellations *epistemes*, arguing that several power-knowledge complexes can co-exist, although in his view only one shapes the non-temporal historical conditions of possibility for an era (Foucault [1966] 2001). In contemporary Russia, the power-knowledge complexes are divided internally but they share interests, ideological perspectives, and in some cases a professional commonality that render them distinctive and coherent. Together they comprise the four pillars of contemporary Russian modernity, creating an "alternative modernity" based not on a single ideological perspective, as in the Soviet era, but on societal responses to "the labyrinth of modernity" (Arnason 2020). The entirety of these responses is what gives the Russian civilizational state its unique character (cf. Coker 2019).

First, the views of the liberals are far more influential than the paltry proportion of votes won in national elections. The bloc is divided between economic liberals, focusing on macroeconomic stability; legal constitutionalists, the inheritors of Boris Chicherin's liberal statism; and radicals, who look to the West for inspiration. They are challenged by the second group, the *okhraniteli-siloviki* (those working in or affiliated with the security apparatus). They consider themselves responsible for "guarding" Russia from domestic and foreign enemies, part of Russia's long "guardianship" (*okhranitel'*) tradition (Ivanov 2007). They view Russia as a besieged fortress, and it is their sacred duty to defend the country from internal and external enemies (Cherkesov 2004: 6). Defending "fortress Russia," they claim certain privileges, including personal enrichment (Yablokov 2018). The bloc is deeply factionalized, with endemic struggles between institutions as well as within them, generating complex mechanisms of internal control (Petrov 2019b). At the margins, they merge with the criminal world (Galeotti 2018). The military is naturally part of this bloc, but their vocation is to defend the country, whereas the *okhraniteli-siloviki* protect the regime. In his Crimea unification speech of 18 March, Putin (2014) adopted some of the language of this faction.

The third macro-faction comprises a diverse bloc of neo-traditionalists, ranging from monarchists, neo-imperialists, neo-Stalinists to Russian nationalists and moderate conservatives (cf. Robinson 2019). They are "traditionalist" because they see Russia's future in representations of the past and "neo" to the extent that the traditionalism is adapted to present-day concerns. The strain represented by Alexander Dugin taps into a deeper well of traditionalism (Teitelbaum 2020) while engaging with the contemporary European new right. Neo-traditionalists defend Russian exceptionalism (hence become nationalists, even when they reject the concept) and assert statism at home and great power concerns abroad (Laruelle 2016). With the onset of the so-called "Russian Spring" in early 2014, some even dreamed of bringing the Donbass insurgency to Moscow to sweep out the liberals and even the endlessly temporizing Putin (Kolstø 2016). Putin fought back and squeezed the genie of Russian neo-nationalism back into the bottle and the neo-traditionalist bid for hegemony was thwarted. The Ukrainian war in 2022 once again inspired neo-traditionalist visions of a renewed Russian Spring.

Eurasianists comprise the fourth category, in part overlapping in personnel and views with the neo-traditionalists. However, while neo-traditionalists are critical of the West, the reference point for their modernization agenda and cultural matrix remains essentially European. They strive to overcome the stigma of backwardness to make Russia a great power within the framework of a Western hierarchy of status and values (Zarakol 2011; see also Morozov 2015). By contrast, Eurasianism as an ideology is rooted in a foundational anti-Westernism (Bassin and Pozo 2016). They have devised a whole ideology explaining why Russia and what they call "Romano-Germanic" civilization are incompatible. Highly factionalized, they are nevertheless united in the view that there is a hermeneutic incompatibility between Russia and the West (Bassin 2016; Pozdnyakov 1994). Thinkers such as Dugin maintain the traditional Eurasianist hostility to the Atlantic powers accompanied by much speculation on geopolitics, the coming apocalypse, and Heideggerian notions of the existential exhaustion of Western civilization (Clover 2016). This faction, too, was inspired by the war with the West.

Putinite managerialism kept competing groups and ideas in permanent balance. The regime drew on all of them but was dependent on none. This applies no less to the *siloviki* despite Putin's background in the security services, and thus refutes the view of him as an instrument of *silovik* revenge (Felshtinsky and Pribylovsky 2012). Putin acted as the arbiter between the macro-factions, mediating between elite groups and institutions to allow each to participate in policymaking and the political process, but allowed none to capture the state or fully impose its policy preferences to create a new historical bloc. The balancing system prevented factions from turning on each other, keeping coercion to a minimum. Intra-elite splits did emerge, notably in the transition to the Dmitry Medvedev presidency in 2007–2008, after Putin came to the end of the two successive terms allowed by the constitution (Sakwa 2011).

As Putin approached the end of his next two successive terms and with presidential elections scheduled for 2024, fear that the trusted methods of elite management would spiral out of control prompted the 2020 constitutional reform, allowing Putin (but not his successor) to run for two more six-year terms. This was accompanied by the shift of the center toward more conservative positions, as the liberals lost influence (except in macroeconomic policy) and the other factions commensurately gained. The administrative regime needed the liberal faction to prevent the Kremlin from becoming hostage to conservative groups of various stripes. This balancing model for most of the Putin era prevented radical policy initiatives such as structural economic reform, but it also restrained hard authoritarianism. From late 2019 the balance broke down, allowing the security bloc to prevail over the others. This entailed severe domestic repression accompanied by the attempt to resolve the security dilemma posed by the expansion of the Atlantic power system to Russia's borders by forceful means. The invasion of Ukraine on 24 February 2022 and the ensuing blockade of Russia marked the end of a whole cycle of history.

The Meso-level: Institutions and Corporations

The meso-level is where interest groups and institutions compete, and where elite analysis, governance studies, and the patronal model come into their own (Colton and Holmes 2006; Hale 2015). Competing economic interests and patron-client relations seek to impose their preferences, the regime-state fights to maintain its autonomy, and Putin struggled to remain the supreme arbiter. The paradoxes of Putinite rule are at their starkest in the meso-level. A system whose legitimacy is based on the restoration of the state in fact governs through the mechanical management of regime relations. Institutionalized governance and informal regime relations are co-dependent, with an unstable balance between them. The long-term trend was toward the erosion of the autonomy of constitutional institutions, and instead, the quasi-independent nodes of the heterarchical state predominated.

The authority of cabinets and prime ministers fluctuated but permanently shared power with the parallel managerial system centered on the Presidential

Administration and numerous security agencies. Regime power was buttressed by network relations with corporations, which include law enforcement agencies, the 85 regions, and the major state-owned companies such as Gazprom, Rosneft, Rostec, Roskosmos, Russian Post, Rostelekom, and Russian Railways, as well as some 1,000 state-owned joint stock companies and over 17,000 unitary enterprises. When combined with government employees in the health, education, security, and other sectors, this complex encompasses some 24 million people, or 30% of employees, funded directly or indirectly by the state. The total is swelled if those employed by politically dependent corporations, such as AFK Sistema, Lukoil, Metalloinvest, Novolipetsk Steel (NLMK), Norilsk Nickel, Sibur, Surgutneftegaz, Transmashholding, and the Urals Mining Metallurgical Company (UMMC), are added. These companies exercise direct power in the regions, and the multiplicity of "verticals" threatens to turn Russia into a "federation of corporations" (Luzin 2019)—the apotheosis of heterarchy.

The Micro-level: Elite Contestation and Control

Group dynamics cut across levels in Russia's heterarchy. Beneath the veneer of monolithic unity, the system is highly personalized and torn by factional conflict, especially among the security services. No sooner is one group marginalized than another takes its place, maintaining factional balance and constraining intra-elite conflict. The administrative regime operated sophisticated mechanisms to manage complex relationships, and it is less surprising that it sometimes failed than it worked at all. At the micro-level, Putin achieved an extraordinary level of elite coherence, positioning himself as the arbiter of elite and corporate disputes. He built connections to all the major elite factions, who trusted him to respect their interests. No faction got all that it wanted, but all received something from remaining loyal. The enduring fear of defection reinforced hierarchical control mechanisms.

These evolved over time. Following the period of contentious politics provoked by Putin's unceremonious return to the presidency and the flawed parliamentary election of December 2011, accompanied by some elite sympathy with the protesters, the regime "nationalized" the elites. The "deoffshorization" campaign imposed much tougher regulations on foreign asset holdings for politicians and other office holders. Purges and repression, typically conducted in the guise of anti-corruption campaigns (as in China), turned the elite into a neo-nomenklatura (Petrov 2019a). Leadership turnover was especially marked in the regions after 2018, and then in government in January 2020. The basic drive was "the center's struggle to restore control over the regional elites and systematic work to weaken them and fit them into a single party of the federal and regional bureaucracy" (Kynev 2019). Putin still struggled to convert policy statements into action, as regularly reflected in his annual address (*poslanie*) to the Federal Assembly. He repeatedly complained about the unjustified imprisonment of businesspeople in economic disputes (Putin 2015), lamenting that "unfortunately, the situation has not improved much" (Putin 2019). The Kremlin had greater freedom to maneuver in foreign policy, and drawing on the great power instincts of three of the four meta-factions and in the absence of the stabilizing role of the liberals, Putin initiated the Ukrainian war.

II. Heterarchy and Governance

Fear of dissolution and disintegration feeds the tutelary impulse. This gave rise to dual state governance regulated by two operative systems: one generated by the constitutional state; and the second spawned by various "regime complexes" of the administrative system, including its para-constitutional and para-statal innovations as well as the three tiers of factional politics. Governance is disaggregated, typically personalized, and consequently fragmented and de-institutionalized. The system is "inherently dynamic, with constant regime change being essential to how the regime operates and survives" (Hale et al. 2019: 168). The constitution acts as an anchor of stability, constraining the arbitrariness of the administrative regime, but the cumulative effect of the 206 amendments enacted in 2020 subordinated the normative order to the needs of regime perpetuation, undermining its regulatory and constraining functions. The shifting boundary between regime and state blurred the line between the public and the private, as in so many late-developing states.

Regime politics seeks to prevent fragmentation from becoming heterarchical segmentation. Federal and business relations had become segmented in the 1990s, and Putin's first measures were designed to counteract this phenomenon. This served performative aspects of regime legitimation (Sharafutdinova 2020), but it was also severely functional. The analogy can be drawn with international relations, where anarchy is tempered by a hierarchy in which the sovereignty of subordinates is in part or wholly ceded to the hegemonic state (Lake 2007, 2009). Equally, the "the Kremlin" (taken as the symbol of authority) imposes hierarchy over the unruly factions and interests in domestic politics. Ever since the Rurikids united the nation, political integration has always been a challenge. The struggle against heterarchy has characterized Russian politics of whatever the regime type—monarchy, empire, Communist state, or republic. However, none could do away with the substantive fact of heterarchy. Putin is in this tradition and has repeatedly argued that Russia had to remain a strongly presidential republic. Questioned about a possible shift to a parliamentary system after his 15 January 2020 *poslanie* announcing constitutional amendments, Putin (2020c) argued that it would be inadvisable: "We should better not carry out any experiments . . . [with its] huge territory, many faiths and a large number of nations, peoples, and nationalities living in the country—you can't even count, someone says 160, someone 190," Russia in his view "still needed strong presidential power." This is why the "zero-option" allowing Putin to run for two more terms was designed to avert a runaway nuclear reaction of elite fragmentation and segmentation (Putin 2020b). The appeal to stability and continuity is the classic call of strongmen (Kribbe 2020), but in Russia's case, it has particular poignancy, given repeated regime collapses: the "Time of Troubles" (*Smuta*) at the beginning of the seventeenth century, the fall of Tsarism in 1917, the dissolution of Soviet Communism in 1989–1990, and the disintegration of the Soviet state in 1991.

The charismatic leader acts as the bulwark against chaos. The president represents "the identity aspirations of different groups in the nation; and through a search for political unity, mobilized above all by the apparent threat from an external enemy" (Lewis 2020: 13). The president acts as the powerbroker rather than taskmaster. Boris Yeltsin worked more through accommodation and concessions, allowing political pluralism to flourish at the regional and corporate levels, but by the same token fostered segmentation that at times veered toward separatism. Despite the extreme powers vested in the state, its inability to stand above competing factions helps explain the emergence of the administrative regime to reassert steering capacity. Putin remorselessly pushed back against segmentation, suppressing separatist impulses along with polyarchy. The regime *vertikal'* subdued the unruly forces that constrained Yeltsin, but the price to pay was the loss of pluralism and political competitiveness. A system based on the regime's ability to exercise discretionary power in the pursuit of control dispersed sovereignty across the heterarchical spectrum. Lewis (2020: 219) notes that "the assertion of exceptionality as the basis of sovereignty—and therefore of political order—has the effect of undermining order in the normal sphere, in everyday judicial processes, business transactions and security operations." The exception threatened to become the norm as the norm itself was subverted by the exception (cf. Jayasuriya 2001).

The three layers of heterarchy and their components engage in policymaking with various levels of commitment, depending on how the issue affects their core concerns. The persistent victory of one group would entail a loss of balance, and the regime "would become dependent on the winners and risk losing the support of rival groups" (Baunov 2020). Factions do not enjoy veto power, as the crushing of the bid for autonomy by the industrial bourgeoisie in the Yukos case demonstrated (Sakwa 2014). However, as relatively autonomous agents, they enjoy the influence that derives from being part of the informal balance of power and enjoy a degree of autonomy as long as they profess loyalty to the regime. This allows personal enrichment, and some political entrepreneurialism. Russia's involvement in the US presidential election in 2016, although its scale and nature are highly contested (Sakwa 2021), had devastating consequences for the relationship. It has been ascribed in part to freelancing activities by agents in which "intelligence and commercial interests are intertwined." This rendered it "difficult for Putin to retain any degree of meaningful control over the individuals who are supposedly serving him" (Marten 2019: 755).

Putin appeared to be tiring of the whole exercise. The 2020 constitutional amendments appeared at first to be designed to achieve greater institutionalization and less personalized elite management (Putin 2020a), although in the end, only timid steps were taken in this direction. Stanovaya (2020: 40) went so far as to argue that Putin deliberately withdrew, allowing inter-elite conflicts free rein: "With Putin increasingly absent from everyday decision-making and rarely available to intervene and arbitrate in these intra-elite battles, the regime is riven by internal conflicts." In pushing through the constitutional changes that allowed him to stay in power up to 2036, Putin admitted that this was to constrain elite contestation. This was the price to pay where regime management rather than free elections regulate factional and elite relations.

Instead of the open struggle for public office and building consensus for favored policies, the factions exercise influence through administrative channels and bureaucratic agencies. Economic liberals shaped macroeconomic policy, while the *silovik-okhranitel'* bloc determined national security issues. The neo-traditionalists enjoyed a moment in the sun in 2014, and remained part of Putin's management of identity issues. They gained an important victory when a 2020 constitutional amendment (Article 68.1) described the Russian language as "state-forming." Pragmatic and technocratic Eurasianist perspectives (techno-Eurasianism) were given institutional form in the creation of the Eurasian Economic Union and contributed to the formulation of the Greater Eurasian Partnership (GEP). The more extreme representations of these blocs have been suppressed. Thus the radical liberals who saw Russia's future as part of the West were marginalized; the more repressive instincts of the *silovik*-guardians constrained (as in their attempts fully to control the internet); the militant Russian nationalists and xenophobes among the neo-traditionalists endured severe police repression and became the largest political group in jail; while the radical Eurasianists, who dream of a decisive breach with the West, basked in Russia's turn to the East. This whole system was thrown into turmoil by the Ukrainian crisis and the balance disrupted.

Conclusion

Transnational webs of power are transforming the way that sectoral and value interest groups and NGOs interact, challenging the traditional prerogatives of the state (Belmonte and Cerny 2021). Heterarchy undermines polyarchy and classical hierarchical Weberian representations of the state as well as customary notions of political pluralism. The enormous diversity of interests, value communities, and actors (distributed on three levels, as described above) renders Russia inherently pluralistic (Chebankova 2020). However, the mechanical quality of interactions between the constitutive ensembles undermined organic integration and instead managerial forms of stability management predominate. The dual state voided constitutional institutions of the autonomy and agency necessary to sustain a functioning political organism. Neopluralism makes interactions between them assume a mimetic character. This is more than the privatization of governance condemned by critics of the neoliberal state, but a qualitative transformation of social and political relationships.

Classic Weberian representations of the modern state gave way to models stressing informality and the diffusion of power and authority. While formally unchanged, the institutions and processes of governance have been hollowed out (Crouch 2004; Mair 2013). The Russian governance model is an extreme version of this. There are many different forms of bad governance (Gel'man 2019), and the Russian case is distinctive because of the coexistence of two operative principles: the legality and procedures of the constitutional state, and the arbitrariness and cronyism of the administrative regime. Actors could not predict which code would operate at any particular time, especially when the two acted simultaneously. Arbitrary acts were couched in the language of legality. However, this is more than the instrumental use of legal institutions to achieve political goals (rule by law), the practice of authoritarians everywhere, but the competitive coexistence of two modes of legitimation—the legality and proceduralism of the constitutional state, and the decisionism that justifies regime forms of governance. The neopluralism of heterarchy is balanced by hierarchy but at the cost of polyarchy. It is not clear how much can be salvaged when the system disintegrates. As pointed out at the beginning of this chapter, the balance has been further—and more seriously—disrupted in Putin's fourth presidential term with the predominance of the security bloc and, most recently, the invasion of Ukraine in 2022, which is the most severe challenge yet.

Note

1 This essay draws from Richard Sakwa, 'Heterarchy: Russian Politics between Chaos and Control', *Post-Soviet Affairs*, Vol. 37, No. 3, 2021, pp. 222–241, and idem, *The Putin Paradox* (London and New York: I. B. Tauris, 2020), pp. 23–57.

References

Arnason, Johann P. (2020) *The Labyrinth of Modernity: Horizons, Pathways, and Mutations.* Lanham, MD: Rowman & Littlefield.

Bassin, Mark (2016) *The Gumilev Mystique: Biopolitics, Eurasianism, and the Construction of Community in Modern Russia.* Ithaca, NY: Cornell University Press.

Bassin, Mark, and Gonzalo Pozo, eds. (2016) *The Politics of Eurasianism: Identity, Culture, and Russia's Foreign Policy.* Lanham, MD: Rowman & Littlefield.

Baunov, Alexander (2020) 'Silencing Dissent: Russian Culture on Trial'. *Carnegie Moscow Center*, July 10. https://carnegie.ru/commentary/82269

Belmonte, Rosalba, and Philip G. Cerny (2021) 'Heterarchy: Towards Paradigm Shift in World Politics'. *Journal of Political Power* 14 (1), January (online).

Brenner, Neil, Bob Jessop, Martin Jones, and Gordon MacLeod (2003) *State/Space: A Reader.* Hoboken, NJ: Wiley.

Cerny, Philip G. (2010) *Rethinking World Politics: A Theory of Transnational Neopluralism.* Oxford: Oxford University Press.

Chebankova, Elena (2020) *Political Ideologies in Contemporary Russia.* Montreal: McGill-Queen's University Press.

Cherkesov, Viktor (2004) 'Nevedomstvennye razmyshleniya o professii: Moda na KGB?'. *Komsomol'skaya Pravda*, December 29.

Clover, Charles (2016) *Black Wind, White Snow: The Rise of Russia's New Nationalism.* London: Yale University Press.

Coker, Christopher (2019) *The Rise of the Civilizational State.* Cambridge: Polity Press.

Colton, Timothy J., and Stephen Holmes, eds. (2006) *The State after Communism: Governance in the New Russia.* Lanham, MD: Rowman & Littlefield.

Crouch, Colin (2004) *Post-Democracy*. Cambridge: Polity Press.

Crumley, Carole L. (1995) 'Heterarchy and the Analysis of Complex Societies'. *Archaeological Papers of the American Anthropological Association* 6 (1): 1–5.

Dahl, Robert (1971) *Polyarchy: Participation and Opposition*. New Haven, CT: Yale University Press.

Felshtinsky, Yuri, and Vladimir Pribylovsky (2012) *The Putin Corporation: The Story of Russia's Secret Takeover*. London: Gibson Square.

Foucault, Michel [1966] (2001) *The Order of Things: An Archaeology of the Human Sciences*. London: Routledge.

Frye, Timothy (2021) *Weak Strongman: The Limits of Power in Putin's Russia*. Princeton, NJ: Princeton University Press.

Galeotti, Mark (2018) *The Vory: Russia's Super Mafia*. New Haven, CT: Yale University Press.

Gel'man, Vladimir (2019) 'Why is Russia so Badly Governed?'. *Riddle*, September 27. https://ridl.io/en/why-is-russia-so-badly-governed/

Hale, Henry E. (2015) *Patronal Politics: Eurasian Regime Dynamics in Comparative Perspective*. New York: Cambridge University Press.

Hale, Henry E., Maria Lipman, and Nikolay Petrov (2019) 'Russia's Regime-on-the-Move'. *Russian Politics* 4 (2): 168–195.

Ivanov, Vitalii (2007) *Okhranitel'*. Moscow: Evropa.

Jayasuriya, Kanishka (2001) 'The Exception Becomes the Norm: Law and Regimes of Exception in East Asia'. *Asian-Pacific Law & Policy Journal* 2 (1): 108–124.

Kolstø, Pål (2016) 'Crimea vs. Donbas: How Putin Won Russian Nationalist Support—and Lost it Again'. *Slavic Review* 75 (3): 702–725.

Kononenko, Vadim, and Arkady Moshes, eds. (2010) *Russia as a Network State: What Works in Russia When Institutions Do Not?* Basingstoke: Palgrave Macmillan.

Kribbe, Hans (2020) *The Strongmen: European Encounters with Sovereign Power*. Edinburgh: Agenda.

Kynev, Alexander (2019) '20 let Vladimira Putina: Transformatsiya regional'noi politiki'. *Vedomosti*, August 15. www.vedomosti.ru/opinion/articles/2019/08/15/808836-20-let-putina

Lake, David A. (2007) 'Escape from The State of Nature: Authority and Hierarchy in World Politics'. *International Security* 32 (1): 47–79.

Lake, David A. (2009) *Hierarchy in International Relations*. Cornell, NY: Cornell University Press.

Laruelle, Marlene (2016) 'The Izborsky Club, or the New Conservative Avant-Garde in Russia'. *The Russian Review* 75 (4): 626–644.

Ledeneva, Alena (2013) *Can Russia Modernise? Sistema, Power Networks, and Informal Governance*. Cambridge: Cambridge University Press.

Lewis, David (2020) *Russia's New Authoritarianism: Putin and the Politics of Order*. Edinburgh: Edinburgh University Press.

Luzin, Pavel (2019) 'Why Corporations are the Kremlin's Best Friends'. *Moscow Times*, September 2. www.themoscowtimes.com/2019/09/02/why-corporations-are-the-kremlins-best-friends-a67106; also available at *Riddle*, August 29. www.ridl.io/en/why-corporations-are-the-kremlin-s-best-friends/

Mair, Peter (2013) *Ruling the Void: The Hollowing of Western Democracy*. London: Verso.

Marten, Kimberly (2019) 'Reckless Ambition: Moscow's Policy toward the United States, 2016/17'. *International Politics* 56 (6): 743–761.

Medvedev, Sergei (2019) *The Return of the Russian Leviathan*. Cambridge: Polity.

Mendras, Marie (2012) *Russian Politics: The Paradox of a Weak State*. London: Hurst.

Morozov, Viatcheslav (2015) *Russia's Postcolonial Identity: A Subaltern Empire in a Eurocentric World*. London: Palgrave Macmillan.

Petrov, Nikolai (2019a) '20 let Vladimira Putina: Transformatsiya elity'. *Vedomosti*, August 16. www.vedomosti.ru/opinion/articles/2019/08/16/808927-20-putina-transformatsiya

Petrov, Nikolai (2019b) '20 let Vladimira Putina: Transformatsiya silovikov'. *Vedomosti*, August 21. www.vedomosti.ru/opinion/articles/2019/08/21/809260-transformatsiya-eliti

Pozdnyakov, E. A. (1994) *Natsiya, natsionalizm, natsional'nye interesy.* Moscow: Progress-kultura.

Putin, Vladimir (2014) 'Address by the President of the Russian Federation'. *Kremlin.ru*, March 18. http://eng.kremlin.ru/news/6889.

Putin, Vladimir (2015) 'Presidential Address to the Federal Assembly'. *Kremlin.ru*, December 3. http://en.kremlin.ru/events/president/news/50864

Putin, Vladimir (2019) 'Presidential Address to the Federal Assembly'. *Kremlin.ru*, February 20. http://en.kremlin.ru/events/president/news/59863

Putin, Vladimir (2020a) 'Presidential Address to the Federal Assembly'. *Kremlin.ru*, January 15. http://en.kremlin.ru/events/president/news/62582

Putin, Vladimir (2020b) 'Speech at State Duma Plenary Session'. *Kremlin.ru*, March 10. http://en.kremlin.ru/events/president/transcripts/62964

Putin, Vladimir (2020c) 'Vstrecha s predstavitelyami obshchestvennosti po voprosam sotsial'noi podderzhki grazhdan'. January 22. http://kremlin.ru/events/president/news/62633

Robinson, Paul (2019) *Russian Conservatism.* DeKalb, IL: Northern Illinois University Press.

Sakwa, Richard (2010) 'The Dual State in Russia'. *Post-Soviet Affairs* 26 (3): 185–206.

Sakwa, Richard (2011) *The Crisis of Russian Democracy: The Dual State, Factionalism, and the Medvedev Succession.* Cambridge: Cambridge University Press.

Sakwa, Richard (2014) *Putin and the Oligarch: The Khodorkovsky–Yukos Affair.* London: I. B. Tauris.

Sakwa, Richard (2020) *The Putin Paradox.* London: I.B. Tauris–Bloomsbury Publishing.

Sakwa, Richard (2021) *Deception: Russiagate and the New Cold War.* Lanham, MD: Lexington Books.

Schedler, Andreas, ed. (2006) *Electoral Authoritarianism: The Dynamics of Unfree Competition.* Boulder, CO: Lynne Rienner.

Sharafutdinova, Gulnaz (2020) *The Red Mirror: Putin's Leadership and Russia's Insecure Identity.* Oxford: Oxford University Press.

Shlapentokh, Vladimir (2007) *Contemporary Russia as a Feudal Society.* New York: Palgrave Macmillan.

Stanovaya, Tatyana (2020) 'The Russian State and Society at a Crossroads: The Twilight Zone'. In Sinikukka Saari and Stanislav Secrieru, eds., *Russian Futures 2030: The Shape of Things to Come.* Paris: European Institute for Security Studies, Chaillot Paper No. 159: 26–42.

Taylor, Brian D. (2018) *The Code of Putinism.* Oxford: Oxford University Press.

Teitelbaum, Benjamin R. (2020) *War for Eternity: The Return of Traditionalism and the Rise of the Populist Right.* London: Penguin.

Yablokov, Ilya (2018) *Fortress Russia: Conspiracy Theories in Post-Soviet Russia.* Cambridge: Polity.

Zarakol, Ayşe (2011) *After Defeat: How the East Learned to Live with the West.* Cambridge: Cambridge University Press.

Zygar', Mikhail (2016) *All the Kremlin's Men: Inside the Court of Vladimir Putin.* New York: Public Affairs.

INDEX

Note: Page numbers in *italics* indicate a figure and page numbers in **bold** indicate a table on the corresponding page. Page numbers followed by "n" indicate a note.

Wengrow, David 30
Westphalian system 20
White, Joyce C. 37
White settlers 62
Widerberg, O. 170

Wigger, A. 194, 198
Wolfers, Arnold 43
World Trade Organization (WTO) dispute
  settlement (as heterarchy case study)
  155–164

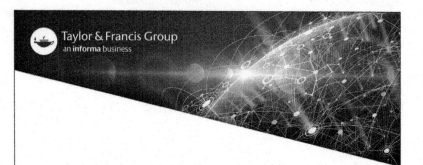

Taylor & Francis Group
an **informa** business

Taylor & Francis eBooks

www.taylorfrancis.com

A single destination for eBooks from Taylor & Francis
with increased functionality and an improved user
experience to meet the needs of our customers.

90,000+ eBooks of award-winning academic content in
Humanities, Social Science, Science, Technology, Engineering,
and Medical written by a global network of editors and authors.

TAYLOR & FRANCIS EBOOKS OFFERS:

A streamlined
experience for
our library
customers

A single point
of discovery
for all of our
eBook content

Improved
search and
discovery of
content at both
book and
chapter level

REQUEST A FREE TRIAL
support@taylorfrancis.com

 Routledge
Taylor & Francis Group

 CRC Press
Taylor & Francis Group